THE PRACTICAL FORECASTERS' ALMANAC

137 RELIABLE INDICATORS FOR INVESTORS, HEDGERS, AND SPECULATORS

THE PRACTICAL FORECASTERS' ALMANAC
137 RELIABLE INDICATORS FOR INVESTORS, HEDGERS, AND SPECULATORS

Edited
by
Edward Renshaw

BUSINESS ONE IRWIN
Homewood, Illinois 60430

This publication is designed to provide accurate and authoritative information in regard to the subject matter covered. It is sold with the understanding that neither the author nor the publisher is engaged in rendering legal, accounting, or other professional service. If legal advice or other expert assistance is required, the services of a competent professional person should be sought.

From a Declaration of Principles jointly adopted by a Committee of the American Bar Association and a Committee of Publishers.

Project editor: Karen Murphy
Production manager: Ann Cassady
Designer: Heidi J. Baughman
Jacket designer: Deborah Becker
Compositor: Eastern Composition, Inc.
Typeface: 11/13 Times Roman
Printer: Book Press, Inc.

Library of Congress Cataloging-in-Publication Data

The practical forecaster's almanac : 137 reliable indicators for
   investors, hedgers, and speculators / edited by Edward Renshaw.
     p.   cm.
   ISBN 1-55623-470-8
    1. Business forecasting—United States. 2. Economic indicators—
United States. 3. Business cycles—United States. 4. Finance—
United States—Statistics. 5. United States—Economic
conditions—1981—Statistics. I. Renshaw, Edward F.
HD30.27.P73   1992
330.973—dc20   92–6758

Printed in the United States of America
1 2 3 4 5 6 7 8 9 BP 9 8 7 6 5 4 3 2

PREFACE

Robert Strauss, the President's special envoy to what used to be the Soviet Union, has lamented that prediction is very difficult—especially if it pertains to the future. The last several years have been trying times for economic forecasters. Most prognosticators were unable to identify the July 1990 peak in business activity until after it occurred. They underestimated the severity of the ongoing employment recession and predicted a stronger recovery from the slump in industrial production than has actually occurred.

Bad news for the economy, however, has provided good news for those investors with a commitment to common stocks and long-term bonds. It has forced the Federal Reserve to lower short-term interest rates more than some of its governors would have liked and set the stage for one of the greatest financial restructurings in U.S. history.

Anyone endeavoring to forecast the future on the basis of statistical indicators is likely to be wrong an uncomfortable proportion of the time. History would suggest, however, that what happens to our economy and its financial markets is "somewhat predictable" and that it can sometimes be injurious to one's financial health to ignore the statistical regularities that have existed in the past.

One of the problems with a new almanac that endeavors to illustrate some of these regularities is the long delay in press. For the skeptical reader and thoughtful investor, however, that might turn out to be a virtue. Economic and financial relationships, which would have predicted the future quite well in the past, do have a tendency to break down. A publication lag will provide an "out of sample" test period that can be helpful in enabling informed readers, conscientious reviewers, and careful updaters to better evaluate the reliability of various indicators and rules of thumb that can be used for forecasting purposes.

An almanac with an emphasis on forecasting that is in need of a little updating can also be of some value to educators in making courses in economics and finance at the high school and college level more interesting. The instructor can put a copy of this almanac, along with the October and more recent issues of the U.S. Commerce Department's *Survey of Current Business*, on reserve in the library and let beginning students become better acquainted with government statistics by updating and evaluating the continuing usefulness of selected tables and forecasting relationships. For the more advanced students there can also be some excitement, challenge, and frustration in trying to improve upon the more interesting relationships in this edition of the *Forecasters' Almanac*.

The tables and commentary in this almanac were delivered to Business One Irwin in August 1991 when consumer confidence was still bolstered by the euphoria surrounding the outcome of Operation Desert Storm, before the stalling out of a rebound in industrial production in response to a slowdown of economic activity in the rest of the world and before it became fashionable for large corporations to announce further layoffs and permanent reductions in their work force. In the interest of a fairer evaluation of the cyclical indicator approach to economic and financial forecasting which was pioneered by the National Bureau of Economic Research in the 1920s and facilitated by the Bureau of Economic Analysis in the 1970s, it was decided not to update the tables in this almanac or the optimism surrounding the associated comments while the almanac was in production.

This almanac is still evolving and went through several unpublished editions in the 1980s. The editor and some of his students, needless to say, are already at work on the next edition, which will provide a more detailed critique of what went wrong with the U.S. economy during the fall of 1991. It should be of particular interest to readers who are familiar with the national income and product accounts since the U.S. Commerce Department is now in the process of gradually unveiling a new measure of economic activity, gross domestic product or GDP. GDP is almost as large as the more familiar GNP (gross national product), which includes income from U.S. capital and resources employed in other countries. GDP has the virtue of being somewhat easier to explain than GNP on the basis of the cyclical indicators which are published in the *Survey of Current Business* and featured in this almanac.

The indicator with the best track record for predicting changes in real GDP is the real money supply, M2 (business cycle indicator series 106). Since 1959 the year-to-year growth rates for real GDP have been about equal to 1.2 percentage points plus 60 percent of the December-to-December growth in real M2 in the preceding year. As of February 1992, M2 was predicting a growth rate for real GDP of only 1.2 percent for 1992. Other indicators, such as the Commerce Department's index of 11 leading economic indicators, were more bullish. The zero growth rate for M2 during 1991 and the stalling out of other leading indicators in the fall of 1991, however, help to explain why the forecasters polled by the National Association of Business Economists reduced their consensus growth rate for real GDP for 1992 from 2.4 to only 1.5 percent over a three-month period.

The possibility that the United States will continue to experience an unusually slow recovery from the economic recession of 1990–91 has made the economy a presidential election issue. The prolonged period of slow growth and recession which has prevailed since the first quarter of 1989 has also made it more difficult to predict what might happen in the financial markets, since there is no close parallel for such a prolonged period of stagnation or such an anemic recovery from a recession in the post-World War II period.

My own interpretation of the evidence presented in this almanac, however, is that the best time to have acquired stock may be over. Since the stock market has often performed worse in post-election years than in election years, and since most equities were generously priced in terms of prospective earnings and dividends as of the end February 1992, it would seem only prudent for investors to proceed with caution.

There has never been a comprehensive critique of the stock market and an evaluation of the forecasting properties of the Commerce Department's cyclical indicators that is as easy to follow and update as the tables in this almanac. The editor is grateful to Business One Irwin for having the courage to publish it and to the many generations of students here at the State University of New York at Albany who have contributed ideas and provided part of the motivation needed to see this edition through to completion.

Edward F. Renshaw
February 1992

CONTENTS

A Guide to Some Great Ideas and Relationships in Economics and Finance   xi

Alphabetical List of the Cyclical Indicators Examined in This Almanac   xiii

Numerical List of the Cyclical Indicators Examined in This Almanac   xv

List of Tables   xvii

CHAPTERS

1   Introduction   1

2   A Users' Guide to Interpreting the Indicators   7

3   Some Lessons from History   13

4   The Commerce Department's Composite Indexes   20

5   Employment and Unemployment   28

6   Production and Income   33

7   Indexes of Consumer Attitudes   37

8   Residential Construction and Investment   39

9   Inventory Investment   41

10   Stock Prices and Economic Activity   43

11   Some Summary Tables for Indicators of Economic Activity   54

12   Identifying Slow Growth Rates   59

13   Inflation and Financial Markets   63

14   Inflation and Its Causes   69

15   Crude Oil Production in the U.S. and the Rest of the World   74

16   Forecasting the Growth Rate for Nominal GNP   78

17   Some International Comparisons   80

18   Some Recessionary Indicators and the Stock Market   81

19	Corporate Earnings and Dividends	86
20	Summary Tables for Some Stock Market Indicators	89
21	Fluctuations in the Daily Closing Values for the S&P Index	92
22	Some Exceptional Days on Wall Street	96
23	Some Additional Crash Indicators	101
24	Stock Market Volatility	106
25	Special Features Section	109
Index		265

A Guide to Some Great Ideas and Relationships in Economics and Finance

Accelerator principle: 1.32

Business cycles: 1.11, 1.30

Business cycle dating: 1.12, 1.26

Consensus forecasts: 2.13, 2.14

Cycles within cycles: 3.05

Demand for money: 1.82

Diffusion indexes: 1.96

Dividend yields that are too low to be sustained: 1.04, 2.85

Economic recovery indicators: 1.16, 1.61, 1.75, 1.94

Employment cycles: 1.22, 1.23

Employment recessions: 1.24, 1.25, 1.26, 1.92, 1.93

Fed's interest rate reaction function: 1.88, 1.89

Financial return equals dividend yield plus the dividend growth rate: 1.04

Formula plans: 2.74, 2.85

GNP growth identity: 2.04

Growth indicators for GNP in 1982 dollars: 1.17, 1.18, 1.41, 1.76, 1.77, 1.91, 1.95, 1.96, 2.01, 2.03

Housing cycles: 1.50, 1.51

Hubbert's remarkable projection: 2.31

Inflation indicators: 2.12, 2.13, 2.14, 2.17, 2.22, 2.24

Inventory recessions: 1.60, 1.61

Inverted yield curve: 1.86

January effect: 3.15

Keynesian multiplier: 1.31

Law of diminishing returns: 3.21, 3.22

Mean reversion: 2.74

Misery index: 2.23

Natural resource scarcity: 2.30, 2.31, 2.32, 2.33

Okun's law: 2.05, 2.06

Phillips curve (equation): 2.21

Potential growth rate: 2.05, 2.06

Presidential election indicators: 2.23

Price-earnings ratios that are too high to be sustained: 2.82

Recession indicators: 1.50, 1.51, 1.75, 1.80, 1.81, 1.83, 1.86, 1.87, 1.90, 1.91, 1.92, 1.93

Risk premiums: 3.24, 3.25

Seasonal patterns to stock prices: 3.15, 3.16

Stock market bubbles and crash indicators: 1.71, 1.86, 1.87, 2.00, 2.74, 2.82, 2.85, 2.92, 3.16, 3.20, 3.21, 3.22, 3.23

Stock market buy indicators: 1.28, 1.31, 1.32, 1.35, 1.36, 1.77, 2.12, 2.15, 2.18, 2.19, 2.70, 2.71, 2.72, 2.73, 2.81, 2.83, 2.84, 2.90, 2.91, 3.00, 3.02, 3.03, 3.04, 3.10, 3.13, 3.14, 3.15, 3.16, 3.30, 3.31, 3.33

Stock market filters: 1.70, 1.73, 3.00

Stock market panics: 1.70, 3.02, 3.04

Supply shocks: 1.18, 2.24, 2.25, 2.26

Switching benefits: 2.74

Time value of money: 1.85

Wage-price spiral: 2.20

Weak recovery hypothesis: 1.02

Alphabetical List of the Cyclical Indicators Examined in This Almanac from the Business Cycle Indicators (BCI) Section of the *Survey of Current Business*

SERIES TITLE AND TABLES IN THIS ALMANAC FEATURING THE INDICATOR	BCI SERIES NO.
Average prime rate charged by banks: 1.87	109
Average weekly hours, manufacturing: 1.20, 1.94	1
Average weekly initial claims for unemployment, 1.29, 1.41	5
Capacity utilization rate for manufacturing: 2.17	82
Change in business inventories, bil. 1982$: 1.60, 1.61	30
Civilian employment: 1.23	442
Civilian unemployment rate: 1.27, 1.28, 1.88, 1.89, 2.03, 2.06, 2.21, 2.23, 2.73	43
Composite index of coincident indicators: 1.12, 1.14, 1.26, 1.94	920
Composite index of lagging indicators: 1.15	930
Composite index of leading indicators: 1.13, 1.16, 1.17, 1.18, 1.95, 2.72	910
Consumer expectations: 1.40	83
Consumer price index for all urban consumers: 1.26, 1.88, 1.89, 1.93, 2.02, 2.10, 2.14, 2.15, 2.17, 2.21, 2.22, 2.23, 2.25, 2.26, 2.80	320
Consumer sentiment: 1.41	58
Diffusion index of 11 leading indicator components: 1.94, 1.97	950
Diffusion index of 4 coincident indicator components: 1.94	951
Discount rate on new issues of 91-day Treasury bills: 1.18, 1.71, 1.76, 1.83, 1.88, 1.89, 1.93, 2.14, 2.17, 2.18, 2.19, 2.73, 2.74	114
Employees in goods-producing industries: 1.23	40

Employees on nonagricultural payrolls: 1.22, 1.24, 1.25, 1.26, 1.88, 1.93,
   1.94   41

Gross national product, bil. 1982$: 1.17, 1.18, 1.41, 1.60, 1.76, 1.95, 2.00,
   2.01, 2.06   50

Implicit price deflator for gross national product, 1982 = 100: 2.12, 2.14   310

Index of stock prices, 500 common stocks: 1.40, 1.70, 1.71, 1.73, 1.75,
   1.76, 1.94, 2.10, 2.60   19

Industrial production: 1.12, 1.16, 1.25, 1.26, 1.34, 1.93, 1.94   47

Industrial production of durable manufactured goods: 1.35   73

Money supply M1, bil. 1982$: 1.18, 1.76, 1.77, 1.80   105

Money supply M2, bil. 1982$: 1.81 1.94, 1.95   106

New private housing units started: 1.41, 1.51   28

Output per hour, all persons, nonfarm business sector: 2.03   358

Personal income, bil. 1982$: 1.12, 1.33   52

Personal income less transfer payments, bil. 1982$: 1.33, 1.94   51

Personal saving rate: 1.89   293

Private housing units authorized by local building permits: 1.50, 1.76, 1.94   29

Producer price index for finished goods: 2.01   336

Ratio, help-wanted advertising to unemployment: 1.76   60

Ratio, mfg. and trade inventories to sales in 1982$: 1.60   77

Stock price index for Canada: 2.60   743

Stock price index for France: 2.60   746

Stock price index for Germany: 2.60   745

Stock price index for Italy: 2.60   747

Stock price index for Japan: 2.60   748

Stock price index for the United Kingdom: 2.60   742

Vendors performance, slower deliveries diffusion index: 2.17   32

Wages and salaries in mining, mfg. and construction in bil. 1982$: 1.36   53

Yield on new issues of high-grade corporate bonds: 1.84   116

Numerical List of the Cyclical Indicators Examined in This Almanac. Listed as They Appear in the Business Cycle Indicators (BCI) Section of the *Survey of Current Business*

SERIES TITLE AND TABLES IN THIS ALMANAC FEATURING THE INDICATOR	BCI SERIES NO.
Composite index of leading indicators: 1.13, 1.16, 1.17, 1.18, 1.95, 2.72	910
Diffusion index of 11 leading indicator components: 1.94, 1.97	950
Composite index of coincident indicators: 1.12, 1.14, 1.26, 1.94	920
Diffusion index of four coincident indicator components: 1.94	951
Composite index of lagging indicators: 1.15	930
Average weekly hours, manufacturing: 1.20, 1.94	1
Average weekly initial claims for unemployment: 1.29, 1.41	5
Ratio, help-wanted advertising to unemployment: 1.76	60
Employees on nonagricultural payrolls: 1.22, 1.24, 1.25, 1.26, 1.88, 1.93, 1.94	41
Employees in goods-producing industries: 1.23	40
Civilian unemployment rate: 1.27, 1.28, 1.88, 1.89, 2.03, 2.06, 2.21, 2.23, 2.73	43
Gross national product, bil. 1982$: 1.17, 1.18, 1.41, 1.60, 1.76, 1.95, 2.00, 2.01, 2.06	50
Personal income, bil. 1982$: 1.12, 1.33	52
Personal income less transfer payments, bil. 1982$: 1.33, 1.94	51
Wages and salaries in mining, mfg. and construction, bil. 1982$: 1.36	53

Industrial production: 1.12, 1.16, 1.25, 1.26, 1.34, 1.93, 1.94   47

Industrial production of durable manufactured goods: 1.35   73

Capacity utilization rate for manufacturing: 2.17   82

Vendors performance, slower deliveries diffusion index: 2.17   32

Consumer sentiment: 1.41   58

Consumer expectations: 1.40   83

New private housing units started: 1.41, 1.51   28

Private housing units authorized by local building permits: 1.50, 1.76, 1.94   29

Change in business inventories, bil. 1982$: 1.60, 1.61   30

Ratio, mfg. and trade inventories to sales in 1982$: 1.60   77

Index of stock prices, 500 common stocks: 1.40, 1.70, 1.71, 1.73, 1.75,
     1.76, 1.94, 2.10, 2.60   19

Money supply M1, bil. 1982$: 1.18, 1.76, 1.77. 1.80   105

Money supply M2, bil. 1982$: 1.81, 1.94, 1.95   106

Discount rate on new issues of 91-day Treasury bills: 1.18, 1.71, 1.76, 1.83,
     1.88, 1.89, 1.93, 2.14, 2.17, 2.18, 2.19, 2.73, 2.74   114

Yield on new issues of high-grade corporate bonds: 1.84   116

Average prime rate charged by banks: 1.87   109

Personal saving rate: 1.89   293

Implicit price deflator for gross national product, 1982 = 100: 2.12, 2.14   310

Consumer price index for all urban consumers: 1.26, 1.88, 1.89, 1.93, 2.02,
     2.10, 2.14, 2.15, 2.17, 2.21, 2.22, 2.23, 2.25, 2.26, 2.80   320

Producer price index for finished goods: 2.01   336

Output per hour, all persons, nonfarm business sector: 2.03   358

Civilian employment: 1.23   442

Stock price index for Japan: 2.60   748

Stock price index for Germany: 2.60   745

Stock price index for France: 2.60   746

Stock price index for the United Kingdom: 2.60   742

Stock price index for Italy: 2.60   747

Stock price index for Canada: 2.60   743

List of Tables

SOME LESSONS FROM HISTORY AND THE RECESSION OF 1990–91

1.01 Avoiding Another Recessionary Surprise, 110

1.02 The Weak Recovery Hypothesis, 110

1.03 Diversity Pays, 111

1.04 Beware of Reflecting Barriers, 112

1.05 The Economic Activity Constraint on Dividend Growth, 112

1.06 The Financial Returns for the S&P Index during Presidential Election Years, 113

THE COMMERCE DEPARTMENT'S COMPOSITE INDEXES

1.11 Business Cycle Expansions and Contractions, 1854–90, 113

1.12 Dating Business Peaks and Troughs, 115

1.13 The Index of Leading Economic Indicators, 116

1.14 The Index of Coincident Indicators, 117

1.15 The Index of Lagging Indicators, 117

1.16 Large Increases in the Index of Leading Economic Indicators, 118

1.17 Identifying Very Poor Growth Years before They Occur, 118

1.18 Very Poor Growth Years Following Oil Price Shocks, 120

EMPLOYMENT AND UNEMPLOYMENT

1.20 The Average Weekly Hours of Production Workers in Manufacuturing, 121

1.21 The Changing Composition of the Employed Labor Force, 122

1.22 Employees on Nonagricultural Payrolls, 123

1.23 Employment in Nonagricultural Goods Producing Industries, 124

1.24 Some Recovery Indicators for Payroll Employment, 124

1.25 Some Recovery Indicators for Payroll Employment, 125

1.26 Some Alternative Ways to Measure the Duration of Economic Recessions, 125

1.27 The Civilian Unemployment Rate, 126

1.28 Unemployment and the Stock Market, 127

1.29 Unemployment Insurance Claims, 127

PRODUCTION AND INCOME

1.30 Recessionary Declines in Real GNP and Its Components, 128

1.31 An Income Expenditure Multiplier Model, 130

1.32 An Aggregate Accelerator Model, 131

1.33 Recessionary Declines in Personal Income, 133

1.34 Industrial Production, 133

1.35 Declines in Durable Manufacturers and the Stock Market, 134

1.36 Molnar's Recessionary Buy Signal, 134

INDEXES OF CONSUMER ATTITUDES

1.40 The Michigan Index of Consumer Expectations, 135

1.41 Poor Growth Years and the Michigan Index of Consumer Sentiment, 135

RESIDENTIAL CONSTRUCTION AND INVESTMENT

1.50 Residential Building Permits, 137

1.51 Housing Starts, 137

INVENTORY INVESTMENT

1.60 Inventory Recessions, 138

1.61 The Duration of Inventory Recessions, 139

STOCK PRICES AND ECONOMIC ACTIVITY

1.70 Stock Market Crashes in Perspective, 139

1.71 Some Lessons from History, 140

1.72 Great Decades to Have Owned Common Stock, 141

1.73 The Stock Market and the Business Cycle, 142

1.74 Stock Market Declines after Business Peaks, 143

1.75 Monthly Lead Times for Stock Prices at Business Peaks and Troughs, 143

1.76 Stock Prices and Poor Growth Years for the U.S. Economy, 144

1.77 The Stock Market's Reaction to Monetary and Fiscal Policy, 146

MONEY AND CREDIT

1.80 The Conventional Money Supply, 148

1.81 M2, 148

1.82 Money and the Bond Market, 149

1.83 The Cyclical Behavior of Short-Term Interest Rates, 150

1.84 The Yield on New Issues of High-Grade Corporate Bonds, 150

1.85 Interest Rates and IRA Investors, 151

1.86 The Highly Inverted Yield Curve, 151

1.87 The Prime Rate, 153

1.88 The Fed's Recessionary Reaction Function, 154

1.89 The Fed's Inflationary Reaction Function, 155

SOME SUMMARY TABLES FOR INDICATORS OF ECONOMIC ACTIVITY

1.90 Identifying Recessions before They Occur, 156

1.91 Forecasting Poor Growth Years, 157

1.92 Forecasting the Duration of Employment Recessions, 158

1.93 Forecasting the Duration of Employment Recessions, 159

1.94 Some Recovery Indicators for Recessionary Troughs, 160

1.95 Forecasting Year-to-Year Growth Rates for Real GNP, 161

1.96 Some Slow Growth Indicators, 163

1.97 Using a Diffusion Index to Identify Unhealthy Expansion Periods, 165

IDENTIFYING SLOW GROWTH RATES

2.00 Stock Returns Associated with Exceptionally Slow Growth Years, 166

2.01 Using Producer Price Acceleration to Identify Slow Growth Years, 167

2.02 Using Real Currency to Forecast Slow Growth Years, 168

2.03 Unused Labor Capacity and the Prediction of Slow Growth Years, 169

2.04 Real GNP and the Labor Force, 170

2.05 Okun's Law, 171

2.06 The Downhill Slide of the Potential Growth Rate, 172

INFLATION AND THE FINANCIAL MARKETS

2.10 Stocks as a Hedge against Inflation, 173

2.11 Gold versus Stock as a Hedge against Inflation, 173

2.12 Inflation and the Financial Returns Associated with the S&P Index, 174

2.13 Are Changes in the Inflation Rate Predictable?, 176

2.14 Some Inflation Indicators for the Implicit Price Deflator for Real GNP, 177

2.15 Deceleration in the CPI Inflation Rate and Stock Returns, 178

2.16 Inflation and the Returns from Holding Corporate Bonds, 179

2.17 Some CPI Inflation Indicators, 180

2.18 Letting the Fed Forecast Good Years to Own Stock, 182

2.19 Letting the Fed Forecast Good Times to Buy Stock, 183

INFLATION AND ITS CAUSES

2.20 Wage and Price Inflation, 184

2.21 The Employment Cost Index, 185

2.22 The Most Volatile Components of the CPI, 186

2.23 Inflation and the Outcome of Presidential Elections, 187

2.24 Double Digit Inflation, 189

2.25 The Price of Imported Oil, 190

2.26 Fluctuations in the Real Price of Imported Oil, 191

CRUDE OIL PRODUCTION IN THE U.S. AND THE REST OF THE WORLD

2.30 Conventional Oil and Gas Resources in the U.S., 191

2.31 Crude Oil Production in the U.S., 192

2.32 Crude Oil Reserves in the Rest of the World, 193

2.33 Non OPEC Crude Oil Production, 194

2.34 OPEC Crude Oil Production, 195

2.35 Disposition of the World's Crude Oil Production, 196

FORECASTING THE GROWTH RATE FOR NOMINAL GNP

2.40 Using a Consensus of Monetary Indicators, 197

2.41 Alternative Preliminary GNP Forecasts, 198

2.42 Consensus Forecast of Nominal GNP, 199

SOME INTERNATIONAL COMPARISONS

2.60 A Comparison of Stock Market Indexes for Various Countries, 200

SOME RECESSIONARY INDICATORS AND THE STOCK MARKET

2.70 Stock Returns during Years Containing a Recessionary Trough, 201

2.71 Taking Advantage of Economic Recessions, 201

2.72 Using Leading Indicators to Identify Safe Years to Be in the Market, 202

2.73 More about Unemployment and the Stock Market, 204

2.74 Switching on a Year-End Basis, 205

CORPORATE EARNINGS AND DIVIDENDS

2.80 Record Earnings for the S&P Index, 206

2.81 Large Declines in Corporate Earnings, 207

2.82 The Peril Associated with High Price-Earnings Ratios, 208

2.83 The Earnings and Dividends Associated with the S&P Index, 209

2.84 Large Increases in the Dividend Yield Associated with the S&P Index, 210

2.85 Stock Market Crashes Associated with Low Dividend Yields, 211

SUMMARY TABLES FOR SOME STOCK MARKET INDICATORS

2.90 Some Indicators That May Help to Propel the Stock Market Upward, 212

2.91 Some "Perfect" Predictors of Good Years to Own Common Stock, 214

2.92 Some Indicators of Stock Market Crashes, 216

2.93 Is Buy and Hold the Best Policy?, 218

FLUCTUATIONS IN THE DAILY CLOSING VALUES FOR THE S&P INDEX

3.00 Major Fluctuations in Stock Prices, 220

3.01 Bear Market Recoveries, 221

3.02 Taking Advantage of Major Bear Markets, 222

3.03 Buying the S&P Index after a Two-Quarter Decline of 14 Percent or More, 223

3.04 Some Panic Days on Wall Street, 223

3.05 Some Cycles within Cycles, 224

3.06 Three Strategies for Acquiring a Portfolio Similar to the S&P Index, 226

SOME EXCEPTIONAL DAYS ON WALL STREET

3.10 One Day Gains of 3.5 Percent or More, 227

3.11 Record Point Increases for the DJIA, 228

3.12 Is the DJIA a Better Value than the S&P Index?, 229

3.13 Advancing Issues on the NYSE, 230

3.14 Record Trading on the NYSE, 231

3.15 The Unappreciated January Effect, 233

3.16 The Silver Lining Associated with Bad Octobers, 235

SOME ADDITIONAL CRASH INDICATORS

3.20 The Prediction of Bad Octobers, 237

3.21 Major Bull Markets and the Law of Diminishing Returns, 237

3.22 Financial Return Cycles, 238

3.23 New Stock Issues, 239

3.24 Old-Fashioned Risk Premiums, 240

3.25 Modern Risk Premiums, 242

STOCK MARKET VOLATILITY

3.30 Stock Market Volatility, 244

3.31 Residual Volatility and the S&P Index, 246

3.32 New Historic Highs for the S&P Index, 246

3.33 Taking Advantage of Bad Years for Stock Brokers, 247

A SPECIAL FEATURES SECTION

3.40 A Chronology of Buy and Sell Signals for the S&P Index, 247

CHAPTER 1

INTRODUCTION

Some six years ago, Albert Sommers wrote with eloquence,

> Immensely powerful, ever changing, pulsating with a hundred different rhythms, and offering every conceivable combination of economic risk and reward, the U.S. economy ranks as one of the wonders of the world. As a subject for detached intellectual study, it offers fascinations and degrees of complexity unsurpassed by any structures in the physical world.[1]

If the U.S. economy is a wonder to behold, this almanac provides some guidance and historical perspective on how to do that.

It is written for busy decision makers, thoughtful investors, harried professors, college students, and economy watchers who must monitor the health of the U.S. economy at different phases of the business cycle or want to predict what might happen in the stock market.

To accomplish its goal, the almanac groups together indicators published by the U.S. Commerce Department and other data-gathering organizations and arranges them in a way that lets them speak for themselves and be more easily interpreted. The net result is a simplification of the art of economic and financial forecasting, which emphasizes time-tested rules of thumb and specialized sets of indicators for different purposes.

I believe the reader won't need a course in statistics or even a personal computer to benefit from the indicators featured in this almanac. It will help generate forecasts that are competitive and in some cases superior to the predictions that are derived from complex models requiring a lot of computer time.

The art of economic forecasting is now heavily influenced by equations that assign a set of fixed weights to different indicators. If the relationships between the various indicators were well behaved and quite stable, this would be an unbeatable approach. In a world where most time series with leading indicator properties are rather volatile and where economic and financial innovation, bad weather, fits of speculative enthusiasm, and political disturbances can distort statistical relationships, however, it is often better to examine pertinent indicators on an individual basis and simply count the number of indicators that seem to be pointing in a particular direction. Disturbances that are peculiar to one or just a few of the relevant indicators will drop by the wayside and not distort the entire forecast.

The collection of data, processing of statistics, and the distribution of economic and financial indicators is undertaken sometimes unwillingly by most businesses, many nonprofit institutions and at all levels of government. Hardly a week goes by without newspapers reporting an addition to at least one of the Commerce Department's more than 600 time series on economic activity—sometimes on the front page! Yet comparatively little has been done to provide ordinary decision makers with some useful guidelines for translating changes in these indicators into reliable predictions. Commentators usually seek—and are quickly provided with—interpretations of the indicators. But it is sometimes difficult to determine whether these pronouncements are off the cuff, motivated by strategic and/or political considerations, or based upon a careful analysis of the historical data.

Consider the rule of thumb that an economic recession is not likely to occur until after the index of leading economic indicators has declined for three consecutive months. It has correctly predicted seven of the nine recessions occurring in the post-1947 period, was four months late in identifying the July 1981 business peak, three months late in predicting the last recession which began in July 1990, and gave signals that were either false or premature in 1951, 1962, 1966, 1978–79, 1984, 1987, and 1989.

The poor performance of this rule in relation to the last two recessions, and the large number of premature signals, suggests some problems with this highly publicized indicator of economic activity. Like most econometric models used for forecasting purposes the index of leading indicators is expected to accomplish too much.

The 11 components in the index of leading economic indicators have been evaluated on the basis of six major characteristics: economic significance, statistical adequacy, consistency of timing at both business cycle peaks and troughs, conformity to business expansions and contractions, smoothness, and prompt availability.[2] By trying to gather together this host of desired characteristics, the index is not very useful in predicting specific developments such as the next economic recession or when it will end.

Economic and financial indicators, like people, are rather diverse and not equally good at accomplishing every objective. As such, they are more helpful when studied individually. Getting to know the particular strengths and weaknesses of each indicator will better protect the decision maker from hasty interpretations of the latest statistics.

The Federal Reserve's index of industrial production is a classic example of a widely publicized indicator that is not equally good at identifying all the things it is asked to identify (Table 1.12).* It is very useful in helping to pinpoint recessionary troughs but has only been coincident (or concurrent) with three of the last nine business peaks dated by the National Bureau of Economic Research (NBER). In contrast, personal income, when expressed in constant dollars, does identify business peaks fairly well but tends to be a leading economic indicator at recessionary troughs.

The discovery that a consensus prediction obtained by polling a number of different professional forecasters is cheaper and theoretically superior to the majority of forecasts has changed the character of business forecasting.[3] According to this theory, a median forecast has to be equal to or better than all forecasts if it turns out to be correct. And if it is way off the mark, the median will still be at least equal to or better than half of the forecasts. In a world where careful evaluation of past forecasts is seldom undertaken, where much of the data is subject to revision, where models and forecasting procedures are continually revised, and where better-than-average forecasts are often simply the result of dumb luck, rather than a superior forecasting technique, busy decision makers are probably well advised to buy into the consensus rather than maintain their own forecasting unit or purchase the myriad of reports of many different forecasting organizations that no one has time to read.

---

*Tables are presented in a separate section at the back of the book.

If everyone subscribed to the consensus and no one invested any effort in trying to improve the art of forecasting, however, the value of the consensus itself would surely deteriorate and might even end up being a lot less reliable than the notion that next year's growth or inflation rate will be equal to last year's rate.

While the flowering of consensus forecasting may have reduced the need for more economists, it also provides a rationale for some new and relatively simple, yet reasonably sophisticated procedures, to check up on professional forecasters. By polling statistical indicators, rather than the people who are in the business of making forecasts, you can quickly see if their predictions are in the right ball park.

There is an old saying that one should "buy low and sell high." Without indicators of what is high and what is low, however, it is very hard to give much meaning to that advice. The application of the indicator approach to stock market forecasting shows that the best buy indicators may be quite different from the best sell indicators. (See summary Table 2.93 for an illustration of this point.)

A particular advantage in polling the indicators is that you may be able to identify a stock market crash before it occurs. In pursuing such a narrow objective, you can make better use of some indicators that are otherwise too volatile, specialized, or misbehaved to be included in a composite index of leading indicators or a general purpose forecasting model.

In 1960 Paul Feldstein and I examined the sorry performance of many mutual funds and made the case for "an unmanaged investment company" that would emulate the behavior of a representative stock price index. That idea lay dormant for about a decade before some Wall Street entrepreneurs decided that the number of converts to the random walk hypothesis made the idea of an index fund profitable. The pendulum of academic opinion, which was so quick to endorse the notion of efficient markets, however, has only recently swung to the recognition that representative stock price indexes move in a cyclical fashion, making year-to-year changes in these indexes somewhat predictable.[4]

In fact, if you make a distinction between crash and good-time indicators, you can easily devise strategies to beat the market that would have provided trading profits over the last four or five decades. (See summary Table 2.93.) The assumption that this is the only way to refute the random walk hypothesis, however, is incorrect. You don't necessarily need to come up with a scheme for moving in and out of the market that is superior to a policy of simply buying and holding a representative stock price index. All you need to show is that you can identify times when the stock market is very likely to perform exceptionally well. By using financial leverage during the most favorable periods, you can outperform the market, on the average, without being very good at identifying stock market crashes before they are over.

In trying to benefit from nonrandomness, individual investors may even have an advantage over professional forecasters and money managers since they have greater flexibility in managing their own portfolio. By confining most purchases and sales to periods of under- and over-valuation—when the odds of being right are fairly high—amateurs may be able to outperform the professionals who have to buy and sell on many days when the economic and financial outlook is extremely murky. As partial proof of that assumption, a study by the National Association of Investment Clubs in 1991 found that 62 percent of the clubs in its sample had lifetime returns equal to or better than the financial returns associated with the S&P composite stock price index.[5]

To benefit from economic and financial indicators, I have found that what you really need is a sense of history and some time-tested rules for deciding which direction the indicators are pointing. That, at least in part, is what this almanac is about. Some other reasons for studying economic and financial indicators are: (1) to better protect one's wealth from the redistributive policies of the Federal Reserve, (2) to guard against an overly optimistic bias that is not only characteristic of most human beings but many of their forecasting systems as well, and (3) to bolster one's confidence and be in a better position to take advantage of tight money, economic recessions, and other disturbances that can cause investors to temporarily lose their nerve and let stock prices decline to bargain levels.

ENDNOTES

1. Albert Sommers, *The U.S. Economy Demystified* (Lexington, Mass.: Lexington Books, 1985), p. xv.

2. Charlotte Boeschan and Victor Zarnowitz, "Cyclical Indicators: An Evaluation and New Leading Indexes," *Business Conditions Digest*, May 1975, pp. v–xiv.

CHAPTER 2

A USER'S GUIDE TO INTERPRETING THE INDICATORS

Carefully examining the indicators in this almanac will quickly get students and other casual forecasters to the point at which the exercise of good judgment, a feel for the data, and luck may be more important determinants of forecasting success than the predictions to be derived from large-scale computer models involving hundreds of equations, sophisticated econometrics, and lots of computer time.

Despite conventional wisdom, you don't need a computer to become a reasonably proficient forecaster. Forecasting based on an interpretation of publicized indicators is something that can easily be learned, in part by reading this almanac. It further can be incorporated into introductory economics and finance courses to make them more interesting and meaningful. The person who aspires to be his or her own forecaster, however, must learn to locate pertinent information.

That's where the almanac comes in. It can be used in several ways. One approach is to get a quick overview by reading the text that accompanies the basic tables to make sure "surprising" relationships are not overlooked. Another strategy is to scan the table of contents, the topical index featuring some ideas and relationships in economics and finance, and the tabular index to the cyclical indicators published by the Commerce Department, which are featured in this almanac, for those tables and relationships of personal interest.

The usefulness of individual indicators depends on the time in which they will be used. It won't be of great value to update indicators that strive to identify a recession before it occurs if, for example, the economy is already in a recession. For that reason, summary tables pertaining to economic activity (Tables 1.90 to 1.97) are arranged in a logical sequence to better facilitate the tracking of business contractions and expansions.

As a useful starting point for the busy investor many of the indicators pertaining to the stock market are summarized in Tables 2.90 to 2.93. It may prove rewarding, for example, to be a contrarian in monitoring the stock market tables, since good years to own stocks are more likely to follow stock market crashes than "great times." An absence of good time signals, however, may be almost as ominous as the signals provided by the less numerous crash indicators.

The investor should also appreciate that financial markets are heavily influenced by anticipations. Readers with money at risk may want to estimate the year-end values for some of the variables themselves or use predictions that appear in the newspaper and forecasts summarized in such places as the *Blue Chip Economic Indicators* newsletter.

In using the almanac for practical investment purposes, it should also be remembered that by the time a statistical yearbook gets published, it will already need some updating. About half of the tables in this almanac involve annual data that are best updated around the middle of February, since the behavior of stock prices in January often sets the tone for what will happen in the remainder of the year (Table 3.15). The remaining tables are based on fluctuations in daily, monthly, and quarterly information that may need to be monitored more continually, especially if changes in the indicators are near an important turning point or a buy/sell signal. Most of the data in these tables can be kept current by reading *The Wall Street Journal*, the business and financial sections of other newspapers, and by subscribing to the U.S. Commerce Department's *Survey of Current Business (SCB)*, available from the U.S. Government Printing Office.

To aid the reader in these efforts, we use an overlapping, three-digit numbering system, the first two digits of which are closely related to the partitioning system in the yellow "business cycle indicator" section of the *SCB*. The statistical series included in this section of the *SCB* have been assigned a "BCI" number by the Department of Commerce and are sometimes referred to by that series number in the footnotes to the basic tables.

The indicated yield series for Moody's bond indexes and S&P's stock indexes can be found in the finance section of the blue pages of the *SCB*. The price-earnings ratios for the S&P index are not published in the *SCB* but can be obtained from Standard & Poor's Corporation. They are also available, somewhat belatedly, from the appendix to the *Economic Report of the President* and the monthly *Economic Indicators*, another document prepared by the Council of Economic Advisors for the Joint Economic Committee of the U.S. Congress and published by the Government Printing Office. Standard & Poor's *Trade and Securities Statistics* and *Security Price Index Record*, which is updated monthly, contains daily closing prices for the S&P index and a great deal of other information going back to the 1920s.

WHAT THE ALMANAC DOES—AND DOES NOT—DO

In compiling this almanac I have tried to limit the discussion to those indicators and relationships among variables that are of primary interest to economists and investors or appear to be of some value in helping to forecast economic activity, employment, inflation, interest rates and the direction of stock prices.

As such, the almanac covers major fluctuations in the indicators and not the trials and tribulations encountered in using economic and financial indicators for short-term forecasting. There are many interesting data series in the *SCB* not considered in this almanac because their movements are so higgledy-piggledy as to not be of very much forecasting value from a cyclical point of view. Some indicators with near perfect forecasting records are also excluded because of changing circumstances, a fear on the author's part that they might not continue to be a reliable indicator or the lack of a good reason for their value to forecasting.

The reader should recognize my predominant bias toward forecasting. I have tuned the signals for some of the indicators to what is easiest to forecast and not necessarily to what one would like most to forecast. Economic theory presumes that tax-exempt retirement accounts should never be invested in stocks unless the expected returns after transaction costs are more than the alternative return on liquid assets. It is easier, though, to differentiate between positive and negative returns than to make fine distinctions about the relative returns from holding different types of assets.

From 1926 to 1990, for example, there were 37 years when the financial returns (including dividends) for the S&P index exceeded 10 percent, 20 years when the returns were negative and only 8 years when the returns ranged from 0 to 10 percent. In large measure, the small number of years showing mediocre returns means that any system that can successfully differentiate between positive and negative return years will not only reduce portfolio risk but almost certainly provide tax-exempt investors with an above average return.

The 1989 edition of *Johnson's Charts* estimates that an investor would have earned a compound average financial return of 9.9 percent by investing in the S&P 500 index from 1926 to 1988. The comparable return for investing in T-bills was only 3.5 percent; for government bonds, 4.5 percent and corporate bonds 5.0 percent.

From 1926 to 1962, there were 12 years when corporate bonds outperformed both T-bills and common stock. In each of these years the S&P index was lower at the end of the year than at the beginning of the year. From 1962 to 1990, however, there were only four years (1970, 1982, 1984, and 1986) when corporate bonds outperformed T-bills and stocks. In each of these years the return on the S&P index was positive. While bonds might outperform other financial assets with greater frequency in the future, we simply don't have enough cases to confidently predict the conditions under which that might occur.

If stocks continue to outperform other assets, on the average, it will not make sense to exit the stock market in response to crash indicators unless you have the intestinal fortitude to reinvest when the market is down and many economic indicators are not very encouraging.

The behavior of the stock market and the economy may still be of value for the reluctant forecaster, who finds it difficult to make financial decisions if it bolsters your confidence when the economic outlook is not very bright and keeps you from getting carried away by mob psychology when the market is booming.

The money game, like baseball or football, has its own peculiarities and can be more interesting—and sometimes rewarding—if you own a fact book and maintain your own score card. Brickman, creator of the small society, has drawn a cartoon with the caption, "Hoo-Boy! The stock market has to be the only place in the world where you can start at the top." By reading the rest of this almanac and learning how to interpret the economic and financial indicators you may be able to better appreciate the sometimes counterintuitive behavior of the market and avoid or at least reduce the risk and disappointment of that type of start.

To base the insights of the almanac as much as possible on solid ground, we have used the technique of informal discriminant analysis to differentiate positive return years from years with a mixture of both positive and negative returns. Informal or "nonparametric" discriminant analysis is a particularly appropriate technique for nonlinear relationships, subject to threshold effects that cannot easily be described by a simple equation. The technique also forces the analyst to take a hard look at the data. In that way, one might learn something new about the character of longer-run changes in stock prices that might have been overlooked if one simply feeds the data into a computer and analyzes it with a standardized data-processing program.

While this approach promotes creativity, it doesn't automatically give you statistical significance. When the proportion of years with negative returns is about 21.3 percent, as was the case from 1942 to 1988, you must identify at least 10 positive returns (and no negative returns) for it to be 90 percent probable that the outcome was not the result of pure chance and at least 13 positive returns and no negatives to be 95 percent confident that a threshold is statistically significant.

Some of the variables in the summary tables don't measure up to these lofty standards but are included anyway because they are important or, at least, seemed interesting and represent the best that this analyst could do with the data. While none of the variables are particularly impressive by themselves, their collective ability to differentiate between generally good and rather poor times to have been in the stock market is rather startling and could be considered statistically significant when compared to the results of a number of other tests developed by statisticians.

In my advanced undergraduate course on economic and financial model building, which has a statistical prerequisite, I often require students to make such tests. But this is simply to ground them in theory. The character of the economic and financial world has been changing so rapidly that the assumptions underlying such tests are not characteristic of the real world. It is more important for students to be comfortable with a particular relationship. Economic and financial indicators are so rowdy, individualistic, and so often ill-behaved that their interpretation will always be more nearly an art than a science.

This analyst, in any event, is more impressed with an indicator if it behaves in a cyclical manner, if its signals are scattered over a long period of time, if it has some diverse but like-minded company, if it has survived some difficult forecasting periods, and if the closest thing to a disastrous signal occurred a long time ago.

Since most users of forecasts are more interested in the future than how accurate last year's forecasts were or how they were derived, many professional forecasters can tout their successes while ignoring their failures. The compiler of this almanac, however, can't hide behind a computerized forecasting box and runs a much greater risk that poor predictions from unruly indicators will not be forgotten.

While there will no doubt be some incorrect forecasts, I don't believe that either the art of forecasting or its usefulness to decision makers will be improved unless users and evaluators have a paper trail that helps determine what went wrong and how they can learn from past errors.

Moreover, since most of the forecasting signals in this almanac are very simple, since publication lags ensure that all of the tables are from three months to about a year out of date and, since a lot can happen in the financial world in that amount of time, the informed reader and the conscientious updater will grasp at least an inkling of how much artistry and real forecasting power there is in a policy of letting the indicators speak for themselves. Let us turn to the rest of the almanac, then, and allow them to speak.

CHAPTER 3

SOME LESSONS FROM HISTORY

The behavior of the U.S. stock market in 1990–91 has reaffirmed an almost ancient pattern of crashing in the vicinity of a business peak (Table 1.70) and being a leading indicator of economic recoveries (Table 1.75).

HOW TO AVOID ANOTHER RECESSIONARY SURPRISE

One of the more important lessons to be learned from the last two economic recessions is that you cannot rely on the Commerce Department's composite index of leading economic indicators to provide as much warning of an impending recession as its individual components. To illustrate this point, we compared the lead times of the index at business peaks with the median lead times for the 11 individual indicators (Table 1.01). The lead times correlated fairly closely with the six peaks in business activity from 1953 to 1980. The median lead time for the individual components, however, has given a much longer period of warning for the last two recessions.

During the last recession, for example, the index of leading economic indicators peaked in July 1990 at about the same time as business activity in general—with no advance warning of an impending recession. The index's failure is due in part to a trend adjustment that was much higher than the economy's sluggish growth rate in the five quarters preceding the July peak in business activity. A bullish stock market and a very strong demand for U.S. exports may have also prevented the composite index from declining before the peak in business activity.

The individual indicators, on the other hand, provided an advance warning of an impending recession. Five of the 11 components peaked at least 76 months in advance of the official peak in business activity and four others peaked from 19 to 25 months in advance of the 1990–91 recession. The S&P composite stock price index is the only component of the index of leading indicators that didn't provide at least seven months' warning.

With so many of the indicators crying wolf for so long—even as the Federal Reserve's index of industrial production continued to set new records—it is not surprising that many professional forecasters were caught unaware by the recession of 1990–91. The July 10 issue of the *Blue Chip Economic Indicators* newsletter, which surveys about 50 forecasters each month, reported that, "The year-ago *Consensus* forecast for 1990 of a 'soft landing' (no recession, but sluggish growth) remains intact."

Some unlucky forecasters have consoled themselves with the idea that the 1990–91 recession was rather unique. They opine that it might never have occurred if it were not for Iraq's unexpected invasion of Kuwait in August 1990 and President Bush's determination to keep Saddam from annexing it. They may be right, but we will never know for sure since the economy had been sputtering along at an unsatisfactory pace long before the invasion.

Since the recession of 1981–82 was also a surprise, however, I believe economy watchers should broaden their horizon and be concerned about the behavior of individual indicators (in summary Table 1.90), which have a better track record at identifying recessions before they occur (Table 1.01).

THE WEAK RECOVERY HYPOTHESIS

Once the recession was underway, economic forecasters deserve some credit for having recognized that a lean inventory picture (Table 1.61) might indicate a short recession. That hypothesis proved correct: the recession that officially began in July 1990 probably ended in April 1991. In fact, only five recessions since 1854 have been shorter and only two recessions since 1947 (Table 1.11). The six-month decline in industrial production from September 1990 to March 1991 also marked the shortest industrial recession in the post–World War II period (Table 1.26).

Just as the indicators did point individually to a shorter-than-usual recession, so they also point to a weaker-than-normal recovery. If you rank post-war recessionary declines in payroll employment in order of their severity and examine the associated increases in employment during the first 12 months of recovery from the recessions (Table 1.02), you will discover that mild recessions are followed by weak recoveries. The rather anemic recovery of the Commerce Department's index of leading economic indicators and its associated diffusion index (Table 1.94) is another reason for being concerned about the vigor of this business expansion.

Heavy debt burdens, a huge stock of unoccupied office buildings, a spread of the U.S. recession to other countries, and structural deficits, which have forced all levels of government to either cut back employment or raise taxes in the midst of a recession, were additional reasons to suggest that the economic recovery of the second half of 1991 would be less brisk than usual (Table 1.02).

DIVERSITY PAYS

The failure of the Commerce Department's index of leading economic indicators to provide some advance warning for the economic recession of 1990–91 and the embarrassing behavior of some individual indicators suggest that it can be quite risky to base one's forecasts and investment decisions on only one index or type of indicator.

This suggestion holds in the case of leading indicator models that gave a lot of weight to the behavior of interest rates and the spread between interest rates of different maturities; in 1990, they performed very poorly (see summary Table 1.90). An experimental leading indicator index, containing such variables, developed for the National Bureau of Economic Research by James Stock of the University of California at Berkeley and Mark Watson of Northwestern University never assessed the probability of a 1990 recession at more than 14 percent.[1] In contrast, the diffusion index for the Commerce Department's index of leading indicators and some adjusted lead times for three types of monetary indicators did a much better job of predicting the recession of 1990–91 before it occurred.

The advantage of forecasts based on a diverse set of indicators is not limited to economic predictions. Years containing a recessionary trough in business activity usually have been very good years to have owned common stock (Table 2.70). One rule for taking advantage of economic recessions, with a very impressive previous track record, is to buy stock two months after two consecutive quarterly declines in real GNP (Table 2.71). This signaling system, however, would have delayed stock purchases until after most stock indexes had fully recovered from the recessionary bear market of 1990–91.

In Table 1.03 we summarize the closing values for the S&P index that are associated with the 23 buy signals given by the various stock market indicators in this almanac during the recession of 1990–91. I first publicized the best signal to have followed—buy after a cumulative decline in the S&P index of 19.4 percent or more—in the January 26, 1989 issue of the *Market Chronicle*. The next best rule to have followed—buy one month after a cumulative decline of 6 percent or more for total wages and salaries (BCI series 53)—was proposed by David Molnar, one of my students, before it became clear that the bear market of 1990 was over and another buy signal had been given.

BEWARE OF REFLECTING BARRIERS

The indicator approach is sometimes criticized because it is rather pragmatic and not very interesting from either a theoretical or a policy perspective. These criticisms are not well founded. Most of the indicators that can help identify economic recessions before they occur, are either directly or indirectly related to the monetary policy of the Federal Reserve (summary Table 1.90). Moreover, the error term for the aggregate accelerator model in Table 1.32 (actual minus predicted) which claims that the growth rate for real GNP should be about equal to minus 6 percentage points plus three times the percentage change in fixed investment, did indicate that 1991 was a good year to own stocks.

The trouble with most of the stock price theories is that they can't really predict year-to-year changes in the value of representative stock market indexes. Most of the more advanced textbooks on corporate finance, however, do devote some space to the interpretation of an actuarial formula that is of some value in projecting the financial returns for the S&P index from the end of one year containing a peak in business activity to the next. According to this formula, if the dividend price ratio remains the same, and if there is no change in the dividend growth rate, the actual financial return (dividends plus price appreciation expressed as a percent of price at the beginning of the period) will be equal to the current dividend yield plus the dividend growth rate.[2]

In Table 1.04 we use this formula to project the financial returns for the S&P composite stock price index between years of peak prosperity. The actual returns in the following period, shown in column (6), assume that all dividends are reinvested at the end of each year and that there are no transaction costs.

Note that the actual return of (− 3.0) percent per year from the end of 1929 to the end of 1937 was much less than the projected average return of 16.5 percent at the end of 1929. From 1937 through the 1960s, when the stock market was still recovering from the trauma of the Great Depression of the 1930s, the actual returns associated with the S&P index were often closely related but consistently greater than the projected returns. Since 1969, the actual returns through the following year containing another business peak have tended, as often as not, to be less than the projected returns.

Assuming that the dividend yield will not be over 3.7 percent at the end of the next year containing a business peak, and that the dividends associated with the S&P stock price index will continue to increase at the same average rate of 6.9 percent experienced from 1981 to 1990, the compound average financial return associated with this business expansion should be at least 10.6 percent. An increase in the dividend yield or a reduction in the dividend growth rate could mean a lower return.

One of the more interesting points to note in Table 1.04 is that there has never been a yield under 3.4 percent at the end of any year containing a peak in business activity. There have been several occasions when investors experimented with dividend yields of less than 3 percent in the midst of recessions and business expansions, but bear markets wiped them all out either before or shortly after the business expansion was over (Table 2.85).

Since the stock market crash of October 1987, I have frequently noted that dividend yields of less than 3 percent for the DJIA and the S&P composite stock price index have been rather ephemeral. From 1988 through the first half of 1991, there were 30 new historic highs for the S&P stock price index (Table 3.32). All of these new highs can be justified on the basis of dividend increases rather than a return to very low yields. While it is always hazardous to predict what might happen to the stock market, you should at least be aware of buy and sell signals that are so well known as to possibly become a barrier seldom, if ever, breached. If the dividend yield associated with representative stock market averages is not pushed below 3 percent, stock market crashes of 19 percent or more will be less justified. Better knowledge about how the stock market has behaved, in other words, might alter its future behavior (Table 1.04).

THE ECONOMIC ACTIVITY CONSTRAINT ON DIVIDEND GROWTH

Before the stock market crash of 1929, the growth of dividends for the S&P index and the growth of economic activity as measured by changes in nominal GNP bore little relationship to one another. Since 1929, the dividend growth rate has been consistently less than the growth of GNP in current dollars from decade to decade (Table 1.05). With the computer industry approaching a condition of saturation and with many large industrial corporations facing formidable competition from foreign producers, this type of constraint on the growth of dividends will likely continue in the 1990s.

The Federal Reserve, after tipping the U.S. economy into two recessions in less than two years in the early 1980s, kept year-to-year inflation rates around 4.1 percent or less during the 92-month business expansion from November 1982 to July 1990 (Table 2.12). Assuming that policy will continue, and that the growth rate for real GNP will recover to the 2.6 percent average rate prevailing from 1979 to 1989 (an optimistic assumption that is not supported by the Okun law relationship in Table 2.05), the average growth rate for nominal GNP in the 1990s should not exceed 6.7 percent. This would suggest that the dividend growth rate for the S&P index will not recover to the 6.9 percent rate experienced from 1981 to 1990. My own guess, in any event, is that the 10.6 percent projected return for the current business expansion in column (5) of Table 1.04 overestimates the actual return. Since the actual return during the first seven months of 1991 greatly exceeded the projected return, my advice to stock market enthusiasts is to proceed with caution (Table 1.05).

THE S&P RECORD DURING PRESIDENTIAL ELECTION YEARS

The financial returns associated with the S&P stock price index were usually better in presidential election years than in post election years from 1928 to 1981.

Hope, it would seem, does spring eternal. To find a negative return for the S&P index associated with a presidential election year you must go all the way back to the turmoil of the Great Depression of the 1930s and the dark days preceding U.S. entry into World War II (Table 1.06). The superior returns in election years were often facilitated by monetary growth rates in excess of those allowed during post election years (Table 1.77). Whether this type of support for "a political business cycle" will continue is one of the more interesting questions to be answered in 1992 and 1993.

ENDNOTES

1. Kajal Lahiri and Geoffrey Moore, *Leading Economic Indicators: New Approaches and Forecasting Records* (New York: Cambridge University Press, 1991) pp. 63–89.

2. Myron Gordon, *The Investment, Financing and Valuation of the Corporation* (Homewood, Ill.: Richard D. Irwin, Inc., 1962), Chapter 4.

CHAPTER 4

THE COMMERCE DEPARTMENT'S COMPOSITE INDEXES

In this section of the almanac, we will review the history of business expansions and contractions since 1854 and the success of the Commerce Department's composite indexes of cyclical indicators in identifying peaks and troughs in business activity since 1947. In the post-1947 period, negative and near-zero U.S. economic growth rates have been synonymous with weak indicators and oil price shocks of varying intensity.

In recent years interest has revived in the cyclical indicators pioneered by the National Bureau of Economic Research (NBER) in the 1920s and 30s, taken over by the Commerce Department's Bureau of Economic Analysis (BEA) in the 1960s, and finally integrated into its *Survey of Current Business* (*SCB*) in April 1990. A three-digit numbering system has been used to update the tables; the first two digits are identical to the partitioning system in the yellow pages of the business cycle indicators section of the *SCB*.[1]

BUSINESS CYCLE EXPANSIONS AND CONTRACTIONS, 1854–90

Wesley Mitchell, one of the founders of the NBER, helped to establish a workable definition of business cycles, which was rephrased by Burns and Mitchell in 1946 as follows:

> Business cycles are a type of fluctuation found in the aggregate economic activity of nations that organize their work mainly in business enterprises: a cycle consists of expansions occurring at about the same time in many economic activities, followed by similarly general recessions, contractions and revivals that merge into the expansion phase of the next cycle; this sequence of changes is recurrent but not periodic. In duration business cycles vary from more than a year to ten or twelve years; they are not divisible into

shorter cycles of similar character with amplitudes approximating their own (quoted in the introduction to *Leading Economic Indicators* by Lahiri and Moore 1991).

Without a doubt economic recessions are occurring with less frequency and are of shorter duration than they used to be. From June 1857 to October 1945, the United States experienced 22 economic recessions with an average duration of almost 21 months. In the post–World War II period no recession has persisted that long. The average duration for the eight recessions from 1947 to 1982 is only 11 months or about 45 percent shorter than the average from 1857–1945.

The longest recorded recession lasted 65 months from October 1873 to March 1879. The next longest persisted for 43 months from August 1929 to March 1933. In the post-Keynesian era, the two longest business contractions were from November 1973 to March 1975 and from July 1981 to November 1982.

In contrast, periods of economic expansion are lasting longer. The eight business upturns from October 1949 to July 1990 have lasted an average of 51.5 months, compared to an average of only 29.3 months for the 23 business expansions occurring from December 1854 to November 1948. The 92-month business expansion from December 1982 to July 1990 has been exceeded only by the 106-month expansion from February 1961 to December 1969 (which may have been extended by the Vietnam War) (Table 1.11).

Dating Business Peaks and Troughs

The Federal Reserve's index of industrial production and BEA's composite index of four coincident indicators (often dominated by wide fluctuations in industrial activity) do a good job of explaining NBER's recessionary troughs from 1949 to 1982. The dating of business peaks, however, is shrouded in greater mystery; neither the index of industrial production nor the composite index of four coincident indicators does a good job. Industrial production peaked from 8 months in advance—to two months behind—NBER's official business peaks. In seven of the last nine recessions, the coincident indicators led in business peaks from one to eight months.

The dating of these peaks may have been influenced by the fact that researchers at the National Bureau of Economic Research invented national income and product accounting at about the same time that cyclical indicators were being studied. In any event, the cyclical peaks in personal income expressed in 1982 dollars have been the best single predictor of business peaks from 1947 to 1990. They have correctly dated three of the last four peaks and were only late by one month in identifying the short-lived recession that got underway in January 1980. (It should be noted that personal income contains some cyclically sensitive transfer payments that moderate declines and usually cause an upturn before a trough in industrial production.)

The *Blue Chip Economic Indicators* newsletter and public opinion polls appear to have preempted NBER's traditional role of announcing an economic recession. Turning points not associated with a particular time series make it unclear how to best measure the severity of a recession or calculate the time to a full recovery. They also divert public attention from the payroll and personal income recessions that hurt people directly. In other sections of this almanac, we will examine cyclical expansions and contractions in these and other indicators of interest to investors and economy watchers (Table 1.12).

LOOKING AT THE INDEXES

In January 1989 the Commerce Department's composite index of leading economic indicators was revised for the 12th time since its release in November 1968.[2] Of the 12 components in the original index only three (the average workweek in manufacturing, residential building permits, and stock prices) have survived virtually intact. The other components of the index of leading indicators are: average weekly initial claims for unemployment insurance (inverted), manufacturers' new orders in 1982 dollars for consumer goods and materials industries, vendor performance (the proportion of surveyed firms reporting slower deliveries), contracts and orders for plant and equipment in 1982 dollars, changes in manufacturers' unfilled orders in 1982 dollars for durable goods industries, changes in sensitive materials prices, the money supply M2, in 1982 dollars, and the University of Michigan's consumer expectations index. The behavior of some of these components is so irregular that the almanac won't even consider them.

The index of leading indicators has several weaknesses. The industrial sector heavily influences it, for example. Thanks to rising exports, industrial production did not peak until two months after the July 1990 peak in personal income (expressed in 1982 dollars). This unusual strength caused the composite index of 11 leading indicators to peak at about the same time as personal income, providing no warning of an impending recession. Since this could happen again in a world where industrial production has become more globalized, economy watchers should better understand the components of the index that are not so sensitive to rising exports.

Another weakness is the propensity to predict recessions that do not occur. Since 1947 the revised index has declined by 2.5 percent or more on 14 occasions, but there have been only nine recessions. To be confident that the economy either was—or soon would be—in a recession, you would have to be certain the United States was not involved in a war (see the two lead times identified with an asterisk in Table 1.13) and only consider cases in which the cumulative index declined by 3.3 percent or more. In five of these cases (presented in the last column of Table 1.13 and showing a zero or negative adjusted lead time) a recession would be unidentifiable until shortly after it had begun. The index of leading indicators, in other words, is more nearly a *coincident* indicator if you adjust it to account for the cumulative decline in the index necessary to avoid large numbers of incorrect forecasts[1] (Table 1.13).

The Index of Coincident Indicators

It is hard to improve upon the index of leading indicators if one's goal is the identification of business peaks at or near their occurrence. Simply compare its adjusted lead times to some adjusted lag times for the composite index of four coincident indicators—the number of employees on nonagricultural payrolls, personal income less transfer payments in 1982 dollars, the Federal Reserve's index of industrial production, and manufacturing and trade sales expressed in 1982 dollars.

To be confident that an official recession was taking place, the composite index of coincident indicators had to decline at least 4.7 percent. The adjusted lag times for such a decline range from only three months for the 1957–58 recession to eleven months for the 1973–75 recession. In none of these cases can the index of coincident indicators identify a recession as quickly as the index of leading economic indicators (see last column of Table 1.13). The index of coincident indicators, however, can confirm that the economy is in a recession, if it has declined by 4.7 percent, and help explain, in restrospect, the recessionary troughs dated by the NBER (Table 1.12). After two consecutive increases in the index of coincident indicators (Table 1.94), an economic recovery is usually underway. (See Table 1.14.)

The Index of Lagging Indicators

The Commerce Department's composite index of seven lagging indicators is most useful at identifying business troughs. The components of this index are: the average duration of unemployment (inverted), the ratio of manufacturing and trade inventories to sales (in 1982 dollars), the change in the index of labor cost per unit of output in manufacturing, the average prime rate charged by banks, commercial and industrial loans outstanding (in 1982 dollars), the ratio of consumer installment credit outstanding to personal income, and the change in the consumer price index for services.

When this index experiences a cumulative decline of 3.7 percent or more, the U.S. economy is usually near a recessionary trough. (See the last column of Table 1.15.)

A large increase in the composite index of leading economic indicators during a recession may also help identify recessionary troughs. In five cases since 1947, a one-month increase of more than 1 percent in the leading indicators occurred immediately after a recessionary trough in industrial production. In three cases, industrial production bottomed out from one to three months after such an increase, and in only one case did the recession persist for much longer.

That exception occurred in February 1982 when the Board of Governors of the Federal Reserve, in a determined effort to end the specter of double-digit inflation, allowed the average yield on new three-month Treasury bills to surge from less than 11 percent in December 1981 to 13.78 percent. The rather unprecedented interest-rate surge during a recession caused stock prices to tumble and business enterprises to almost steadily reduce their orders for new plant and equipment until August 1982. At that point, easier credit set the stage for a great bull market and the longest peacetime expansion of the U.S. economy in the history of business cycle analysis. (See Table 1.16.)

IDENTIFYING VERY POOR GROWTH YEARS
BEFORE THEY OCCUR

In his 1988 assessment of the accuracy of macroeconomic forecasts, McNees notes, "In contrast to the results frequently obtained for auction market financial variables (such as interest rates, exchange rates, or stock prices), the evidence suggests that 'experts' do predict important macro-economic variables (like real GNP growth and the inflation rate) more accurately than extrapolative, statistical models (such as the 'random walk' or ARIMA models)."

The evidence to support this conclusion is most impressive in predictions of the year-to-year percentage changes in real GNP. From 1969 to 1989 the average absolute forecasting error for the median forecast from the NBER/ASA business outlook survey was less than half as large as the forecasting errors for both the long-term growth rate and the more recent four-quarter growth rate for real GNP.

While the overall record of business economists is quite impressive, their forecasting errors have tended to be exceptionally large during those years when real GNP dropped (1970, 1974, 1975, 1980, and 1982). The mean absolute error (MAE) in these years is 1.9 percentage points and can be compared to an MAE of only .6 percentage points for the 16 years of expanding economic activity.

In many respects, near zero or negative growth years are the most interesting. Since 1948, the four best years to have owned a portfolio of stocks resembling the S&P composite stock index (1954, 1958, 1975, and 1980) have been no-growth years. The worst year to have owned stocks (1974) was also a no-growth year. But that may have been because of an unusual combination of events such as the four-fold increase in the price of OPEC oil in January 1974, the lifting of most wage and price controls in April, and a tendency then (but now discredited) for financial analysts to discount corporate earnings and dividends with a nominal rather than a real rate of interest.

Since missing a very poor growth year might be both costly and embarrassing, specialized tests must be used to determine whether economic forecasts are in the right ball park. All of the near zero-or-negative growth rates for real GNP can be identified if the December-to-December, June-to-December, and September-to-December declines in the revised index of 11 leading economic indicators are all equal to 1.0 percent or more. (See those growth rates identified with a double asterisk in column 4 of Table 1.17.)

This forecasting rule would have incorrectly predicted a very poor growth year after the credit crunch of 1966, which occurred during the escalation phase of the Vietnam War. Since the financial return for the S&P index was a very respectable 23.7 percent in 1967, however, this forecasting error is not a very serious matter from a financial point of view. You can also verify that the financial returns associated with the S&P index have been positive in any year following a decline in the index of leading economic indicators of 1.9 percent or more on either a December-to-December basis, a June-to-December basis, or a September-to-December basis (Table 1.17).

Very Poor Growth Years Following Oil Price Shocks

Crude oil prices were once included in a component of the Commerce Department's index of leading economic indicators called the *change in sensitive material prices*. They have since been deleted from that series because they can no longer be relied on to turn down before the composite index of coincident indicators. All of the eight very poor growth years for the U.S. economy from 1948 to 1989, however, were preceded by a year-to-year increase in the average first purchase price of domestic crude oil of 5 percent or more.

Since 1947, the U.S. economy has been able to absorb a large increase in the price of crude oil without getting bogged down or remaining in an economic recession in only a few years. They have always occurred when the economy was operating at a condition of less than full employment and the revised index of 11 leading economic indicators was increasing at a modest rate. Every year when crude oil prices increased by more than 5 percent and the index of leading indicators declined by at least 1 percent has been followed by a very poor growth year for the U.S. economy.

The importance of how complementary these two series are is shown by the fact that there have been six years (1951, 1956, 1960, 1966, 1970, and 1984) when the index of leading economic indicators declined by more than 1 percent and real GNP actually increased in the following year.

While higher oil prices may not be the cause of economic recessions, they can lead to restrictive monetary policies that will help to tip the economy into a recession. Except for 1953 (when the consumer price index was still increasing at a modest .7 percent annual rate) and 1971 and 1976 (when the U.S. economy was beginning to recover from economic recessions), the Federal Reserve has not allowed the conventional money supply M1 to increase as rapidly as the consumer price index when crude oil prices were increasing at an average rate of 5 percent or more. It should also be noted that, if the economy was not already in an economic recession, the Fed has often resisted the inflationary effect of large increases in crude oil prices by allowing short-term interest rates to rise at a very rapid rate (Table 1.18).

ENDNOTES

1. Current and and historical data for the series shown in the C-pages of the *SCB* are also available on printouts, diskettes, and the Commerce Department's Economic Bulletin Board. For more information about their timely availability, you can write to the Statistical Indicators Branch, Business Outlook Division (BE-52), Bureau of Economic Analysis, U. S. Department of Commerce, Washington, D. C. 20230.

2. Marie Hertzberg and Barry Beckman, "Business Cycle Indicators: Revised Composite Indexes," *Survey of Current Business*, January 1989, pp. 23–28.

CHAPTER 5

EMPLOYMENT AND UNEMPLOYMENT

The labor market is such a large part of the U.S. economy that no one can afford to ignore it. More than 75 percent of the net domestic product generated by nonfinancial corporations in 1990 was used to compensate employees. Despite its importance, extracting useful predictions from employment and unemployment statistics is not easy. But when you investigate what happens in the labor market, you will find it a better predictor of what will happen in the stock market than the economy.

THE AVERAGE WEEKLY HOURS OF PRODUCTION WORKERS IN MANUFACTURING

One of the problems with the index of leading indicators is that it contains too many components with very short or otherwise unreliable lead times. The average weekly hours of nonsupervisory workers in manufacturing provide good examples of an enduring component of the index that has always peaked out in advance of an economic recession but has sometimes not declined enough to provide a reliable warning of its occurrence.

In the 1947–89 period, you can correctly identify all of the NBER recessions by considering fluctuations of 1.1 hours or more in this series. The adjusted lead times for this decline percentage, however, range from a high of nine months for the 1980 recession to a lag of six months for the 1981–82 recession—even if you ignore the extraordinarily long lead times of 15 and 34 months for the 1.1 hour work week declines preceding the recessions following the Korean and Vietnam Wars. During the mild recession of 1990–91, U.S. exports pulled the economy along so strongly that weekly manufacturing hours only declined by one hour.

At the business peaks identified by the National Bureau of Economic Research, the cyclical work week declines in manufacturing have varied from only 0.2 hours for the 1973–75 recession to a decline of 1.2 hours for the 1957–58 recession.

While average weekly hours are generally not reliable predictors of economic recessions, there is at least one curious point to note in connection with Table 1.20. Apart from cyclical variations, no evidence supports a downward trend in the average number of hours worked in manufacturing. The November 1988 peak of 41.2 hours is exceeded only by the February 1966 peak when the Vietnam War was escalating rapidly. Factory automation may have reduced the need for production workers but not the hours of those workers employed during periods of economic prosperity.

The Changing Composition of the Employed Labor Force

The share of the employed labor force in agriculture has trended down from 13.8 percent in 1947 to only 2.7 percent in 1990. Higher energy prices caused the number of persons employed in mining to increase faster than total employment during the 1970s. By 1990, when about half of the oil consumed in the United States was imported, the share of employed labor in mining was only about a third of what it was in 1947, when the United States was almost completely self-sufficient in energy. Because labor productivity in manufacturing improved substantially, the share of employment in this industry declined by 11 percentage points from 1947 to 1990. The shrinking share of the labor force employed in the volatile manufacturing sector has made the U.S. economy less vulnerable to severe employment recessions (Table 1.21).

Employees on Nonagricultural Payrolls

The most encouraging aspect in the payroll data in Table 1.22 is that periods of employment expansion seem to be getting longer. The three expansions from October 1949 to April 1960 only lasted 33 months on average. In contrast, the five expansions since February 1961 have lasted twice as long on average—63 months. The 90-month expansion from December 1982 to June 1990 is the longest peacetime expansion on record, and was only exceeded by the 109-month expansion from February 1961 to March 1970. (That upturn may have been prolonged by the procurement increases associated with the Vietnam War and the gradual buildup of U.S. military forces preceding that war.)

The length of employment recessions in Table 1.22 has ranged from only 4 months for the recession of 1980 to 17 months for the 1981–82 recession. The employment decline percentages are inversely related to the peak dates and positively related to the length of the employment recessions. While employment recessions are milder than they used to be, no evidence supports the hypothesis that it takes less time for total payroll employment to recover from a recession to a new historic high.

Job losses during employment recessions have been disproportionately concentrated in manufacturing, mining, and construction—the three components of the Labor Department's time series on employees in goods-producing industries. Employment in some service-related industries has continued to increase during economic recessions.

With total employment in service-related industries almost four times as great as total employment in goods-producing industries, it is unreasonable to expect much improvement in overall labor productivity unless greater efficiency can be achieved outside of the nation's factories. If improvements in white-collar efficiency are delayed until the economy is in a recession, future recessions might turn out to be painfully long. (See Table 1.23.)

Some Recovery Indicators for Payroll Employment

Those recessions that have begun with at least one monthly decline in payroll employment of .4 percent in the first three months of the recession have ended much sooner, on the average, than those cases in which the initial declines were smaller (see Table 1.24). Employment recessions have also been significantly shorter when the peak in industrial production occurred at least three months before the monthly peak in non-agricultural employment (see Table 1.25). The data in these two tables support the hypothesis that policy makers will ignore an employment recession unless it is rather precipitous or has been confirmed by a prolonged decline in industrial activity. The recession of 1990–91 may have been an exception, however, since the peak in the yield on 91-day Treasury bills occurred 15 months before the June 1990 peak in payroll employment. The data presented in summary Table 1.93 suggest that this might have helped to shorten the employment recession more than would be indicated by Tables 1.24 and 1.25 but as of mid-1991 it was still too early to tell.

SOME OTHER WAYS TO MEASURE ECONOMIC RECESSIONS

While it may be partly a coincidence, you cannot help but be impressed by the fact that the three shortest employment recessions since 1947 have been associated with high inflation rates. The Federal Reserve may have been more concerned with keeping the unemployment rate from soaring upward than in bringing down the inflation rate. (See the last two columns of Table 1.26.)

The six-month decline in industrial production from September 1990 to March 1991 was much shorter than any of the other industrial recessions experienced in the post-1947 period.

The Civilian Unemployment Rate

A cumulative increase in the civilian unemployment rate amounting to .6 percentage points or more used to be a fairly reliable predictor of an impending recession. During the last five recessions, however, this signal has either been coincident with the NBER business peak or has lagged somewhat behind the peak. Increases in the civilian unemployment rate during the eight recessions from 1947 to 1988 ranged from a low of 2.2 percentage points for the short-lived recession of 1980 to a high of 4.5 percentage points for the 1948–49 recession. The highest unemployment rate in the post–World War II period was 10.8 percent for December 1982 and can be compared to an average unemployment rate of 24.9 percent for all of 1933 (Table 1.27).

Unemployment and the Stock Market

In the 1947–89 period, a portfolio like the S&P composite stock price index purchased at the end of the month after a cumulative increase in the civilian unemployment rate equal to .9 percentage points or more (for the preceding month) would have appreciated at least 14.8 percent one year later. In half of these recessionary cases, you would have acquired the S&P index after its bear market trough and in the other four cases it would have been better to wait for a cumulative increase in the unemployment rate in the 1.2 to 1.8 percentage point range. Over the .9 to 1.8 range there was remarkably little difference in the average following-year price appreciation associated with the S&P index.

The advantage in buying stock after an increase in the unemployment rate of only .9 percentage points is that the second-year price appreciation has been better, on the average, than for larger increases in the unemployment rate. The second-year price appreciation of 9.1 percent, however, was only about one third as great, on the average, as the first-year appreciation of 26.4 percent.

An investor following the .9 percentage point rule before the January 1991 upward seasonal revision in the initial 5.0 percent unemployment rate for March 1989 to 5.1 percent could have benefited from the 5.9 percent unemployment rate for November 1990 by acquiring a no-load index fund at the end of December when the S&P index closed at 330.22. The revised statistic for the March 1989 unemployment rate (reported in Table 1.27 and used as a more conservative reference point in Table 1.28) delays the purchase signal to the end of January 1991 when the S&P index had increased to 343.91. The recessionary trough for the S&P index occurred way back on October 11, 1990, when it closed at a value of 295.46.

Institutional investors are so aware of the extraordinary gains from acquiring stock during a recession that others may want to invest in equities even before convincing evidence of a recession exists. Of course, there must also be a bear market and the Federal Reserve must not be determined to keep the economy in a recession for a prolonged period of time to reduce inflation.

Unemployment Insurance Claims

Inverted unemployment insurance claims are a relatively new and somewhat controversial component of the Commerce Department's index of 11 leading economic indicators. There have been several occasions when this indicator did not turn up before a recessionary trough and one occasion (July 1981) when it did not turn down before a business peak.

When average weekly initial claims for unemployment insurance have experienced a recessionary increase of 150,000 claims or more, however, the U.S. economy has always been bogged down in a recession. During the last four economic recessions, moreover, this indicator confirmed the existence of a recession before the index of coincident indicators declined by 4.7 percent. It therefore merits some attention as an early bad news confirmation signal (Table 1.29).

CHAPTER 6

PRODUCTION AND INCOME

To anticipate the best time to purchase stocks, investors should understand a basic tenet of macroeconomics, called the *accelerator principle*. It states that real GNP must grow at a fairly rapid rate just to keep investment from falling and boomeranging on income, employment, stock prices, and other economic indicators. If the economy falls into recession, the investor should be ready to buy stock.

Economic recessions come in all shapes and sizes. Recessionary declines in real GNP in 1982 dollars have ranged in severity from only 1 percent for the 1960 recession to a high of 4.3 percent for the 1973–75 recession. The only major component of real GNP that has consistently declined during post-1947 recessions is gross private domestic investment (GPDI). The associated decline in GPDI has always been at least 2.5 times as severe as the decline in real GNP. The volatility of investment and its sensitivity to declines in real GNP led John Maynard Keynes to develop a theory of income determination that is based, in part, on this multiplier effect. Others, following Keynes, have invented a theory of investment behavior that emphasizes an accelerator principle (Table 1.30).

AN INCOME EXPENDITURE MULTIPLIER MODEL

While most large-scale econometric forecasting models are basically Keynesian in character, there has been a notable reluctance on the part of textbook writers to confront economic theory with fact. Part of the reason may be related to how difficult it is to establish plausible direct multiplier relationships between aggregate income and the two most important fiscal policy variables, government spending and taxes. The absence of easily verified multipliers in the early post–World War II period led Milton Friedman to conclude in the words of Paul Samuelson, "that fiscal policy per se has essentially no predictable effect of any significance on the prospects for inflation or deflation, for high employment or mass unemployment."

Keynesian economics is basically disequilibrium or depressionary economics. Resulting theories are less reliable when the economy is in a period of reasonably full employment. The analyst can use production possibility curves trading off in theory, between guns and butter to seriously question the notion of sizeable multiplier effects for government spending. Three economic recessions in less than one decade, the monetary revolution of 1979, and the Economic Recovery Tax Act of 1981, however, have made it easier to explain changes in the national income and product accounts on the basis of a rather simple Keynesian type of multiplier model.[1]

The calculations in column (6) of Table 1.31 can be derived from a multiplier model that assumes personal consumption will be equal to 50 percent of disposable income (defined as nominal GNP minus net taxes minus net imports) plus a variable percentage of nominal GNP in the preceding year.

This formulation of the consumption function allows the derivation of a multiplier equation showing the possible impact of large trade and government budget deficits on the economy. Since the recession of 1953–54, the government deficit in the national income and product accounts has increased fairly dramatically during a recessionary trough, helping to offset both the direct and indirect effects of a decline in gross private domestic investment.

The residual propensity of consumers and business enterprises to spend out of the previous year's GNP in column (6) was remarkably stable from 1953 to 1986. During this period, the following year financial returns for the S&P stock price index were always positive whenever this residual was less than 50 percent of the previous year's GNP. Increases in the government deficit that help to offset weak spending will then, sometimes signal a good time to own common stock (Table 1.31).

An Aggregate Accelerator Model

One of the great ideas in macroeconomics is the notion of an accelerator principle. Table 1.32 illustrates that the year-to-year growth in real gross private fixed domestic investment has often been about equal to three times the growth rate for real GNP minus 6 percentage points. This relationship implies that real GNP must increase by about 2 percent just to keep private investment from falling and negatively affecting economic growth.

This accelerator relationship helps to explain why economic recessions often follow slow growth rates for real GNP. The instability of the GNP growth rate in the 0 to 2.0 percent range makes it very difficult for the Federal Reserve to effectively fight inflation without pushing the economy into a recession.

When the actual growth of real fixed investment has been at least 2.2 percentage points greater than the expected increase predicted by the accelerator model, the following year returns for the S&P index have all been positive, at least in the years from 1948 to 1991. The following year financial returns have also been positive after a decline in real GNP expressed in 1982 dollars of minus .3 percentage points or more (Table 1.32).

Recessionary Declines in Personal Income

The 1990–91 recession was the third worst recession in the post–1947 period as far as personal income less transfer payments is concerned. The harm done to consuming power is even more disturbing when the associated inflation-adjusted decline in personal income with transfer payments is considered. A smaller proportion of the labor force, it would seem, is now eligible for unemployment insurance than was the case in the 1970s and early 80s. This fraying of the safety net is disturbing since it might help to prolong future recessions (Table 1.33).

Industrial Production

About the middle of each month, the Board of Governors of the Federal Reserve releases its monthly index of industrial production for the preceding month. This index, which measures output in manufacturing, mining, and utilities, is among the most watched of all business statistics. Since April 1960, the U.S. economy has never been able to avoid a recession after a cumulative decline of 2 percent or more in the industrial production index.

Industrial production usually peaks out before the rest of the economy. The economic recession of 1990–91, however, was unusual in that industrial production (thanks to a weak dollar and a strong demand for some exports) did not decline until four months after the June employment peak. Recessionary declines in industrial production have ranged from a low of 5.1 percent for the 1990–91 recession to a high 14.8 percent for the 1973–75 recession. Troughs in industrial production help identify the recessionary troughs dated by the National Bureau of Economic Research (Table 1.12). A recovery from an NBER recession is usually in progress after two consecutive monthly increases in the industrial production index (Table 1.94). See Table 1.34.

Declines in Durable Manufactures and the Stock Market

One of the more interesting ways to take advantage of economic recessions is to buy a portfolio similar to the S&P index at the end of those years in which the December-to-December value of the durable manufactures component of the index of industrial production has declined by two percent or more. Since 1947, the following year financial returns for the S&P index have (so far) always been in the double-digit range (Table 1.35).

Molnar's Recessionary Buy Signal

David Molnar, an undergraduate in my economic and financial modeling course, has proposed another interesting rule for trying to take advantage of economic recessions. In his approach, the investor purchases the S&P index one month after a recessionary decline of 6 percent or more in total wages and salaries in mining, manufacturing, and construction, adjusted for inflation. Price appreciation in the following year has so far always been of double-digit proportions (Table 1.36).

ENDNOTE

1. Edward Renshaw, "A Keynesian View of the U. S. Budget and Trade Deficits," *Public Finance* 45, No. 30, pp. 440–48.

CHAPTER 7

INDEXES OF CONSUMER ATTITUDES

Some analysts have claimed that changes in consumer attitudes and expectations are better predictors of what will happen to the economy than professional economists and all of their assorted indicators. But the actions of consumers are about as difficult to interpret as what happens in the stock market.

THE MICHIGAN INDEX OF CONSUMER EXPECTATIONS

In January 1989 the University of Michigan's index of consumer expectations (which focuses on expected economic changes) was included in the components of the Commerce Department's index of leading economic indicators. It is rather fortunate that the behavior of consumers is not always influenced by their expectations. Since February 1953, while there have only been 8 recessions, the index of consumer expectations has suffered 18 cumulative declines of 7 percentage points or more.

In fact, consumer expectations are more reactive than predictive. Many of the same variables and developments that propel the stock market probably influence consumers. From 1953 to 1990 very large declines in the consumer expectations index (amounting to 19 percent or more) were associated with bear markets (Table 1.40).

Very Poor Growth Years and the Michigan Index of Consumer Sentiment

The index of consumer sentiment has two major components: a component reflecting consumers' assessments of current economic conditions and a component now included in the Commerce Department's index of leading economic indicators that focuses on expected economic changes.

While the index of consumer sentiment is not a very reliable predictor of economic activity, it can help differentiate between very poor and more satisfactory growth rates for real GNP if increases in unemployment insurance claims or a decline in housing starts also signal a recession. The financial returns associated with the S&P stock price index have so far been positive in the year after a November-to-November increase in unemployment insurance claims of 16 percent or more (Table 1.41).

CHAPTER 8

RESIDENTIAL CONSTRUCTION AND INVESTMENT

Since World War II difficulties in the residential housing industry have been leading predictors of an economic recession.

RESIDENTIAL BUILDING PERMITS

The Commerce Department's index of new private housing units authorized by local building permits (1967 = 100) is the only component of the leading economic indicators that has declined consistently before the nine post–World War II economic recessions. At each business peak, the number of building permits has been down at least 20 percent from its cyclical high. At only one time—during the Vietnam build-up year of 1966—did building permits decline by more than 20 percent and then recover to a new cyclical high before the occurrence of another recession.

The main problem with using building permits to forecast business recessions is their variable lead times. The lead times have ranged from only 10 months before the 1981–82 recession to 78 months for the 1990–91 recession. I have found that the forecaster can alleviate the problem by using a 20 percent decline in the permit index to signal a recession if the permit peak was less than 150 and a decline of 35 percent if the permit peak was over 150. All of the adjusted lead times in the last column of Table 1.50 are either zero or positive and, in most cases, they are highly coincident with the actual peak in business activity.

HOUSING STARTS

There have been dramatic fluctuations in the number of new housing units started in the United States for more than a century. Since 1947 housing starts have usually fallen by more than 40 percent before a recession was over. Since the January 1969 peak in housing starts, the U.S. economy has either been in a recession or very close to a recession once the number of starts declined to 1,350,000 units for two months in a row (Table 1.51).

CHAPTER 9

INVENTORY INVESTMENT

In trying to predict the duration of a recession, one should watch the behavior of business inventories.

INVENTORY RECESSIONS

Economic recessions can sometimes be triggered by an oversupply of business inventory. The subsequent reductions in inventory accounted for more than 40 percent of the real GNP decline in each of the nine recessions since 1947. In the recessions of 1948 and 1960, all of the decline in real GNP can be attributed to a drop in inventory investment to negative levels.

Higher real rates of interest associated with a tighter monetary policy have caused business enterprises to adopt new inventory strategies, such as 'just-in-time' delivery, to minimize the inventory of parts and materials. Another development in maintaining acceptable levels is the willingness of automobile manufacturers and other producers of durable goods to use rebates and discounts to reduce excess inventory. This type of marketing appears to have restored a more appropriate balance between inventory and sales (Table 1.60).

The Duration of Inventory Recessions

Fluctuations in business inventories have enjoyed a central role in the theory of business cycles ever since *The General Theory of Employment, Interest and Money* by John Maynard Keynes was published in 1936 (Metzler 1947). In Table 1.61 post-1947 recessions are rank ordered on the basis of the four-quarter change in business inventories in 1982 dollars ending with the first decline quarter after a recessionary peak in business activity. When the cumulative buildup of inventory has been less than $20 billion, the recessions in real GNP have (so far) lasted only one or two quarters. When the inventory buildup has exceeded $100 billion, on the other hand, the recessions have lasted five quarters.

Five of the eight recessions from 1947 to 1989 have "double bottoms" related to one-quarter "up-ticks" in GNP (using 1982 dollars) in the midst of a more prolonged decline in real GNP. The upticks in GNP can largely be explained by less severe reductions in inventory investment in the uptick quarter than in the preceding quarter. For the three cases where the four-quarter change in business inventory was less than $40 billion, there are no double bottoms. For the five cases where the four-quarter change in inventory was greater than $40 billion, the recessions all have double bottoms. The implication is that the recession of 1990–91 is not likely to be characterized by a "double bottom" (Table 1.61).

CHAPTER 10

STOCK PRICES AND ECONOMIC ACTIVITY

The stock market is a more reliable predictor of economic recoveries than peaks in business activity.

STOCK MARKET CRASHES IN PERSPECTIVE

On October 16, 1987, after a loss of more than 9 percent in the preceding eight trading days, the S&P composite stock price index lost another 5 percent of its value and closed more than 16 percent below the historic high of 336.77, achieved on August 25, 1987. This was the fastest 16 percent decline in the S&P index from a new historic high since it was first compiled on a daily basis in 1928. The speed of this decline helps explain the panic of October 19, when the index plunged more than 20 percent in a single trading session. It also explains why the stock market is now perceived—unjustly—to be more unstable than it used to be.

The crash of 1987 has to be put in historic context. While it made headlines across the nation and around the world, it was not the worst bear market since World War II. If you define a "crash" as a downward plunge of 10 percent or more in the average monthly values for the S&P composite stock price index, 1987 was the *third* worst bear market since World War II and only the 15th most severe bear market since the S&P index was extended back to the 1870s by the Cowles Commission. (See Table 1.70.)

If anything, the stock market has become more rather than less, stable. In the 12 decades since the Civil War, only the 1950s and 1980s stand out as having no stock market peak followed by a bear market with a decline greater than the 26.8 percent drop in the S&P index after the August 1987 peak.

Moreover, prolonged bull markets are often followed by bear markets of uncomfortable severity. The 61-month expansion in stock prices from July 1982 to August 1987 is exceeded only by the all-time great bull market of the 1920s, which persisted for 71 months without a contraction in monthly average stock prices of 10 percent or more. For the five bull markets persisting for 43 months or more, the crash magnitudes that followed ranged from 17.3 to 35.6 percent, with an average of 27.4 percent—only slightly greater than the 1987 drop in stock prices.

During the Great Depression of the 1930s, there were eight crashes in the S&P index, ranging from 15 to 72.8 percent. In all of the other decades since the Civil War, there have been from two to four peaks in the S&P index followed by declines of 10 percent or more. Stock market instability, it would seem, is a well-entrenched phenomenon that investors have always had to cope with.

Recessions accompanied 29 of the 42 crashes in Table 1.70. The other 13 bear markets, including the crash of 1987, occurred in the midst of prosperity. These kinds of crashes tend to be shorter than those associated with recessions. (See those declines identified with a # mark in column 4 of Table 1.70.)

Only three economic recessions since 1873 have not been accompanied by stock market declines of 10 percent or more. Two of these recessions occurred toward the end of World Wars I and II. The only other recession without a stock market crash was from October 1926 to November 1927, during the United States' greatest bull market.

Some Lessons from History

Henry Kaufman has suggested that part of the blame for the crash of October 19, 1987, should be placed on "a failure of market participants either to learn from or remember the lessons of history." He believes that during the euphoria of the spectacular rise in stock prices over the first eight months of 1987, the warnings of low dividend and earning yields on stocks were ignored. "It was assumed that yields would rise along with expected large increases in corporate earnings."

This is good advice. If you were to select one variable besides stock prices upon which to determine whether the stock market is under- or overvalued, you would probably choose the dividends associated with the S&P stock price index. In September 1929, for example, the monthly dividend yield had fallen to 2.92 percent. At 6 of the 14 stock market peaks experienced in the post-1947 period, the dividend yield on the S&P index was under 3.2 percent. Before the four most severe bear markets, the yield had declined to less than 3 percent. (See Table 2.71.)

It should be noted that overvaluation can sometimes persist for a considerable period of time without being corrected by a stock market crash. In both 1964 and 1965 the dividend yield on the S&P index averaged only about 3.0 percent. When low yields are accompanied by a policy of tight money and rising short-term interest rates, however, all the ingredients for a major bear market exist (Table 1.71).

Great Decades to Have Owned Common Stock

Great bull markets and great decades to have owned common stock generally occur when the stock market is substantially undervalued before the advance. Table 1.72 shows end-of-the-decade values for the S&P index and associated dividend yields from 1879 to 1989. In three decades, the S&P index more than doubled in value (the 1920s, 1950s, and the 1980s), and during each the preceding yield on the S&P index exceeded 5 percent.

As of December 1989, the yield on the S&P index had declined to 3.33 percent. If history continues to be a fairly reliable guide to the future, stock prices are not likely to double in the 1990s.

You can verify history with some statistical analysis. If the dividend yield remains constant, stock prices can be expected to increase at the same rate as dividends. From 1981 to 1989 the dividends associated with the S&P index increased at a compound annual rate of 6.6 percent. If they continue to increase at that rate and there is no change in yield, the S&P index can be expected to increase only 89.5 percent during the 1990s. A decline in the dividend growth rate or an increase in the dividend yield would reduce the projected gain.

THE STOCK MARKET AND THE BUSINESS CYCLE

The National Bureau of Economic Research provides some of the most persuasive evidence in support of a longer-run pattern to stock prices. In a massive compendium published in 1961, Geoffrey Moore found that only the net change in the number of operating businesses was a better leading indicator of business cycles.[1] Stock prices were classified as being a leading indicator 31 times, roughly coincident 14 times, and a lagging indicator only 5 times.

The most publicized weakness of stock prices as an indicator is that they predict more economic recessions than actually occur. Table 1.73 uses cumulative reversals amounting to 5.5 percent or more in the monthly average daily closing prices for the S&P composite 500 stock price index to define peaks and troughs in the index. This reversal percentage is the smallest you can use and still eliminate all of the abortive stock market rallies occurring in the midst of recent economic recessions. Once the economy is in a recession and the stock market has recovered 5.5 percent on a monthly average basis, the S&P index has consistently gained at least another 25 percentage points before heading downward by 5.5 percent. (See the gains in column 5 of Table 1.73, marked with a double asterisk.)

Since May 1946, there have been 24 downside reversals and only 9 recessions. Fifteen of these downside reversals occurred in the midst of a business expansion and were followed by an upside reversal of at least 5.5 percent before the economy went into recession. In seven cases, a downside reversal of 5.5 percent was followed by a recession, and in two cases, a reversal of this magnitude did not occur until after the business peaks of January 1980 and July 1991.

Stock Market Declines after Business Peaks

Suppose you could identify business peaks at the end of the month in which they occurred. Should you purchase common stock? The data presented in Table 1.74 show that the S&P index has then proceeded to lose from 3.8 to 35.1 percent of its value on a daily closing value basis before bottoming out during the nine recessions since 1947.

Monthly Lead Times for Stock Prices

While much attention has been paid to the unreliability of stock prices in predicting economic recessions, it is less well appreciated how well the stock market predicts economic recoveries. Ignoring the money supply, M2, which is so trendy as not to have exhibited a distinct trough during some recessions, stock prices are the only component of the index of leading economic indicators consistently leading economic recoveries since World War II. The unadjusted lead times for stock prices fall in a comparatively narrow range of from three to eight months.

In contrast, the unadjusted recovery lead times for the revised index of 11 leading economic indicators range from a low of one month for the 1973–75 recession to a high of 10 months for the 1960–61 and 1981–82 recessions (Table 1.75).

STOCK PRICES AND VERY POOR GROWTH

While the stock market is not a very reliable predictor of economic recessions, it can identify very poor growth years, if other indicators point in the same direction. In Table 1.76, we use a November-to-November decline of .854 or less for residential building permits and December down ratios for stock prices and three other indicators to identify poor growth years. The down ratio is defined as the December value of the indicator expressed as a proportion of its previous cyclical high. A very poor growth year is predicted by a down ratio of .890 or less for the ratio of help-wanted advertising in newspapers to persons unemployed; a ratio of .969 or less for the conventional money supply M1 expressed in 1982 dollars; a ratio of .950 or less for stock prices; and .450 or less for the inverted yield on new 91-day Treasury bills. Perfect discrimination has so far been achieved when three or more of these indicators point in the same direction.

The Stock Market's Reaction to Monetary and Fiscal Policy

Former CEA Chairman Beryl Sprinkel was among the first economists to publicize a positive relationship between changes in the money supply and changes in stock prices.[2] In fact, if you could accurately predict what would happen to the real value of the conventional money supply in a certain year, you could also identify which year would be good to own stocks. Since the beginning of World War II, M1 expressed in 1982 dollars has increased by 1.6 percent or more on a December-to-December basis in 23 years; in each, the financial return for the S&P index was positive. (See those cases marked with a double asterisk in column 4 of Table 1.77.)

In a similar way, when the first differences in the growth rates for the real money supply in column (5) were four percentage points or more, the financial returns have also been positive for the S&P index in the following year. (See the 10 returns in column 6 identified with a hatch mark.)

The stock market crash of October 19, 1987, shifted the attention of Wall Street to Washington, D.C., and quickly became an indictment of the economic policies of the United States and some of its trading partners. While some economists assumed that large trade and budget deficits caused the crash, historical data suggest that the stock market debacle may have more nearly resulted from a rapid *reduction* in the federal deficit rather than an accurate reflection of its unconscionably high level.

Since the beginning of World War II, the financial returns associated with the S&P index have always been positive when the federal budget deficit in the National Income and Product accounts equalled 3.25 percent or more of nominal GNP. This point can be verified by comparing columns (1) and (6) of Table 1.77 for the years 1942–45, 1975, and 1982–87. For the 13 years when the federal budget surplus as a percent of nominal GNP deteriorated by at least one full percentage point, the financial returns for the S&P index are also positive. (See those surpluses or deficits in column (1) that are identified with an asterisk.)

Before the enactment of the Economic Recovery Tax Act of 1981, which slashed tax rates while allowing national defense spending to almost double, most large budget deficits occurred either during wars or economic recessions. Many economists believe large budget deficits in the midst of a recession are stabilizing and help shorten the economic decline.

MONEY AND CREDIT

Martin Zweig, whose stock market newsletter has outperformed 24 other newsletters in the past decade, has developed a complicated set of economic and financial indicators to predict what will happen in the stock market.[3] In his book *Winning on Wall Street*, Zweig's main advice to investors is, "Don't Fight the Fed." The reason is directly tied to the correlation between the money supply and the market.

The Conventional Money Supply

No variable has a more distinguished record in identifying post-World War II recessions than the conventional money supply. M1 expressed in 1982 dollars has turned down at least nine months before each of the last nine recessions, experiencing a cumulative decline of 1.5 percent at least five months before each. Short-term changes in the conventional money supply have been so unpredictable in recent years, however, that the Fed has sometimes refused to establish a target growth rate for M1 (Table 1.80).

M2

Instability in the demand for M1 has caused many economists to focus their attention on broader measures of the money supply. M2, including savings and small time deposits at financial institutions as well as currency and checkable deposits, has been included in the Commerce Department's index of leading economic indicators since 1976. This aggregate was late in identifying the recession of 1957–58 and did not decline in a meaningful way either before or during the recession of 1960–61. A decline of 1.5 percent or more in M2 expressed in 1982 dollars, however, has provided from 3 to 17 months warning for the last five recessions (Table 1.81).

Money and the Bond Market

There is not much doubt that changes in the money supply affect long-term interest rates. A model used by Baumol to explain why the demand for money should be a function of the interest rate presumes that real money balances will be directly proportional to the square root of economic activity and indirectly proportional to the square root of the interest rate.[4] With a little manipulation, you can use this formula to show that the percentage change in long-term interest rates might be about equal to two times the percentage change in the inflation rate plus the percentage change in real GNP minus two times the percentage change in the money supply.

In 85 percent of the time since 1968, this formula has correctly explained the direction of the average change for Moody's high-grade corporate bond index and has sometimes come very close to predicting the magnitude of the actual yield change (Table 1.82).

The Cyclical Behavior of Short-Term Interest Rates

The discount rate on new issues of 91-day Treasury bills has increased at least 70 percent before each of the last nine recessions. The adjusted lead times for this degree of cyclical acceleration have ranged from 8 to 20 months, ignoring the longer lead times associated with the two business expansions prolonged by the Korean and Vietnam wars. This analyst has not discovered a more promising early indicator of a possible recession (Table 1.83).

The Yield on New Issues of High-Grade Corporate Bonds

The yields on new issues of high-grade long-term corporate bonds have so far always increased at least 25 percent from their cyclical lows since 1947. In two cases, though, that degree of cyclical acceleration did not occur until after a peak in business activity.

Corporate bonds have been classified as a lagging indicator at both business peaks and troughs, but the classification does not always hold up. During the 1982–90 business expansion, the yield on new corporate bonds did not reach its cyclical low until February 1987. The Fed then proceeded to tighten credit to the point at which new issue yields quickly moved upward more than 2 percentage points to a very early peak of 10.80 percent in October 1987 (Table 1.84).

Interest Rates and IRA Investors

If long-term interest rates recover enough to remain in the vicinity of 9 percent or more, young people could become millionaires simply by investing $2,000 per year in an IRA account. Enhancing the average return from say 9 to 11 percent would shorten the time required to achieve this objective from 45 to 39 years (Table 1.85).

The Highly Inverted Yield Curve

Interest rate spreads have sometimes helped to predict economic activity.[5] Six of the last nine economic recessions in the United States were preceded by a tight money condition in which the average monthly yield on three-year Treasury securities was at least 4.5 percent greater than the comparable yield on 10-year Treasury bonds for one or more months. The adjusted lead times for this indicator fall in the comparatively narrow range of from three to nine months ignoring the time in which a highly inverted yield curve occurred during the Vietnam War build-up year of 1966.

The lead times for this indicator have been sufficiently uniform to make the inverted yield curve one of the more interesting predictors of stock market crashes. Selling the S&P index after the first monthly inversion of 4.5 percent or more would have enabled an investor to have re-purchased the index during the next bear market at a discount of 13 percent or more on six occasions and at a more modest discount of 3.5 percent in March 1980. The inverted yield curve may have performed poorly at that point partly because of mad speculation in oil stocks following the Iranian revolution and a quick reversal of the Fed's tight money policy after the economy slipped into an unwanted recession in the first half of 1980.

During the 92-month business expansion from November 1982 to July 1990, the Fed never allowed the yield curve to invert enough to signal a recession (Table 1.86).

The Prime Rate

At least one monthly increase in the average prime rate charged by commercial banks of 9.6 percent or more preceded seven of the nine postwar recessions. The adjusted lead times for this recessionary indicator range from 0 to 14 months. The failure of this and some other interest-rate signals to provide a warning for the 1990–91 recession may imply that business expansions can sometimes die of old age rather than be bludgeoned to death by rapidly escalating interest rates (Table 1.87).

THE FED'S RECESSIONARY REACTION FUNCTION

Section 2A of the Federal Reserve Act, as amended, requires the Board of Governors "to promote effectively the goals of maximum employment, stable prices and moderate long-term interest rates." Moreover, in carrying out monetary policy the Fed is to take "account of past and prospective developments in employment, unemployment, production, investment, real income, productivity, international trade and payments and prices."

Robert Black, president of the Federal Reserve Bank of Richmond, has criticized this mandate as too sweeping and unrealistically general, particularly if viewed as a set of short-run objectives. He believes that price stability is the only sensible objective for the Fed to try to achieve with monetary policy.[6]

The evidence suggests, however, that the Fed has paid at least as much attention to the problem of unemployment as inflation. Since the

Fed stopped pegging interest rates in 1951, it has always allowed the discount rate on new issues of 91-day Treasury bills to decline by at least 20 percent during employment recessions (Table 1.88) and has almost always allowed the yield to decline during any year when the unemployment rate increased by more than .1 percentage points. The only exception is 1980 when a brief recession failed to reduce the CPI inflation rate below the double-digit level. (See columns 1 and 4 of Table 1.89.)

Since World War II, however, the Fed's policy with regard to the real, inflation-adjusted return on Treasury bills during employment recessions has varied considerably. The average real rates of return have differed by more than 9 percentage points and have ranged from a negative return of 5.00 percent for the 1974–75 recession to a positive return of 4.18 percent for the 1981–82 recession. From a forecasting point of view, the real rates of return on T-bills are interesting since they help explain the length of recessions. (See also summary Tables 1.92 and 1.93.) The higher the real rate, the longer the recession. The preliminary real rate of 1.14 percent for the 1990–91 recession was second in magnitude only to the extraordinary real rates prevailing during the protracted 17-month recession from July 1981 through December 1982 (Table 1.88).

THE FED'S INFLATIONARY REACTION FUNCTION

The Fed's response to accelerating inflation has varied more than its response to unemployment but is almost as predictable. Except for the 1974 and 1990 recessions, the T-bill rate has been pushed upward whenever the acceleration in the CPI inflation rate amounted to .3 percentage points or more.

For monetary policy to regulate the economy, consumers should increase their saving rate as short-term interest rates rise and decrease it when they fall. In the last 40 years, this sort of response has only occurred about two thirds of the time. (See columns 4 and 5 of Table 1.89.) The unresponsiveness of saving is related in part to the huge federal budget debt and the fact that households now receive far more interest income than that paid out as interest on housing and consumer debt. For those persons with most of their financial assets in savings accounts and money market funds, tight money and the prospect of rising interest rates might presage a consumption boom. In that event the Fed may have to restrict credit and raise interest rates to fight inflation, practically destroy the new housing industry and, in the bargain, risk tipping the economy into an unwanted recession.

Residential building permits and new housing starts, in any event, are the only economic indicators that have consistently declined substantially before each of the last nine economic recessions. (See Tables 1.50 and 1.51.)

In 1952 Nobel Laureate Jan Tinbergen was able to show that, in the absence of wonder drugs that can cure more than one disease and very special interrelationships between variables, there is a need for at least as many instruments of economic control as there are goals or objectives to be achieved.[7] The political gridlock emerging in connection with higher taxes and the undesirable side effects and uncertain effectiveness of fluctuating interest rates in regulating the economy suggest a need for some new instruments of control. The United States might want to emulate some of the Scandinavian countries and mandate the withholding of some salary payments for investment in government securities during periods of excess demand to be released for consumption during periods of weak demand (Table 1.89).

ENDNOTES

1. Geoffrey Moore, *Business Cycle Indicators* (Princeton: Princeton University Press, 1961), vol 1, table 3.2, p. 56.

2. Beryl Sprinkel, *Money and Stock Prices* (Homewood, Ill.: Richard D. Irwin, Inc., 1964).

3. Tom Herman, "Buy Stocks Now, Say the Gurus at Two Top Rated Newsletters," *The Wall Street Journal*, July 18, 1991, pp. C1 and C12.

4. William Baumol, "The Transactions Demand for Cash: An Inventory Theoretic Approach," *Quarterly Journal of Economics*, November 1952.

5. Ben Bernanke, "On the Predictive Power of Interest Rates and Interest Rate Spreads," *New England Economic Review*, November/December 1990, pp. 51–68.

6. Richard Black, "The Fed's Mandate," *Economic Review*, Federal Reserve Bank of Richmond, July 6, 1984, p. 6.

7. Jan Tinbergen, *On the Theory of Economic Policy* (Amsterdam: North Holland Publishing Co., 1952).

CHAPTER 11

SOME SUMMARY TABLES FOR INDICATORS OF ECONOMIC ACTIVITY

These summary tables should get the harried professor, his or her students, and other casual forecasters quickly to the point where the exercise of good judgment, a feel for the data, and luck may be more important determinants of forecasting success than the predictions to be derived from large-scale models of the U.S. economy involving hundreds of equations, sophisticated econometrics, and lots of computer time.

IDENTIFYING RECESSIONS BEFORE THEY OCCUR

It is not easy to identify economic recessions before they occur. McNees has noted that before the two most prolonged recessions in the post–World War II period (the recessions of 1973–75 and 1981–82), forecasters were not able to identify the peak until "about the time that it was occurring."[1] In the July 10, 1990, issue of *Blue Chip Economic Indicators*, it was reported: "The year-ago CONSENSUS forecast for 1990 of a 'soft landing' (no recession, but sluggish growth) remains intact. The economy in 1991 is projected to be a shade better, but the prognosis is still largely 'more of the same.'" This was the month in which the longest peacetime expansion of the U.S. economy came to an end.

Table 1.90 shows the adjusted lead times for 11 indicators that can be used to monitor the health of the U.S. economy. Three of these indicators (the Treasury bill rate, M1 expressed in constant dollars, and residential building permits) were included in an earlier warning system that successfully predicted the 1990–91 recession several months before it occurred.[2]

If only one of the 11 indicators in Table 1.90 is pointing in the direction of a recession, it probably won't happen soon. When three of the indicators signal a peak in business activity, however, it may not be far off. The adjusted lead times for three recessionary signals have ranged from a low of only three months for two of the last seven recessions to a high of 11 months. By the time five of these indicators signal a state of ill health, the economy may already be in a recession. When seven of these indicators point in that direction, you can be pretty confident that a business expansion is over.

Forecasting Poor Growth Years

The longest consistent set of forecast data available for the U.S. economy has been compiled by the Research Seminar in Quantitative Economics at the University of Michigan. From 1953 to 1987, there were seven years when real GNP declined on a year-to-year basis. In every one of these years, forecasts made in the preceding November either missed the recession altogether or underestimated its severity by amounts ranging from only .1 percentage points for the 1980 recession to 4.5 percentage points for the recessionary year of 1974.

Roy Webb has concluded that for horizons of several quarters ahead, it is hard to beat a simple forecasting rule of never predicting a recession. At the four-quarter horizon he found that several forecasting services using econometric models did no better than a simple no-recession forecast. "The very low number of long range forecasts of recession may be an implicit acknowledgement by the forecasting services of the low accuracy of such forecasts. It is also possible that false predictions of recession were perceived to be more costly than false predictions of expansion."[3]

The optimistic bias of most forecasting organizations makes it desirable for risk-averse users of real GNP forecasts to monitor economic and financial indicators for signs that the economy may not be as robust as most business forecasters care to predict. The 14 poor-growth indicators that are summarized in Table 1.91 may be of some value in that regard.

FORECASTING HOW LONG EMPLOYMENT RECESSIONS WILL LAST

Employment recessions have lasted from only 4 months to 17 months. A forecasting equation, which adjusts the lead times for industrial production and the average return on T-bills for the T-bill lead time at employment peaks, would support the hypothesis that the employment recession that began in June 1990 may have reached its low point in April 1991. See Table 1.93. Employment is generally a lagging indicator, however, and sometimes has a double bottom. When labor productivity is increasing rapidly, industrial production and economic output can increase without increasing employment. If the three indicators summarized in Table 1.92 are right, the employment low for this recession won't occur until sometime in the second half of 1991.

It should be noted that statistics pertaining to payroll employment are subject to a great deal of revision. When a firm goes out of business, the loss of jobs is immediately noticed by a failure to report their continued existence. It may be a long time, however, before jobs created by new firms get reported to the Bureau of Labor Statistics.

Some Recovery Indicators for Recessionary Troughs

A recovery from an official NBER type of recession is usually in progress after two consecutive monthly increases in the Commerce Department's composite index of four coincident indicators, after two consecutive monthly increases in the Federal Reserve's index of industrial production, or after nine or more monthly increases over a two-month period in the seven cyclical indicators: average weekly hours in manufacturing, stock prices, residential building permits, employees on nonagricultural payrolls, industrial production, personal income less transfer payments in 1982 dollars, and the money supply M2 in 1982 dollars.

You can obtain a diffusion index for these seven indicators by calculating the percentage that is rising over a two-month span. This mixture of leading and coincident indicators does a better job of avoiding abortive rallies in the midst of a recession and identifying recoveries in economic activity than the diffusion indexes for the Commerce Department's leading and coincident indicators. The Commerce Department's diffusion indexes were slow to recover from the economic recession of 1990–91 and may indicate a weak expansion of both output and employment (Table 1.94).

Forecasting Year-to-Year Growth Rates for Real GNP

For seven years, the economists surveyed by the *Blue Chip Economic Indicators* newsletter did a marvelous job of forecasting the preliminary year-to-year growth rates for real GNP. Since 1983, however, they would have been better off, on average, to have mothballed their favorite forecasting models and simply assumed that next year's growth rate would equal the annualized percentage change in real GNP from the current year's second quarter to its fourth quarter. (A two-quarter growth rate is annualized by simply multiplying it by 2.)

If this type of projection continues to predict the year-to-year growth rates for real GNP with the same accuracy, it could put a lot of more complicated forecasting models out of business. In January 1990 the Bureau of Economic Analysis in Washington, D.C., decided to deactivate its quarterly econometric model of the U.S. economy so that more resources could be devoted to the task of improving the national income and product accounts. The downsizing of Data Resources and the merger of Chase Econometrics with the Wharton economic forecasting organization provide additional evidence in support of the conclusion that the predictions from large-scale econometric models are not necessarily superior to the predictions to be derived from a careful monitoring of economic and financial indicators (Table 1.95).

SOME SLOW-GROWTH INDICATORS

From 1929 to 1990 real GNP expressed in 1982 dollars is estimated to have increased a little over 2.9 percent per year. In the rather turbulent period from 1929 to 1955, there were no cases of a below-average positive growth rate. In this period the economy either grew at an above-average rate or became mired down in a recession.

Since 1955 there have been 12 cases of a below-average growth rate in the 0 to 2.9 percent range. When two or more of the slow-growth indicators in Table 1.96 point in that direction and the 14 poor-growth indicators in Table 1.91 are used to screen out negative and near-zero growth years, 11 of these slow-growth cases can be identified without any false signals.

Poor- and slow-growth indicators are particularly useful in helping to determine whether other forecasts, such as those presented in Table 1.95, are in the right ball park. They also help identify economic recessions before they occur. Six of the last seven expansionary peaks in business activity have either followed or occurred during slow-growth years.

Using a Diffusion Index to Identify Unhealthy Expansion Periods

Readers who are worried about the possibility of an economic recession should keep a wary eye on the diffusion index for the 11 leading economic indicators (the percentage rising over a six-month span). Since 1947, the U.S. economy has never experienced a peak in business activity until at least one month after a decline in the noncentered value for this index to less than 30 percent.

There have been four years (1951, 1962, 1966, and 1984) when this diffusion index plunged below 30 percent for four or more months and then gradually recovered to 90 percent or more for at least one month without a recession occurring. To protect yourself from low diffusion values that are decidedly premature or may only be signaling a "growth recession," you should try to confirm the risk of an official NBER recession by carefully monitoring other recessionary indicators such as those that are listed in Table 1.90.

ENDNOTES

1. Stephen K. McNees, "Forecasting Cyclical Turning Points," in *Leading Economic Indicators: New Approaches and Forecasting Records*, Kajal Lahiri and Geoffrey Moore, eds. (New York: Cambridge University Press, 1991), p. 204.

2. Ibid.

3. Roy H. Webb, "On Predicting the Stage of the Business Cycle," in Lahiri and Moore, pp. 113–115.

CHAPTER 12

IDENTIFYING SLOW GROWTH RATES

In 1857 John Stuart Mill noted: "It must have been seen, more or less distinctly by political economists, that the increase in wealth is not boundless; that at the end of what they term the progressive state lies the stationary state, that all progress in wealth is but a postponement of this and that each step in advance is an approach to it." The 1990s might turn out to be the decade when growth-minded economists and investors begin to appreciate what Mill said.

Stock Returns Associated with Exceptionally Slow-Growth Years

From 1929 to 1990, there were only six years when the growth rate for real GNP was both positive and less than 2.5 percent. And in every one of these very slow-growth years it was a trying time to have owned common stock. In five of these years (1957, 1960, 1969, 1981, and 1990), there was a recessionary peak in business activity and in the nonrecessionary year of 1956, the financial return for the S&P index was only 6.4 percent.

While economic forecasters have often warned businessmen about the possibility of an exceptionally slow-growth year, they have not been very able to identify these years before they happen. From 1969 to 1989, the forecasters surveyed by the National Bureau of Economic Research at the end of the year predicted that the economic growth rate would be positive but under 2.5 percent eight times. They were right in only two years (1981 and 1990) (Table 2.00).

Using Producer Price Acceleration to Identify Slow-Growth Years

When the December-to-December growth rate for the producer price index for finished goods has increased .7 percentage points or more faster than the year-to-year growth rate, the U.S. economy has usually grown at a negative or below-average rate in the following year. The only exceptions to this conclusion since 1955 (when real GNP is measured in 1982 dollars) are the growth rates following the Vietnam build-up year of 1965 and the first full year of peacetime wage and price controls in 1972 when the Fed may have been more concerned about getting President Nixon reelected than in fighting uncontrolled food and energy inflation (Table 2.01).

Using Real Currency to Forecast Slow-Growth Years

Whenever the growth rate for real currency was 1 percent or less, the U.S. economy has either been in a recession or would soon slip into one since 1959. Under this situation, the United States never experienced an economic growth rate above the long-term average of 2.9 percent from 1929 to 1990 (Table 2.02).

Unused Labor Capacity and the Prediction of Slow-Growth Years

Table 2.03 uses the civilian unemployment rate and the growth of output per hour in the nonfarm business sector of the U.S. economy as the basis for an index of unused labor capacity. Since 1955, real GNP has never grown more than 2.9 percent in a year after one in which the sum of these two rates was less than 6.9 percent—with the exception of 1967, when military procurement was still rapidly increasing.

A slump in the growth of labor productivity preceded three of the last five recessions (the recessions of 1969–70, 1980, and 1990–91). Lackluster productivity and a slower growth of the labor force are likely to guarantee many more slow-growth years (Table 2.03).

REAL GNP AND THE LABOR FORCE

The average growth rate for real GNP has drifted down from about 4.0 percent in the 1950s and 60s to a little less than 2.6 percent in the 1980s. The main reason for the plunge is a drop in the growth of output per worker from more than 2 percent to less than 1 percent in the 1970s and 80s.

In an interesting 1967 article on the anatomy of urban crisis, William Baumol argued that many urban problems result from differentially low productivity in some rapidly growing service industries, suggesting that the ongoing transition to a service economy could lead to an eventual end to economic progress.[1] If output per worker doesn't rebound, real GNP's average growth could easily slump to less than 2 percent in the 1990s (Table 2.04).

Okun's Law

In 1962 Arthur Okun published a path-breaking paper on "Potential GNP: Its Measurement and Significance," which has since achieved the distinction of being considered a law. While no law has been subject to more breakdowns, there is one version of this law formulated by Stephen McNees that has continued to explain the historical data rather well.[2]

In Table 2.05 we show a parsimonious version of the Okun-McNees formula explaining year-to-year changes in the civilian unemployment rate. Since 1966 these changes have almost equaled 70 percent of the year-to-year growth rate for the civilian population 16 and over—minus 40 percent of the growth rate for real GNP.

When the change in the unemployment rate is set equal to zero and this formula is solved for an adult population growth rate of .9 percent, you find that the full-employment U.S. growth rate may have already declined to about 1.8 percent per year. It should be noted that most business forecasters are more optimistic. A survey by the *Blue Chip Economic Indicators* newsletter in February 1990 concluded that real GNP is likely to increase at an average rate of 2.6 percent during the 1990s (Table 2.05).

THE DOWNHILL SLIDE OF THE POTENTIAL GROWTH RATE

In 1963 this analyst examined various factors contributing to a dramatic "substitution of inanimate energy for animal power" (such as the speed, scale, and efficiency of converting energy into useful working effects).[3] I noted that none of these factors seemed to be open ended or exempt from the law of diminishing returns, and suggested that real wages, which had doubled, redoubled, and then redoubled for a third time in the space of about one century might "never double again." The average hourly earnings of production workers in 1982 dollars peaked out a decade later in 1973 and were only about 5 percent greater, on the average, in 1990 than in 1963. The working class population in the United States, it would seem, can no longer count on an improved standard of living as it grows older.

In the last several editions of his textbook *Macroeconomics*, Robert Gordon has assumed an inverse relationship between unemployment and the ratio of actual to potential GNP of minus 40 percent.[4] In Table 2.06 we use this "Okun law" coefficient and a variable constant term equal to the change in the unemployment rate plus 40 percent of the current growth rate for real GNP to calculate annual estimates of the potential growth rate for the U.S. economy. While the yearly estimates are not very stable, there has been a marked propensity for the seven-year median rate in column (5) to drift downward since 1961 with only two minor upticks in 1978 and 1980. By 1987 this estimate of the potential growth rate for the U.S. economy had declined by more than 50 percent from 4.1 percent in 1961 to only 2 percent. The downhill slide in the potential growth rate is of more than academic interest since it appears to have been roughly coincident with a peaking out of the inflation-adjusted value of the S&P stock price index in December 1968 (Table 2.06).

ENDNOTES

1. William Baumol, "Macroeconomics of Unbalanced Growth," *American Economic Review*, June 1967, pp. 419–20.

2. Stephen McNees, "How Much Growth Is Too Much?" *New England Economic Review*, January 1984, p. 84.

3. Edward Renshaw, "The Substitution of Inanimate Energy for Animal Power," *Journal of Political Economy*, June 1963, pp. 284–92.

4. Robert Gordon, *Macroeconomics* (Boston: Little, Brown, 1990), Chapter 11.

CHAPTER 13

INFLATION AND THE FINANCIAL MARKETS

While stocks are not a very reliable hedge against inflation, it is questionable whether there is any better one.

STOCKS AS A HEDGE AGAINST INFLATION

The official consumer price index of the Bureau of Labor Statistics was initiated in 1904 with a food index. Supplementary price information was collected over the years, and at the end of World War I a comprehensive index was compiled back to 1913. From 1913 to 1968, the inflation-adjusted value of the S&P index increased 230 percent. There have been four occasions (1916–21, 1929–32, 1936–42, and 1968–82), however, when the S&P index adjusted for changes in the consumer price index plunged downward by more than 50 percent. Since 1963 there have never been more than two years in a row when the December-to-December percentage gain in stock prices has exceeded the inflation rate. Timing, it would seem, is essential if an index fund resembling the S&P index is to be a hedge against inflation.

In April 1991 the value of the S&P index in 1982–84 dollars was still more than 6 percent below the all-time peak occurring in December 1968. In fact, the inflation-adjusted value of the S&P index has remained under 300 for so long that this number may turn out to be one of those reflecting barriers or "value-related ceilings" that will be very difficult, if not impossible, to penetrate. The percentage increase in the earnings associated with the S&P index from 1968 to 1990, in any event, was almost exactly the same as the increase in the CPI (Table 2.10).

Gold versus Stock as a Hedge against Inflation

In 1990, the average value of the S&P composite stock price index was more than 75 times as great as in 1875. Gold and silver, on the other hand, were only about 19 and 4 times as expensive. Many stocks promise dividends as well as some protection against consumer price inflation. In 9 of the 11 years from 1980 to 1990 the financial return associated with the S&P index was greater than the percentage change in the price of gold (Table 2.11).

Inflation and the Financial Returns Associated with the S&P Index

A number of analysts have been perplexed by evidence that common stock returns and changes in the inflation rate have been negatively related to each other over long periods of time. Eugene Fama notes that "these results are puzzling given the previously accepted wisdom that common stock, representing ownership of the income generated by real assets, should be a hedge against inflation."[1] The inflation-fighting policies of the Federal Reserve, however, will probably always make it safer to invest in stocks and bonds when other prices are increasing at a slower rate than when their inflation rates are accelerating.

Table 2.12 shows the historical advantage of owning stocks when the inflation rate is stable or declining as measured by the average first purchase price of U.S. crude oil at the well head and the year-to-year percentage changes in the implicit price deflator for real GNP.

From 1942 to 1990, the price of crude oil remained the same or declined during 17 years; in each of these years, the financial return on the S&P index was positive. The data generally support a negative relationship between stock returns and changes in the inflation rate. The U.S. stock market, however, can sometimes respond favorably to a large increase in the price of oil as was the case during the 1947–48 and 1978–80 periods when the price of crude oil nearly doubled—and more than doubled.

Since World War II the financial return on the S&P index has been positive whenever the inflation rate for the implicit price deflator for real GNP declined.

Some evidence now suggests, however, that stocks are a better hedge against inflation than they used to be. Since the last great inflationary bear market of 1973–74, seven years of accelerating inflation (1975, 1978, 1979, 1980, 1987, 1988, and 1989) have seen positive financial returns for the S&P index. In the longer period from 1942 to 1974, only six years of positive returns (1942, 1945, 1951, 1956, 1968, and 1971) could not be connected with a decline or no change in at least one of the inflation indicators in Table 2.12.

ARE CHANGES IN THE INFLATION RATE PREDICTABLE?

In an analysis of annual and quarterly forecasts, Victor Zarnowitz concluded that: "Forecasts of inflation are not much better than projections of the most recently observed inflation rates, and they lag behind the actual rates much like such projections."[2]

Forecasted inflation rates are sometimes compared to a model that assumes that there will be no change in the year-to-year growth rate for the implicit price deflator (IPD). These growth rates, however, are slow to turn around. A more rigorous performance test is the assumption that there will be no change in the latest four-quarter inflation rate. In Table 2.12 this assumption and preliminary estimates of the inflation rate are used to evaluate the year-to-year consensus forecasts for the IPD inflation rate compiled by *Blue Chip Economic Indicators* for the years 1977–90. In only 6 of the 14 years could professional forecasters muster a consensus superior to the four-quarter projections in column (3).

Why is it so difficult for professional forecasters to outperform the assumption that there will be no change in the latest four-quarter inflation rate? Part of the explanation may lie in the random or highly unpredictable character of supply shocks, especially for oil and agricultural products (Table 2.13).

Some Inflation Indicators for the Implicit Price Deflator for Real GNP

During the 1970s, a consensus forecast based on the December T-bill yield, the annual growth rates for the conventional money supply (M1), hourly earnings, and the consumer price index often outperformed a projection based only on the preceding four-quarter growth rate of the implicit price deflator for real GNP. While this model (first publicized in

1990) didn't outperform a projection based on the preceding four-quarter inflationary rate during the 1980s, it has got off to a good start in the 1990s and deserves some attention because it includes a number of variables that may determine the inflation rate (Table 2.14).

Deceleration in the CPI Inflation Rate and Stock Returns

Some of the best years to own common stock since the beginning of World War II follow years when the December-to-December growth rate for the consumer price index was at least 1.4 percentage points less than the year-to-year growth rate for the CPI. The following year returns for those years have all been positive and have an average value of 20.4 percent (Table 2.15).

Inflation and the Returns from Holding Corporate Bonds

The value of correctly forecasting changes in the December-to-December CPI inflation rate is most apparent for the long-term bond market. From 1955 to 1990, when the first differences in this inflation rate exceeded .7 percentage points, the financial returns from holding corporate bonds ranged from a loss of 8.1 percent in 1969 to a high of only 6.8 percent in 1990; the average value is minus .77 percent. The comparable return from holding the S&P stock price index during these years was a slightly better average gain of only 1.7 percent.

After the .7 percentage point threshold has been reached, however, there is little correlation between the magnitude of the first differences in the CPI inflation rate and the associated returns from holding bonds (Table 2.16).

SOME CPI INFLATION INDICATORS

Disillusionment with the predictions derived from theory-based models of inflation has led some analysts to search for inflation indicators.[3] It is still very much an open question, however, as to whether this new approach will improve the art of inflation forecasting.

In Table 2.17 a consensus of five different inflation indicators is used to identify large increases in the December-to-December CPI inflation rate in the following year. The five inflation indicators are: (1) a December capacity utilization rate for manufacturing of 85 percent or more; (2) a vendors' performance rating (percent of companies receiving slower deliveries) over 55 percent; (3) a first difference in the average December yield on new three-month Treasury bills of .9 percentage points or more; (4) an acceleration in the half-year inflation rate for the CPI of .18 percentage points or more; and (5) an annual inflation rate for the food component of the consumer price index that is 1.2 percentage points greater than the annual inflation rate for the whole index. On a collective basis, however, the record of these indicators is not exemplary—they only identify 9 of the 13 increases in the CPI inflation rate of .9 percentage points or more occurring since 1954.

None of these indicators could predict the 1.5 percentage point inflation rate for 1990. The annualized inflation rate in the six months prior to Iraq's unexpected invasion of Kuwait in August 1990 was only slightly above the inflation rate for 1989. A more than doubling of the cost of imported oil between June and October, however, caused the annualized inflation rate to leap upward to about 6.4 percent in the six months ending in January 1991 from about 4.7 percent in the prior six months. Inflation forecasters, it would seem, must be prepared to quickly change their predictions when major disturbances occur in the oil market (Table 2.17).

LETTING THE FED FORECAST GOOD YEARS TO OWN STOCK

The Federal Reserve has a tendency to lean against the wind and presumably wouldn't let short-term interest rates decline or increase moderately if it believed that the inflation rate was likely to accelerate rapidly. In 21 of the years between 1948 and 1989 the December-to-December percentage change in the average monthly yield on new issues of three-month Treasury bills was negative or less than 10 percent. Only two of these years (1976 and 1989) were followed by negative returns for the S&P index. In both of these cases, the inflation rate accelerated by at least 1.5 percentage points in the following year (Table 2.18).

LETTING THE FED FORECAST GOOD TIMES
TO BUY STOCK

The data in Table 2.19 are based on fluctuations of 20 percent or more in the average monthly discount rate on new issues of 91-day Treasury bills. Buying the S&P index after a downside reversal of this magnitude and holding it for one year would have always enabled a no-load investor at least to break even one year later and in most cases benefit from a double-digit return.

ENDNOTES

1. Eugene Fama, "Stock Returns, Real Activity, Inflation and Money," *American Economic Review*, 1981, pp. 545–65.

2. Victor Zarnowitz, "An Analysis of Annual and Multiperiod Quarterly Forecasts of Aggregate Income, Output, and the Price Level," *Journal of Business*, January 1979, pp. 1–33.

3. Stephen McNees, "How Well Do Financial Markets Predict the Inflation Rate?" *New England Economic Review*, September–August 1989, pp. 31–46.

CHAPTER 14

INFLATION AND ITS CAUSES

While inflation is sometimes characterized as too much money chasing too few goods, the relation between changes in the money supply and the price level is not very predictable in the short run. In this Chapter we examine some other sources of inflation.

WAGE AND PRICE INFLATION

In the long run, the most important determinant of inflation is wage growth. From 1954 to 1972, the adjusted hourly earnings of production workers on private, nonagricultural payrolls increased about 1.3 percentage points more rapidly than the implicit price deflator for real GNP. Since 1972, most of the productivity benefits from improved technology have accrued to production workers in the form of higher fringe benefits rather than hourly earnings. Moreover, year-to-year increases in real GNP of 5.5 percent or more and very rapid increases in the price of energy have usually caused the implicit price deflator to temporarily increase more rapidly than hourly earnings (Table 2.20).

The Employment Cost Index

From 1980 to 1990, the average inflation rate was closely aligned to the BLS employment cost index. The average growth rate for the all item CPI was only about .4 of a percentage point less than the 5.6 percent growth rate for the new employment cost index for total compensation in private industry.

The good news with regard to the wage-price spiral is that cost-of-living escalator clauses have gone out of fashion, making wage inflation less responsive to food and energy price shocks. The number of workers benefiting from COLA's has declined by more than 60 percent since 1977, and many of the remaining cost-of-living clauses have been weakened significantly. High unemployment in Europe and most developing countries and the globalization of manufacturing have made many industrial unions more concerned about job security than a possible resumption of wage-price inflation. In 1990, for the first time since 1960, the growth of average hourly earnings slowed during a year containing a peak in business activity.

In the last decade, employment cost inflation has been roughly equal to four percentage points plus 20 percent of the previous year's CPI inflation plus 80 percent of the preceding year's employment cost inflation minus 70 percent of the December unemployment rate. The negative relationship between the growth of compensation (or the inflation rate) and the unemployment rate, when other variables are held constant, is sometimes referred to as the Phillips curve (Table 2.21).

The Most Volatile Components of the CPI

Food, energy, shelter, and medical care have been the most volatile components of the CPI. Over time, the impact of this volatility has been lessened somewhat. For example, the weight given to food prices in the CPI has been significantly reduced over time. In December 1972, before the worldwide drought and food shortage of 1973–74, the relative importance of food was 22.4 percent. In January 1987, when the CPI was revised to reflect spending patterns shown in the test years 1982–84, the weight given to the food component was reduced to nearly 16 percent. Since a higher proportion of the remaining 16 percent is now spent on packaging and advanced food processing, a large increase in the price of basic food stuffs will not raise the all-item CPI as much as was formerly the case.

Despite the decrease in volatility stemming from food prices, the impact is still potentially adverse. For example, we seem to have returned to a less benign era in which large reductions in crop yield occur more frequently. From 1910 to 1936, there were six declines in crop yields per acre amounting to 10 percent or more. From 1936 to 1972, there were no declines of this magnitude. Since 1972 the United States has had four declines in crop production per acre amounting to more than 10 percent.

The impact of housing costs on inflation has also been mitigated. While consumers now spend a higher fraction of their income on housing, some much needed stability has been imparted to the home ownership component of the CPI cost-of-shelter index as a result of a shift to a rental equivalent measure of homeowner costs. The old procedure was to measure the average monthly price of new houses, mortgage interest rates, and other cost elements. This made the cost of home ownership extremely sensitive to changes in monetary policy. In 1970, 1975, 1978, 1979, 1980, 1981, and 1982 the official CPI increased from 1 to 2.5 percentage points more rapidly than an experimental rental equivalent CPI. Tight money, instead of curing inflation, probably helped make it worse in some of these years.

Using the rental equivalent, however, will mean that the inflation rate for shelter will not likely come down as much in response to economic recessions. This component of the consumer price index, moreover, is likely to continue to increase more rapidly, on the average, than the CPI as a whole.

Medical care services are another inflation-prone component of the CPI that ought, in principle, to be more controllable. In the 1990s many older persons are quitting smoking, drinking more moderately, getting more exercise, and about to shrink in numbers as a result of the baby bust occurring during World War II and the Great Depression of the 1930s. The AIDS epidemic and many new and more costly medical procedures, however, are likely to make health care cost containment one of our most enduring and frustrating problems (Table 2.22).

Inflation and the Outcome of Presidential Elections

Since President Wilson promised to keep the United States out of World War I in 1916, no political party has been able to get reelected when the annual inflation rate for the CPI in the election year exceeded 4.6 percent. The electorate also seems to be uncomfortable with big increases in the misery index, which is the sum of the unemployment and the inflation rates. By adding one variable—the four-year increase in personal consumption expenditure—you could have predicted the outcome of every election since 1916, with the exception of 1952 when a popular general promised to get the United States out of an unpopular war. Whether this model will continue to explain the outcome of presidential elections is one of the more interesting questions to be answered in 1992 (Table 2.23).

Double-Digit Inflation

Since the CPI was extended back to 1913, the United States has not experienced a year of double-digit inflation unless it was preceded by double-digit inflation for such basic food stuffs as wheat and corn. Large increases in the price of crude oil have also either preceded or accompanied double-digit inflation. Since World War II the Federal Reserve has always tried to end the specter of double-digit inflation by keeping the growth of the conventional money supply, M1, substantially under this scary rate (Table 2.24).

The Price of Imported Oil

The last two bouts of double-digit inflation might have been avoided if it were not for a two-fold increase in the price of imported oil in January 1974 and a doubling of imported oil prices in 1979–80. The good news with regard to the price of imported oil is that the CPI does not react to large increases in the price of imported oil as it did in the 1970s and early 80s. Mandated improvements in the fuel efficiency of new automobiles and other types of energy conservation helped to reduce the weight given to motor fuels in the CPI from 3.8 percent in 1972 to only 2.9 percent in January 1987 (Table 2.25).

Fluctuations in the Real Price of Imported Oil

Energy conservation and a large increase in oil production in non-OPEC countries reduced the real price of imported oil more than 75 percent from $44.37 per barrel in 1982–84 dollars in January 1981 to only $9.96 in July 1986. Even so, the United States and most other large non-OPEC producers are running out of conventional oil resources, and if unconventional oil can't be cheaply microwaved out of shale and heavy oil deposits, the real price of imported oil could easily set new records long before most of today's teenagers end their driving career.

The real cost of imported oil, in any event, has been trending upward since July 1986 and in the next few years will be heavily influenced by the oil production policies of Saudi Arabia. Saudi Arabia has sometimes adjusted its production to moderate price changes and can now play the role of a swing producer again. If worldwide demand for oil continues to increase and if oil production outside the Middle East continues to shrink rapidly, however, it is doubtful whether Saudi Arabia will be both willing and able to stabilize the price of oil for many more years (Table 2.26).

CHAPTER 15

CRUDE OIL PRODUCTION IN THE UNITED STATES AND THE REST OF THE WORLD

Since U.S. oil production peaked in 1970, the United States has never experienced a recession that wasn't associated with a large increase in the price of crude oil (Table 1.18). With our own prosperity so dependent on an exhaustible resource, you would think that energy conservation would be a serious matter. In 1989, however, petroleum consumption in the United States almost reached the levels of 1973, before the Arab oil embargo and the tripling of imported oil prices.

CONVENTIONAL OIL AND GAS RESOURCES IN THE UNITED STATES

In 1989 the U.S. Department of Interior lowered its estimate of the undiscovered conventional oil resources that might eventually be added to U.S. petroleum reserves by more than 40 percent to 49.4 billion barrels. If this oil and all of the measured, indicated, and inferred reserves estimated to have existed at the end of 1989 could be produced at the production rate for that year, we would use up all of the conventional oil resources in the United States and its adjacent coastal waters in less than 33 years. The outlook for natural gas is not much better (Table 2.30).

Crude Oil Production in the United States

Oil production in the lower 48 states has been trending downward since 1970. From 1977 to 1986, less than two billion barrels of recoverable oil were found in new fields despite the greatest U.S. well-drilling effort in history. This can be compared to more than 20 billion barrels of reserves added in and around old oil fields. By engaging in infill drilling and quickly utilizing secondary and tertiary production technology, oil companies were able to speed the recovery of oil from both new and old oil fields and temporarily halt the downward plunge in oil production in 1983 and 1984. This made the United States more energy self-sufficient in the short run but will not be helpful in the long run. If the remarkable 1962 projection by the noted petroleum geologist M. King Hubbert continues to explain the data fairly well, U.S. oil production outside of Alaska will continue to decline and be only about a third of what it once was by the end of this century.

Alaskan oil production increased more than 10 fold from 1976 to 1988 but has now declined by almost 10 percent. The Alaska Department of Natural Resources has estimated that oil production in our northernmost state will also be only about one third of what it once was by the end of this decade. There is a possibility of moderating this decline somewhat after the year 2000 by opening up the Alaskan National Wildlife Refuge to near term petroleum exploration. The ANWR is the only unexplored region of the United States that might contain a large oil field. Drilling activity needed to ascertain its potential, however, has so far been successfully opposed by environmentalists (Table 2.31).

CRUDE OIL RESERVES IN THE REST OF THE WORLD

One problem with the world's oil resources is that they aren't distributed very fairly in relation to population. Five relatively small countries located in the Persian Gulf, with less than 2 percent of the world's population (Saudi Arabia, Iraq, Kuwait, Iran, and the United Arab Emirates), are believed to control almost 65 percent of the world's conventional oil resources (Table 2.32).

Non-OPEC Crude Oil Production

Crude oil production in the six largest non-OPEC producing countries (the USSR, USA, China, Mexico, the United Kingdom, and Canada) increased more than 40 percent from 1973 to 1985 but has since been declining. Oil production in other non-OPEC countries has continued to increase, but in 1989 and 1990 this increase was not sufficient to offset production declines in North America, the UK portion of the North Sea, and the USSR.

The rapidity with which some oil fields can be exhausted is awesome. Oil production in the United Kingdom was negligible in 1974. With the development of oil fields in the British sector of the North Sea total oil production jumped to more than 2.5 million barrels per day in 1985–86 but has since declined by almost 30 percent. Part, but not all, of the decline is related to platform rebuilding and improving the safety of oil production in a hostile environment (Table 2.33).

OPEC Crude Oil Production

Energy conservation measures, the substitution of coal and other types of energy for oil, and increases in crude oil production in non-OPEC countries reduced the demand for OPEC oil by about 47 percent from 1977 to 85 and helped to set the stage for a dramatic collapse of oil prices. Since total crude oil production peaked out in the six largest non-OPEC producing countries in 1985, however, the demand for OPEC oil has increased by more than 7 million barrels per day. More than 80 percent of this increase in demand has been supplied by the five largest producers in the Persian Gulf.

The eight other members of the Organization of Petroleum Exporting Countries (Algeria, Ecuador, Gabon, Indonesia, Libya, Nigeria, Qatar, and Venezuela) increased their output a little in response to the cutoff of oil from Iraq and Kuwait but as a collective will probably never again be both willing and able to exceed their all-time record of 11.0 million barrels of oil per day established in 1973. Only one of these countries, Venezuela, has the potential to become a major oil producer again. Most of Venezuela's oil resources are high-sulfur crudes that are not in great demand, however.

The most troubling aspect to oil production in the Persian Gulf is that those countries with the greatest potential for increasing their output won't have a very compelling need to do so if oil prices remain in the vicinity of $20 or more per barrel. Since the Islamic revolution, Iran has been a leading price hawk and will certainly not want to restore its output to the profligate levels achieved under the Shah. Following years of war, Iraq has a job ahead in rebuilding its economy and will probably continue to be one of the most vocal advocates of restricted production to raise prices.

The key to price stability remains Saudi Arabia. If that desert Kingdom were to limit production for the benefit of future generations, to lessen the danger of global warming or to improve relations with its neighbors and other members of the Organization of Petroleum Exporting Countries, the age of rapid economic advance in most oil importing countries could quickly come to an end (Table 2.34).

Disposition of the World's Crude Oil Production

In examining the disposition of the world's crude oil output, it is quite clear that the United States is at least as responsible for the revival of OPEC power and influence as other oil poor countries. From 1982 to 1989, the apparent consumption of crude oil in the United States increased 14 percent compared to an increase of 11 percent in the rest of the world. To support its addiction to petroleum in the wake of declining domestic production, the United States had to increase its net imports of crude oil and refined petroleum products by about 65 percent from 4.3 million barrels per day in 1982 to 7.1 mb/d in 1990 (Table 2.35).

CHAPTER 16

FORECASTING THE GROWTH RATE FOR NOMINAL GNP

In this section we build on the information given in the first part of the almanac to go out on a macroeconomic limb and test the indicator theory. We use economic and financial indicators to forecast the year-to-year growth rates for GNP in current prices. We can then get indirect estimates of the growth rate for real GNP by subtracting the expected inflation rate from the predicted growth rate for nominal GNP.

PUTTING THE QUANTITY THEORY OF MONEY TO WORK

If the forward-looking velocity of money is constant, next year's growth rate for GNP in current prices will be equal to this year's December-to-December growth rate for the money supply. During the 1960s and early 1970s, the December-to-December growth rates for M2 did the best job of explaining the growth rates for nominal GNP in the following year. From 1974 to 1980, M3 has a better track record than M2, and from 1981 to 1989, the currency growth rate does the best job of explaining year-to-year changes in the Commerce Department's revised estimates of GNP for the following year.

While M2 has a slightly better forecasting record than either currency or M3 from 1960 to 1989, even better predictions of future GNP can be obtained, on the average, by basing your forecast on the median growth rate for currency, M2 or M3, rather than sticking with a favorite definition of the money supply (Table 2.40).

ENHANCING THE ABILITY OF MONEY TO FORECAST NOMINAL GNP

In Table 2.41 we use the median growth rate for currency, M2 or M3, and two other indicators to predict the preliminary year-to-year growth rates for GNP in current prices. The four-quarter growth of personal consumption plus expenditure for residential construction, known as a leading economic indicator, has the best forecasting record over a long period of time. Since 1983 the annualized growth of nominal GNP from the second quarter to the fourth quarter of the current year does a very remarkable job of predicting the growth rate for GNP in current prices in the following year. For the years since 1978, however, a consensus forecast based on the median of these three indicators does the best job of projecting GNP on a yearly basis.

INDIRECT ESTIMATES OF THE GROWTH RATE FOR REAL GNP

You can make an indirect estimate of the growth rate for real GNP by subtracting an expected inflation rate from the forecasted growth rates for nominal GNP. In Table 2.42 the median growth rate for the prediction variables in the first three columns of Table 2.41 is used to forecast the growth rate for GNP in current prices. The expected inflation rate is assumed to be equal to the annualized growth rate for the implicit price deflator from the second quarter of the year in question to the fourth quarter of the same year.

This method of estimating the future inflation rate doesn't have a very good forecasting record before the 1980s. Since 1981, however, it helps to produce real GNP forecasts that are about as good as any other inflation indicator such as the fourth-quarter-to-fourth-quarter growth rate for the IPD in Table 2.14 or the consensus forecast for the IPD in that table. It also has the distinction of generating the most optimistic forecast for real GNP for 1991 of any of the indicators considered in this almanac. While the economic recession of 1990–91 may have ended in March or April, there will probably be little or no growth in real GNP on a year-to-year basis.

CHAPTER 17

SOME INTERNATIONAL COMPARISONS

Despite what you might read or hear, the grass is not always greener on the other side of the ocean. The stock markets in other countries can also go down.

A COMPARISON OF STOCK MARKET INDEXES FOR VARIOUS COUNTRIES

While the performance of many no-load international mutual funds was very impressive from 1986 to 1988, the stock markets of most other industrialized countries haven't outperformed the U.S. market over long periods of time, if you adjust their record for changes in the value of foreign currencies. Even the star of the international markets—Japan—has shown that that which goes up the most can also decline the most in early 1990 and the spring of 1991. The stock markets of Canada, France, Germany, Italy, and the United Kingdom have underperformed the S&P in at least half of the years since 1953 (Table 2.60).

CHAPTER 18

SOME RECESSIONARY INDICATORS AND THE STOCK MARKET

Economic recessions are often great times to buy common stock. This section uses the indicators to show how and why.

STOCK RETURNS DURING YEARS CONTAINING A RECESSIONARY TROUGH

If you could have correctly forecasted all those years containing a trough in business activity since 1929, and invested in a portfolio similar to the S&P index at the beginning of the year, the average financial return for the year (including dividends) would have been 31.7 percent (from 1929 to 1990) versus an average return of only 10 percent for the year after a recessionary trough in business activity. Since the great recession of 1929–33, all of the recessionary troughs in business activity have occurred not later than the year after a peak in economic activity—if the peak occurred before November (Table 2.70).

TAKING ADVANTAGE OF ECONOMIC RECESSIONS

The stock market's propensity to explode upward at a very rapid rate before the economy has bottomed out means that, for best results, an investor should buy stock while the economic outlook is still rather bleak. In 1977 Alfred Moran suggested that investors should wait two months after two consecutive quarterly declines in real GNP and then buy stock. A person who used this signal to acquire a no-load index fund for the S&P index on May 28, 1982, could have obtained a gain of 45.1 percent on his or her portfolio one year later. For the seven qualifying recessions in the 1947–89 period, the following year price appreciation for this strategy has always exceeded 20 percent and has an average value of 31.3 percent.

While the minimum gain from following Moran's recessionary rule is almost three times as great as the compound average gain of 7.15 percent for the S&P index from 1947 to 1989, it is uncertain whether this rule will be of much value to future investors. Moran's rule of thumb missed the short-lived recession beginning in February 1980. Changes in the methodology and some of the data used to calculate GNP, moreover, have altered the decline patterns for some recessions. When real GNP is expressed in 1982 dollars, there is no longer a buy signal for the recession of 1960–61. There is also a second-quarter uptick in real GNP for the recession of 1973–75 that delays the buy signal until almost the end of that recession.

Besides these changes, professional investors are now so aware of the extraordinary returns possible from buying stock in the midst of a recession that by the time the economy has declined for almost three quarters, it may be too late to benefit from the Moran strategy (Table 2.71).

USING LEADING INDICATORS TO IDENTIFY SAFE YEARS TO BE IN THE STOCK MARKET

The 1989 revision of the Commerce Department's index of leading economic indicators replaced two components with more timely indicators, modified other components, and assigned equal weight to the 11 indicators now in the index. These changes have enabled the revised index to do a slightly better job of isolating relatively safe years to have invested in common stocks than the old index of leading indicators.

In column (2) of Table 2.72, we show the annual December-to-December percentage changes in the index of leading economic indicators. For the 16 years from 1948 to 1990 when these changes were *over* 13 percent or *under* minus 1.8 percent, financial returns for the S&P composite stock price index in the following year were always positive. Most of the returns in column (3) identified with an asterisk occurred either during or shortly after an economic recession.

The index of leading economic indicators can also help predict recoveries from stock market crashes occurring in the midst of prosperity. In column (1) of Table 2.72 we calculate a cyclical down ratio for the S&P index defined as the average December value of the index expressed as a proportion of its previous average monthly cyclical high. For the nine years when the December down ratio for the S&P index was less than .984 and the annual percentage change in the revised index of 11 leading economic indicators in column (2) was positive, the financial returns for the S&P index in the following year were also positive. See those returns identified with a # mark in column (3).

The most important lesson to be learned from Table 2.72 is that the relationship between stock prices and leading economic indicators is not linear. This complexity may help to explain why structural models of the U.S. economy have not successfully forecasted the direction of stock prices and why many economists still believe that long-run changes in stock prices resemble a random walk.

The usefulness of large declines in the Commerce Department's Index of Leading Economic Indicators at predicting stock market recoveries, however, might be seriously impaired if the U.S. economy were to again get bogged down in a very prolonged recession similar to that which occurred from 1929 to 1933.

It should also be noted that some of the components in the revised index cannot be accurately estimated on a timely basis and, as such, are often substantially revised. This type of uncertainty makes it important to examine individual time series with leading indicator properties and give extra weight, other things being equal, to those series that aren't revised much.

MORE ABOUT UNEMPLOYMENT AND THE STOCK MARKET

Evidence supporting the nonrandom stock price theory is easy to overlook because it usually involves first or second differences and is likely to be both nonlinear and nonsymmetric. The validity of this conclusion is illustrated to some extent by the data in Table 2.73 on changes in the civilian unemployment rate and the financial returns associated with the S&P composite stock price index.

Table 1.28 shows that relatively safe years to own common stock follow cumulative increases in the unemployment rate of from .9 to 1.8 percent in the post-1947 period. It is less well appreciated that large declines in the unemployment rate can also indicate good years for common stock. Since the beginning of World War II, the unemployment rate declined on the average by 1 percentage point or more in nine separate years, and each was followed by a positive return for the S&P index. (See those returns in column 3 of Table 2.73 identified by a hatch mark.)

In seven other years, the unemployment rate increased by 1.4 percentage points or more and each was followed by a positive return for the S&P index. (See those returns identified with a single asterisk.) The good performance of the stock market reflects the fact that all of the economic recessions occurring since World War II have been comparatively short.

While the stock market sometimes performs very well after a small change in the unemployment rate, it has been much more risky to have owned stock in these years. In fact, in almost 50 percent of the 33 years following relatively small changes in the unemployment rate you would have been better off to have owned Treasury bills or a money market mutual fund than to have had your tax-exempt retirement funds invested in an index fund linked to the S&P average. (See those T-bill yields in column 4 that are identified by a double asterisk. Only one of these superior T-bill yields occurred after an exceptionally high or low change in the unemployment rate.)

SWITCHING ON A YEAR-END BASIS

The Economic Recovery Tax Act of 1981, which authorized people with earned income to establish tax-deferred retirement accounts that can be shifted back and forth between stock and money market funds, and new regulations that permit college professors belonging to TIAA-CREF to manage their own retirement funds in the same way have made it worth while for almost every working person to be better informed about the behavior of stock prices and to consider the possibility of being a market timer if stocks seem overvalued.

Being a good market timer can pay off. If an investor had been able to switch perfectly at the end of a year to end up in that asset, stocks or T-bills, with the highest return for the year, he would have enhanced the expected return on his portfolio by about 2.0 percentage points during the great bull market of the 1950s. This same successful market timing would have increased the expected return by more then 5 percentage points during the more turbulent decade of the 1970s, when the compound average financial return associated with the S&P index turned out to be less than the average yield on Treasury bills.

During the 1980s, and so far during the 1990s, a tax-exempt investor with the option of switching back and forth between a no-load mutual fund resembling the S&P index and a money market fund could have obtained these kinds of results simply by exiting the stock market after two consecutive years of financial returns exceeding 10 percent and remaining in a money market fund until after one yearly return of less than 10 percent for the S&P index. While this switching system wouldn't have worked during the 1940s and the first half of the 1950s, when the stock market was still recovering from the loss of confidence experienced during the Great Depression, its overall record for the last six decades is positive. The data in Table 2.74 provide a practical example of how it might be possible to benefit from cyclical fluctuations in stock prices and a recently discovered phenomenon that is sometimes referred to as *mean reversion*.

CHAPTER 19

CORPORATE EARNINGS AND DIVIDENDS

Experiments have shown that inexperienced investors often lose sight of fundamental determinants of stock market value and may help generate a stock market boom that will almost certainly lead to a crash.

RECORD EARNINGS FOR THE S&P INDEX

While record earnings are the stuff that propels the stock market up, in the long run they are often anticipated and, as such, not a very reliable guide to future price appreciation. In 8 of the 23 years of record earnings since 1928, the financial returns associated with the S&P index have been negative, and in four of these years, the return including dividends was positive but less than 10 percent. On average, you would have been better off to have been in the market in the year after a new earnings record than during the year the record was achieved. This was especially true from 1978 to 1989. Since 1979 there has been no improvement in the CPI inflation-adjusted earnings associated with the S&P index (Table 2.80).

LARGE DECLINES IN CORPORATE EARNINGS

Since World War II, it has been rewarding to be in the stock market in those years when the earnings associated with the S&P index declined by 6 percent or more. During these eight years, the average return for the S&P index was 25.4 percent. When economic recessions and growth recessions are short, declining earnings can apparently be a useful indicator of stock market recoveries. The average return in the year following a decline in earnings of 6 percent or more was also a very respectable 19.1 percent (Table 2.81).

THE PERIL ASSOCIATED WITH HIGH
PRICE-EARNINGS RATIOS

Very high price-earnings ratios for the S&P index indicate that the stock market may be overvalued. Since this index was first computed on a daily basis in 1928, the end of the quarter P/E ratio increased to a value exceeding 20.50 five times. After each of these experiments with high P/E ratios, you could have sold a portfolio similar to the S&P index and repurchased it during the next bear market at a discount of at least 16 percent or more. The crash magnitudes for high P/E ratios tend to be inversely proportional to the time interval between sell signals. One reason the crash of October 19, 1987, was so severe is that it had been more than 26 years since the last experiment with very high P/E ratios in 1961 (Table 2.82).

EARNINGS AND DIVIDENDS ASSOCIATED WITH THE
S&P INDEX

If you could have accurately forecasted both the earnings and the dividends associated with the S&P index (a doubtful assumption), the dividend payout ratio would usually have helped identify relatively safe years to have been in the market. Since 1941, there have been 18 years when the payout ratio increased 3.2 percentage points or more, either because earnings declined or dividends increased more rapidly than earnings. In 17 of these years, the financial returns for the S&P index were positive.

While there aren't many cases, declining dividends have consistently signaled stock market recoveries since the beginning of World War II. Negative first differences amounting to 3.2 percentage points or more in the year-to-year growth rates for dividends have also predicted good years to invest in the stock market (Table 2.83).

Large Increases in the Dividend Yield Associated with the
S&P Index

Most large increases in the dividend yield result from a pronounced bear market rather than a rapid increase in corporate dividends. The S&P index financial returns have been very good in the year after a 24-basis-point increase in the index's average dividend yield (Table 2.84).

Stock Market Crashes Associated with Low Dividend Yields

Since 1871, the dividend yield for this index dipped below 3 percent on nine occasions. On each a tax-exempt investor should have moved out of stock into liquid assets and waited until an ensuing bear market caused the yield to rise above 3.5 percent before repurchasing stock.

From April 28, 1961, to November 30, 1987, the capital appreciation associated with this type of switching strategy is 587.7 percent compared to 252.6 percent for a buy-and-hold strategy. The higher dividends associated with the accumulation of relatively more shares would have been more than sufficient to compensate for transaction costs. During out-of-market periods from 1964 to 1987, switchers would have benefited from higher yields on Treasury bills than the dividend yields associated with buy and hold.

The profits from the end of the month transactions in column (5) of Table 2.85 are higher, on the average, the longer the interval and the larger the percentage gain in stock prices between sell signals. If we equate inexperience with the time interval between signals, this finding supports Professor Vernon Smith's contention that booms followed by sudden crashes are more likely if a market becomes dominated by inexperienced traders.[1]

Smith's experiments are designed to test the theory that a stock's price is determined by investors' expectations of what dividend the share will pay. He and his associates have found that inexperienced traders tend to lose sight of such fundamental determinants of value, speculate on whether price trends will continue, and, as such, help generate a boom followed by a crash.

ENDNOTE

1. Vernon Smith, *et. al.*, "Bubbles, Crashes and Endogenous Expectations in Experimental Spot Asset Markets," *Econometrica*, 1988, pp. 1119–51.

CHAPTER 20

SUMMARY TABLES FOR SOME STOCK MARKET INDICATORS

While the pendulum of academic opinion has now swung back in support of the nonrandom stock market theory, the history of attempts to model the market and benefit from this structure has not been very encouraging.

The formula plans emerging in the 1940s to capitalize on the wide swings in stock prices occurring in the 1930s, for example, were soon discredited by the great bull market of the 1950s. The updating of the forecasting rules devised by Touhey in 1980 to explain the stock market turmoil of the late 1960s and 1970s is also discouraging. By 1990 a lack of timely signals had induced the producers of the television series *Wall Street Week* to abandon their statistical elves in favor of a new index based on a survey of professional opinion.

While investors should be a bit skeptical of any indicator or statistical system that purports to "beat the market," the repetitive aspects of the stock market crash of 1987 and the recession of 1990–91 suggest it may be even more perilous to your wealth to ignore history altogether.

SOME INDICATORS THAT MAY HELP TO PROPEL THE STOCK MARKET UPWARD

Table 2.90 brings together some lower-inflation, surplus-liquidity indicators that are quite useful in helping to identify good years to have owned common stock. All of these indicators require an accurate forecast of one or more variables to be practical. In some cases it may be fairly easy to guess what will happen to the inflation rate, the real money supply, the federal deficit expressed as a percent of nominal GNP, and the dividend payout ratio for the S&P index. In others, accurate predictions may be next to impossible. All of these variables are of some value, however, in helping you appreciate the conditions most favorable to an increase in stock prices.

When two or more of these indicators signal a good year, the financial returns for the S&P index have so far always been positive. Except for 1979, when mad speculation in oil stocks propelled the S&P index upward, the years with no signals have been trying times to own common stock.

SOME "PERFECT" PREDICTORS OF GOOD YEARS TO OWN COMMON STOCK

Table 2.91 brings together some of those leading indicators with a perfect history since World War II of identifying positive financial returns for the S&P index in the following year. By indulging in a little fine tuning, you can identify 37 of the 38 positive return years from 1942 to 1990 with the seven indicators in this table. There is enough redundancy, however, so that only four of these indicators are needed to accomplish this feat. They are: (1) big increases in the growth rate for the real money supply, (2) large changes in the unemployment rate, (3) the Commerce Department's index of 11 economic indicators, and (4) downside reversals in the annual high-low ratio for the S&P index. While some of these variables may eventually lose the distinction of being a perfect indicator of good years to own stock, you can probably be fairly confident that the market will move up if several of these indicators point in that direction.

SOME INDICATORS OF STOCK MARKET CRASHES

The crash indicators in Table 2.92 were first publicized by the author in the March/April 1990 issue of the *Financial Analysts Journal* and have weathered the following July–October crash better than I would have expected. The three most severe bear markets since the beginning of World War II, as well as the seventh most severe bear market, were predicted or at least identified by four of the five crash indicators in this table. For the eight cases in which at least three of the indicators signaled a bear market, you could have sold the S&P index after the third sell signal and bought it back during the following bear market at a 12 percent discount.

IS BUY AND HOLD THE BEST POLICY?

Table 3.40 in the special features section of this almanac provides a chronological overview of most of the buy and sell signals for the S&P index. To be included in the chronology, each indicator had to have numerous signals and not more than one bad prediction in recent decades. Good crash indicators, which are the key to a successful trading strategy, are so scarce as to deserve careful monitoring.

In compiling summary Table 2.93, we have ignored the 400 trading day exit signal since it is too periodic and not sufficiently value oriented to be a good crash indicator. Equal weight is given to all of the other buy and sell signals in the chronology in deciding whether a transaction should take place.

While most of the gains and losses associated with the assumed transactions in Table 2.93 are rather small and capture only a portion of the profits to be expected from avoiding major bear markets, their cumulative impact is rather startling. A tax-exempt investor in a no-load index fund resembling the S&P index—with a propensity to switch—could have obtained, at least in theory, 5.3 times as much price appreciation since June 28, 1946, as would have been obtained from a buy-and-hold policy. Judicial use of financial leverage during the most favorable holding periods could have considerably enhanced the gains from trading. And in recent decades, an investor could have benefited from yields on liquid assets exceeding dividends to be expected from the companies in the S&P index during out-of-market periods.

It should be emphasized that systems for beating the market that would have worked well in the past do break down and don't perform as well in the future. The main advantage to a chronology containing numerous buy indicators, each with a pretty good track record, is that it is rather robust. One could miss or simply throw away the first buy signal following each of the 19 sales in Table 2.93 and obtain results that are about the same, on average, as were obtained for the first buy signal. By giving more weight to the best indicators and by exercising good judgment, it might be possible for a thoughtful switcher with a sense of history to obtain better results than are indicated by the simple trading system in this table. The data in summary Table 2.91 and chronology Table 3.40 indicate that very few year-end buy signals can sometimes be as bearish as an actual sell signal.

CHAPTER 21

FLUCTUATIONS IN THE DAILY CLOSING VALUES FOR THE S&P INDEX

While there are some exceptions to this rule, history would suggest that an investor will usually be better off to acquire stock after a bad day (or period) on Wall Street than to jump onto a bull market band wagon that is already in motion.

MAJOR FLUCTUATIONS IN STOCK PRICES

Table 3.00 shows major peaks and troughs in the value of the daily S&P index for the period 1946–90. All of the peaks and troughs since 1961 are identified on the basis of a 15 percent reversal of the index. A reversal percentage of this magnitude is needed to "filter out" an abortive rally in the midst of the more pronounced bear market from August 2, 1956, to October 22, 1957. The peaks and troughs associated with two smaller contractions are also included in this table to reflect the economic recessions beginning in July 1953 and April 1960.

The most interesting point to note in connection with this table is that once the market has experienced a pronounced bear market and begun to increase by 15 percent, it has usually risen at least another 15 percentage points before another downside reversal of this magnitude occurs. The only exception in the post–World War II period is the bear market of 1946–47 when the following recovery was only 24 percent.

If an investor had purchased the S&P index at the end of the day it first closed 15 percent above the preceding trough value, he or she would have always been able to have sold the index at a slight profit one year later. Holding the index for a second year would have sometimes resulted in a loss (Table 3.00).

BEAR MARKET RECOVERIES

Once the stock market has bottomed out and begins recovering from a major bear market, it has usually exploded upward at a very rapid rate during the first (or second) quarter of the recovery. (See Table 3.01.) Price appreciation in the first quarter after a major bear market has been almost twice as much, on average, as the price appreciation in each of the next three quarters. This is not something you would expect on the basis of the random walk theory.

TAKING ADVANTAGE OF MAJOR BEAR MARKETS

On September 7, 1929, the S&P index registered a new all-time high and then proceeded to lose more than 86 percent of its value in a series of wild downward gyrations before bottoming out at a historic low for this century at 4.40 on June 1, 1932. In the next three months, this index more than doubled in value to 9.31 on September 7, 1932. Since that spectacular rally, an investor could have obtained average price appreciation amounting to 15.5 percent by simply buying a portfolio similar to the S&P index after a cumulative decline in the index of 19.4 percent or more and holding it for one year. (See Table 3.02.) In the post-1948 period, the average first year gain of 16.7 percent could have been supplemented with an additional gain of 17.5 percent by holding the portfolio for a second year. If you assume that there won't be any more recessions comparable to those experienced in the 1930s and the mid-1970s, buying after a large percentage decline in the closing values for the S&P index would appear to be a good way to take advantage of more than one bad day on Wall Street.

BUYING THE S&P INDEX AFTER A TWO-QUARTER DECLINE OF 14 PERCENT OR MORE

Another interesting way to profit from a major bear market is to buy stock at the end of the first quarter after the S&P index has declined by 14 percent or more over six months. Since World War II, you could have realized a gain during the next quarter and enjoyed positive price appreciation over a two-year holding period on eight separate occasions (Table 3.03).

SOME PANIC DAYS ON WALL STREET

If there is an important lesson to be learned from panic days on Wall Street it is that you should be very cautious about investing in the stock market when the dividend yield for the S&P index is 3 percent or less. Seven of the eight largest one-day declines for this index have followed a dividend yield of less than 3 percent.

The pattern of very bad days on Wall Street is not exactly random. All of the one-day declines of 6 percent or more for the S&P index since 1928 have either been isolated events or have come in clusters spread over a fairly short, one-to-six month period. All of the clusters, with the exception of the two declines in 1940, during one of the darkest periods of World War II, can be linked to low dividend yields or a very rapid increase in stock prices.

Since President Eisenhower's heart attack in 1955 one-day declines of 6 percent or more have usually come fairly close to marking a bear market low. In the years since 1946, the next cumulative move of 6 percent or more for the S&P index after a one-day decline of that magnitude or more has been up (Table 3.04).

SOME CYCLES WITHIN CYCLES

While it is no longer very fashionable to assume that fluctuations in stock prices can be adequately described by cyclical movements over a fixed time interval, there is some evidence in support of the notion that bull markets will (usually) be nicked by several minor "corrections" before giving way to a major bear market. This point is most easily verified by considering cumulative declines of 3 percent or more for the S&P composite stock price index after it has registered a new historic high.

There have been 11 occasions since it was first computed when the S&P index lost 13.9 percent or more of its value after climbing to a new all-time high. (See Table 3.05.) For the 10 completed bull markets following bear markets of this magnitude there have always been at least three minor new high declines of from 3 to 10.6 percent before the stock market entered a more pronounced bear market of greater severity.

There is no assurance, of course, that history will repeat itself. Table 3.05, however, is one of the easiest technical data bases to maintain and possibly one of the most useful from the point of view of quickly obtaining some historical perspective and identifying times when it may be especially worthwhile to try to determine whether the stock market is under- or overvalued.

After the great bull market peak experienced on September 7, 1929, the stock market did not recover to a new high until September 22, 1954, a period of more than 25 years. Since 1954, the longest interval between new peaks was the seven-and-one-half-year interval from January 11, 1973, to July 16, 1980. The next longest bear market was the three-and one-third-year interval from November 29, 1968, to March 6, 1972. The crash of 1987 has the distinction of being the fourth most severe new high bear market but only took the sixth longest time (23 months) to recover to a new peak. The other pronounced bear markets following new historic highs persisted from a little less than seven months (for the bear market associated with Iraq's invasion of Kuwait) to a little over two years before the S&P index reached a new high.

THREE STRATEGIES FOR ACQUIRING A PORTFOLIO SIMILAR TO THE S&P INDEX

During the summer of 1988, I had my son compare three strategies for acquiring a portfolio similar to the S&P index. The first was a strategy of buying an equal number of shares at the end of every trading day. The second was to buy an equal number of shares at the end of every day the index rose 1 percent or more and the third was to buy shares after the market had declined by 1 percent or more.

For the 63-year period 1928–90, the best strategy would have been to buy stock after a bad day on Wall Street. There have been 46 years when the least-cost strategy was to purchase stock after a market decline of 1 percent or more and only two years (1943 and 1964) when this policy would have turned out to be the high-cost strategy. Buying stock after a one-day decline of this magnitude would have been the least-cost strategy in 1990 and during 12 of the 13 years from 1978 to 1990.

Since the arrival of stock index futures and program trading in mid-1982, it has consistently been more worthwhile, on the average, to have bought stock after a one-day loss of one percent than to have purchased equities after a one-day increase in the S&P index of this magnitude (Table 3.06).

CHAPTER 22

SOME EXCEPTIONAL DAYS ON WALL STREET

Yes, some days on Wall Street are worth remembering.

ONE-DAY GAINS OF 3.5 PERCENT OR MORE

While you are usually better off to buy stock after a bad day on Wall Street, there are some exceptions. There have been 23 days since the beginning of World War II when the S&P index increased 3.5 percent or more in one day, and in every case that can (now) be evaluated, the index was higher one year later than at the end of this one-day advance. Advances of this magnitude are a by-product of severe bear markets and are usually a sign that the plunge in stock prices is over or at least nearing an end (Table 3.10).

RECORD POINT INCREASES FOR THE DJIA

During the first 10 months of 1987, the DJIA increased by a record number of one-day closing points seven times. This contrasts with only seven other record-setting days over the much longer period from October 1929 through 1986. For those six cases since the Great Depression of the 1930s when the one-day record point increase for the DJIA left this index at least 6 percent below its preceding high (see those cases identified with an asterisk in column 2 of Table 3.11), the following-year gains for the broader S&P index are 36.6, 13.1, 5.9, 51.6, 19.4, and 9.8 percent. The following-year percentage changes for the seven other cases are 18.0, 14.4, 2.6, −8.7, −9.2, −13.8, and −15.7 percent.

The large record-setting gains of 5.9 percent and 10.1 percent occurring on October 20 and 21 of 1987 can now be considered a response to panic selling and the undervaluation of some stocks after the Dow's record 502.67 point drop on the 19th. The percentage changes associated with this decline and the 186.84 record point increase set on October 21 are so large that they may not be exceeded for a very long time.

IS THE DJIA A BETTER VALUE THAN THE S&P INDEX?

The S&P composite stock price index has outperformed the DJIA over long periods of time. There have been numerous years when this was not the case, however. During the 1980s the DJIA increased 228.3 percent while the S&P was increasing 227.4 percent, a difference of only .9 percentage points (Table 3.12).

ADVANCING ISSUES ON THE NYSE

From 1968 through October 1988, there were 113 days when the S&P composite stock price index increased more than 2 percent but only 39 days when the number of advances also exceeded 1,300. If an investor had purchased a portfolio similar to the S&P index at the end of these 39 days and held it until the next daily change of plus or minus 2 percent, he or she would have enjoyed an average gain of 2.69 percent. This can be compared to an average gain of only .08 percent for the other 74 days when the S&P index increased by more than 2 percent and the number of advances was less than 1,300.

Days with a gain of 2.8 percent or more for the S&P index and 1,300 or more advances on the NYSE have so far always indicated a positive gain for the S&P index in the following year. Two or more one-day gains of 2 percent or more over a 15-day period with advances in excess of 1,300 on both days have also signaled a safe year to have owned the S&P index (Table 3.13).

RECORD TRADING ON THE NYSE

On October 29, 1929, after losing 28.8 percent of its value in less than two months, the S&P index lost another 10 percent of its value and the New York Stock Exchange experienced a record trading volume of 16.41 million shares that was not to be exceeded for almost 40 years.

Since panic selling can generate new trading records that may not be broken for a long time, we have assigned an asterisk to all of those post-World War II daily trading records in column (1) of Table 3.14 that may have been distorted upwards by panic selling and have ignored these cases in compiling subsequent records.

After President Truman's statement on June 26, 1950, that involved the United States in the Korean War, the S&P index declined 5.4 percent. It lost another 1.1 percent of its value the following day when the NYSE set a trading record that was not exceeded until the mid-1950s.

The next bout of panic selling followed President Eisenhower's heart attack on September 26, 1955, and left a trading record that was not exceeded until the panic of May 28, 1962. The next-day buying spree, which followed the loss of 6.7 percent on May 28, established a trading record that was not exceeded until March 1967.

History suggests that panic selling can create some wonderful buying opportunities. An investor who bought the S&P index at the end of the stock market collapse on October 29, 1929, could have realized a profit of 18.2 percent two days later. The S&P index was up 4.0 percent two days after the panic following Eisenhower's heart attack, 7.4 percent two days after the selling panic of May 28, 1962, 14.9 percent two days after the spectacular crash of October 19, 1987, and 2.8 percent one day after the minicrash of October 13, 1989, when the S&P index lost 6.1 percent of its value.

For those investors with a longer-term horizon and a fascination with trading records one of the more interesting rules is to acquire stock *if the closing value for the S&P index is below the closing value for the preceding record trading day*. In the post-World War II period this type of buying strategy would have always insured a positive return (including dividends) in the following year (Table 3.14).

THE UNAPPRECIATED JANUARY EFFECT

January and December are probably the most interesting months to study the stock market. By the mid-1970s, statisticians were beginning to conclude that there might be some seasonality to the monthly rates of return from holding common stock due primarily to large January returns, and by the early 1980s it was appreciated that most of the exceptional returns in this month were associated with small firms.

While much has been written about the January size effect, it is less well appreciated that this month often sets a tone for the market that will carry forward to the end of the year. From 1947 to 1989 there were 23 years when the S&P composite stock price index increased by more than 1 percent in January, and in every one of those years the financial return for the entire year was positive. (See those cases marked with an asterisk in columns (2) and (3) of Table 3.15.)

The financial return for the entire year also exceeded the January gain in all but one of these years. The notable exception is 1987 when the S&P index, after the largest January gain in its history (13.2 percent), increased another 22.9 percent before getting involved in the most spectacular new-high crash in the history of the NYSE.

The identification of relatively safe years to have invested in the stock market can be improved somewhat by combining the gains for both January and the preceding December. For the 25 cases where the combined gain exceeded 3 percent for these two months, the full-year return for the S&P index also has always been positive.

The unresolved question is whether this success story is an accident or whether there is something special about January that enables investors to more accurately anticipate the behavior of stock prices in the remainder of the year. It has been noted that January is the start of the tax year for investors and the beginning of the tax and accounting years for most firms. If this month gets off to a good start, some funds that were taken out of the market in connection with tax-loss selling in the preceding year may be reinvested.

Preliminary and, in many cases, final announcements of previous calendar (fiscal) years' sales and earnings are often made in January. Some analysts have suggested that the extra information that is available at this time of the year from both government and the private sector may allow investors to more accurately forecast the future.

Except for the short-lived recession from January 1980 to July of that year, when there was some mad speculation in U.S. oil companies following the Iranian revolution, the U.S. economy has never experienced a peak in business in any year since 1945 when the January gain in stock prices was over 1 percent.

THE SILVER LINING ASSOCIATED WITH BAD OCTOBERS

During the 63 years from 1928 to 1990 the S&P index declined 30 times from the end of August to the end of October and only increased 33 times. While bad Octobers can be rather nerve racking, they can also help to create some very fine buying opportunities.[1] Since the beginning of World War II, investors could have obtained annualized price appreciation amounting to more than 30 percent, on the average, by simply buying a no-load index fund similar to the S&P index after every September–October decline amounting to 4.8 percent or more and holding it until the end of the following January. Holding the index fund for an additional seven months until the end of August would have provided the investor with a less spectacular but still rather respectable annualized return of about 15 percent once dividends are taken into consideration.

The emphasis to this point has been on losses experienced during September and October. This emphasis is a bit unfair to the 33 years when the S&P index increased during these two months and the 10 years since 1945 when the September to October gain exceeded 5 percent. In the next three months, after these rather astonishing gains, the S&P index always continued up for at least three more months before getting involved in another bear market.

Since 1946 the S&P index has also performed impressively well in the seven-month period following October–January gains of 8 percent or more. The marked propensity for the market to continue upward at a rapid rate after a very good August-to-October showing or an exceptional gain from the end of October through January no doubt helps to explain why speculative enthusiasm is so often carried to the point of insuring some very bad days in September and October (Table 3.16).

ENDNOTE

1. M. Kaimakliotis and E. Renshaw, "Some Self-Perpetuating Patterns in the Stock Market," *Journal of Portfolio Management*, Winter 1991, pp. 41–43.

CHAPTER 23

SOME ADDITIONAL CRASH INDICATORS

Crash indicators are not as numerous as good-time indicators. When the following indicators do issue a warning, however, you should be rather cautious.

THE PREDICTION OF BAD OCTOBERS

The best predictor of bad Octobers that I have found is the preceding gain in stock prices from the end of January to the end of August. There have been eight occasions since 1928 when the S&P index increased 15.5 percent or more from February through August (Table 3.20). After seven of these spectacular gains, the S&P index declined from 1.9 percent in 1955 and 3.2 percent during 1989 in the following two months to more than 19 percent during 1929, 1933, and 1987.

This method of identifying bad times to have been in the stock market helps to explain three of the four most spectacular stock market declines since program trading was invented. The first of these occurred in September 1986. On September 4 of that year, the S&P index closed at a new historic high of 253.83 and then proceeded to lose more than 9 percent of its value in the next six trading days before gradually recovering to another new high 89 days later. This was the 16th largest new high decline and the worst six-day decline after a new high since 1928.

On October 16, 1987, after a loss of more than 9 percent in the preceding eight trading days, the S&P index lost another 5 percent of its value and closed more than 16 percent below the historic high of 336.77, which was achieved on August 25, 1987. This was another fast-decline record after a new historic high. The speed of this decline may help to explain the panic of October 19, when most stock market indexes plunged more than 20 percent in a single trading session. During the crash of 1929, it took two trading days for the S&P index to lose that much value.

On Friday the 13th of October 1989, the Dow Jones Industrial Average lost more than 190 points and raised fears that there might be another crash similar to that experienced in 1987. Four days earlier, on October 9, the S&P index had recorded a new historic high of 359.80 before proceeding to lose more than 7 percent of its value by the end of the week. This was yet another new high decline record.

The one thing that the crash of 1929 and these new high decline records have in common is speculative gains of 18 percent or more in the preceding February-to-August period. In only two of these years (1929 and 1987), however, was all of the gain achieved from February through August wiped out in the ensuing crash. The wipeout in these two years can probably be attributed to overvaluation. When the stock market was not overvalued in terms of earnings and dividends or caught up in a recession (as was the case from 1929 to 1933, during 1937, 1957, and 1980), the net losses experienced by investors in September to October have usually been minor. (See Tables 3.16, 2.82, and 2.85.)

MAJOR BULL MARKETS AND THE LAW OF DIMINISHING RETURNS

Many tables in this almanac (such as Table 3.01) help illustrate a law of diminishing returns applicable to major bull markets, but none more vividly than the 400-trading day exit depicted in Table 3.21. For all of the bull market advances amounting to at least 24 percent following declines of 13 percent or more in the post-World War II period, you could have reduced portfolio risk and obtained a higher return in most cases by exiting the market for a time and shifting from stocks to Treasury bills or a money market fund 400 days after the bear market trough. The main difficulty with this indicator is that it is too periodic and not sufficiently value oriented to be a good crash indicator by itself (Table 3.40).

FINANCIAL RETURN CYCLES

There have been 13 occasions since the beginning of World War II when the financial returns in the last column of Table 2.90 increased from less than 10 percent to over 10 percent. During this long period, there has only been one year (1961) when the switch to a double-digit return was followed by another return of less than double-digit proportions. The year 1961 remains the only switching year when the average yield on the S&P index was less than 3 percent.

The high probability that the market will continue to perform very well for at least another year makes it quite rational for technically oriented portfolio managers and upside trend chasers to bid up the price of common stocks after a first double-digit return, even when such behavior makes the market vulnerable to another crash.

Since the S&P index recovered to a new historic high after the crash of 1929, a policy of selling this index after two double-digit returns in a row and repurchasing it during the next bear market could have provided investors with a discount ranging from a low of 7.5 percent at the end of 1986 to a high of 47.2 percent at the end of 1972 (Table 3.22).

NEW STOCK ISSUES

Some of the more painful crashes since the mid-1950s have occurred after years when new offerings of common stock increased 50 percent or more and set new dollar records. Since it can be advantageous for corporations and original shareholders to sell stock when the prevailing outlook is bullish and to refrain from issuing new stock in a depressed market, it makes sense for astute investors to keep a wary eye on the new-issue market and to not assume that what is good for Merrill Lynch is necessarily good for one's own longer-run financial health.

The stock market crash of 1962 that followed the growth-stock boom of 1961, the 1969–70 crash that followed the conglomerate-merger boom of the late 1960s, the 1981–82 crash that was preceded by an oil-drilling boom, and the new-offering boom that preceded the stock market crash of 1987 are good examples of the way business enterprises sometimes take advantage of an overly enthusiastic market and help set the stage for a stock market debacle.

Years with relatively little new-issue activity, on the other hand, can sometimes be great times to own stock. There have been five cases of a cumulative decline in new stock offerings of more than 45 percent since 1957 and in each case the price appreciation for the S&P index exceeded 8 percent in the following year (Table 3.23).

OLD-FASHIONED RISK PREMIUMS

From 1961 to 1981, you can identify all of the loss years for the S&P index with a simple risk premium defined as the earnings-price yield on the S&P (measured by the average earnings over the last three years divided by the closing price in the last year) minus the yield on Moody's high-grade corporate bond index, with only a few false signals. (See those years identified with an asterisk in column (6) of Table 3.24.)

In 1979 Nobel Laureate Franco Modigliani and Richard Cohn criticized financial analysts for using a nominal rate of interest to capitalize corporate earnings and suggested that investors had been systematically undervaluing the stock market by about 50 percent. "In the presence of inflation," they argued, "one properly compares the cash return on stocks, not with the nominal returns on bonds, but with the real return on bonds."[1] The gradual acceptance of this new standard for valuing corporate earnings helped to set the stage for the bull market of the 1980s, which is the second-best decade to have owned stocks since the S&P index was extended back to the 1870s.

While the nominal risk premium approach to stock market evaluation has been properly criticized, there are probably some three-year average earnings to closing price ratios and some old-fashioned risk premiums that are simply too low to indicate good times to be in the stock market. The stock market did not perform very well in 1984, after an old-fashioned risk premium of −4.08 percentage points at the end of 1983, and in October 1987, after the premium had sunk to the lowest level in the post-World War II period, it suffered the biggest one-day decline ever.

MODERN RISK PREMIUMS

Table 3.25 shows a more modern year-end risk premium for the S&P composite stock price index, which assumes that earnings should be discounted by a real interest rate. We start by calculating an earnings-price ratio for the index based on the highest earnings for the current or any previous year expressed as a percent of the closing value for the index. A real risk premium is then obtained by subtracting the December yield for Moody's Aaa corporate bond index from the high earnings-price ratio and adding to this residual the December-to-December inflation rate for the consumer price index.

A real risk premium less than 1.35 percentage points preceded two of the three poorest years to have owned a portfolio similar to the S&P index since the recession of 1982 (1984 and 1987) and would have also protected an investor from the stock market crash of 1962.

ENDNOTE

1. F. Modigliani and R. Cohn, "Inflation, Rational Valuation and the Market," *Financial Analysts Journal*, March 1979, pp. 24–44.

CHAPTER 24

STOCK MARKET VOLATILITY

Since the demand for equities is less stable than the supply, bad years for brokers can sometimes signal very good years for courageous investors.

STOCK MARKET VOLATILITY

While financial analysts are not in complete agreement as to whether the stock market has become more or less volatile since the advent of program trading, the historical data suggest that it has generally been less risky to have invested in the stock market after a reduction in year-to-year volatility than after an increase in the yearly high-low ratio for the S&P index. There have been 17 downside reversals for the annual high-low ratio for this index since the beginning of World War II, and every one of these years has been followed by a positive financial return (Table 3.30).

Residual Volatility and the S&P Index

Volatility is not necessarily bad for investors if the stock market has been declining or going nowhere. In Table 3.31 we calculate a residual volatility measure for the S&P index by subtracting the absolute value of the current year's financial return for the index from its annual high-low ratio expressed as a percentage point range. When the residual volatility has exceeded 16 percentage points, the financial returns for the S&P index in the following year have always been positive since the beginning of World War II.

New Historic Highs for the S&P Index

In his testimony before the House Subcommittee on Telecommunications on May 19, 1988, Federal Reserve Chairman Alan Greenspan accepted the idea that financial innovations such as stock index futures, options, and computerized programmed trading can destabilize the market and suggested: "In the end, we must be prepared to accept a different pattern of behavior in our equity markets and our objective must be to enhance their ability to accommodate change and withstand bouts of volatility."

There is not much doubt that the U.S. stock market has become more volatile on a day-to-day basis than was the case during the 1950s and 1960s. Four of the seven largest one-day losses for the S&P index since the beginning of World War II occurred after trading began in stock index futures in June 1982. (See Table 3.04.) Since the arrival of this innovation, it has been consistently more worthwhile on a year-by-year basis to buy stock after a one-day loss of 1 percent or more than to buy stock after a one-day increase in the S&P index of this magnitude (Table 3.06).

The evidence in support of increased daily volatility is even more striking if attention is focused on those days when the S&P index achieved a new historic high. In 1928–29, when speculative fever was very high and many people were buying stock on extremely low margins, 27.4 percent of the new historic highs for this index were achieved on a daily gain of more than 1 percent. After the implementation of much higher margin requirements in the wake of the stock market crash of 1929, this percentage plunged to less than 4 percent in the 1950s, 1960s, and 1970s. In 1986–87, before the largest one-day plunge in stock prices in the history of the New York Stock Exchange, almost 40 percent of the new historic highs were achieved on a daily gain of more than 1 percent. And in 1989, before the 190 point drop in the DJIA on Friday the 13th of October, this percentage had increased to 46.2 percent. You should be wary of new highs achieved on large daily gains since they sometimes indicate a very good time to get out of the market (Table 3.32).[1]

Taking Advantage of Bad Years for Stock Brokers

While good days for Merrill Lynch are sometimes good days to invest in the stock market (Table 3.14), an investor will often be better off to buy stock after a bad year for brokers. There have been 10 years since the beginning of World War II when the volume of trading on the NYSE declined by 10 percent or more on a December-to-December basis, and

CHAPTER 25

SPECIAL FEATURES SECTION

Nowhere is the advantage of having *diverse* but *highly specialized* sets of cyclical indicators more apparent than in the merger of good and bad signals for the S&P index to illustrate the possibility of profitable trading opportunities.

A CHRONOLOGY OF BUY (+) AND SELL (−) SIGNALS FOR THE S&P INDEX

A successful trading strategy is not nearly as dependent on having good buy signals as it is on having timely sell signals. Good crash indicators are so scarce as to deserve to be carefully monitored and given more weight than other indicators.

Table 3.40 provides the reader with a chronological overview of most of the buy and sell signals for the S&P index contained in this almanac. To be included, each indicator had to have numerous signals and not more than one bad prediction in recent decades. The 400 trading day exit signal, however, is too periodic and not sufficiently value oriented to be a good crash indicator by itself. The more selected set of buy indicators in summary Table 2.91 and the data in this chronology indicate that an absence of several year-end buy signals can sometimes be more bearish than an actual sell signal.

This type of chronology can be useful in assessing the worth of stock market indicators not examined in this almanac and appraising the comparative benefits that might have been obtained from more complex buy and sell signals that can be derived from moving averages and other types of computer-based trading strategies. Summary Table 2.93 illustrates a simple trading strategy that would have been superior to buy and hold in the past. There is no guarantee, of course, that this strategy will continue to identify mostly profitable trades in the future.

TABLE 1.01

Lead Times for the Commerce Department's Index of 11 Leading Economic Indicators at Official Peaks in Business Activity and the Median Lead Times for Its Components, 1953–1990

Date of Business Peak	Lead Time in Months from Own Peak to Business Peak	
	Leading Indicators	Components[a]
July 1953	5	5
Aug. 1957	20	21
Apr. 1960	10	12
Dec. 1969	8	10
Nov. 1973	8	8
Jan. 1980	15	13
July 1981	2	7
July 1990	0	21

[a]The median lead time for the seven business peaks experienced from 1953–1981 is calculated from the specific peak and trough dates for selected indicators reported on page C–46 of the business cycle indicator section of the *Survey of Current Business*, October 1990. The median lead time for the July 1990 business peak is based on the peaks for the individual components reported in the footnotes to the business cycle indicator section of the same issue of the *SCB*.

TABLE 1.02

Recessionary Declines in Payroll Employment Ranked in Order of Severity and the Percentage Increase in Employment during the First 12 Months of the Following Recovery in Business Activity

Date of Recessionary Trough in Economic Activity	Decline in Payroll Employment (%)	Percentage Increase in Payroll Employment First 12 Months of Economic Recovery
July 1980	1.43	2.0
Apr. 1991p	1.54	?
Nov. 1970	1.54	2.1
Feb. 1961	2.18	3.0
Mar. 1975	2.88	3.1
Nov. 1982	3.09	3.5
May 1954	3.46	3.2
Apr. 1958	4.32	4.7
Oct. 1949	5.19	8.7

p equals a preliminary estimate.

Source of basic data: BCI series 41.

TABLE 1.03

Buy Signals in This Almanac for the S&P Composite Stock Index That Were Associated with the Economic Recession of 1990–1991

Indicator	Basic Table	Buy Date	Closing Value S&P Index
NYSE advances over 1,300 and S&P up 2.8%	3.13	8/27/90	321.44
Wages and salaries down 6%	1.36	9/28/90	306.05
S&P index down 19.4%	3.02	10/11/90	295.46*
August to October decline of 4.8%	3.16	10/31/90	304.00
Nov.–Nov. unemployment claims up 16%	1.41	11/30/90	322.22
Leading indicators down 1.9%	1.17	12/31/90	330.22
Accelerator residual over 2.2% points	1.32	12/31/90	330.22
Industrial production down 2%	1.35	12/31/90	330.22
Dec.–Dec. T-bill rate down 10%	2.18	12/31/90	330.22
Cumulative decline T-bill rate of 20%	2.19	12/31/90	330.22
Dividend growth rate decline of 3.2% pts.	2.83	12/31/90	330.22
Downside reversal for high-low ratio	3.30	12/31/90	330.22
Residual volatility signal	3.31	12/31/90	330.22
One day gain for S&P of 3.7%	3.10	1/17/91	327.97
NYSE advances over 1,300 and S&P up 2.8%	3.13	1/17/91	327.97
S&P index up 15 percent from trough	3.00	1/30/91	340.91
Unemployment rate up .9% points	1.28	1/31/91	343.93
December and January effect signals	3.15	1/31/91	343.93
October to January gains of 8%	3.16	1/31/91	343.93
Unemployment rate up 1.2% points	1.28	3/28/91	375.22
Unemployment rate up 1.5% points	1.28	4/30/91	375.35
Buy two months after a two-quarter decline in real GNP	2.71	5/31/91	389.83
Unemployment rate up 1.8% points	1.28	6/28/91	371.16

*Lowest closing value for the S&P index during the recession of 1990–91.

TABLE 1.04

Actual and Projected Rates of Return Associated with the S&P Composite Stock Price Index Which Bridge Years of Peak Prosperity, 1929–1990

Years of Peak Prosperity	S&P's Composite Stock Price Index		Yield in Percent[a] (3)	Dividend Growth Rate in Percent per Year[b] (4)	Projected Average Return for the Following Period[c] (5)	Actual Average Return in Following Period[d] (6)
	Year-End Price (1)	Associated Dividends (2)				
1926		$.69				
1929	21.45	.97	4.5	12.0	16.5	−3.0*
1937	10.55	.80	7.6	−2.4	5.2	9.6
1944	13.28	.64	4.8	−3.1	1.7	8.6
1948	15.20	.93	6.1	9.1	15.2	17.1
1953	24.81	1.45	5.8	9.3	15.1	17.2
1957	39.99	1.79	4.5	5.4	9.9	16.9
1960	58.11	1.95	3.4	2.9	6.3	8.5
1969	92.06	3.16	3.4	5.5	8.9	4.6*
1973	97.55	3.38	3.5	1.7	5.2	6.5
1979	107.94	5.70	5.3	9.1	14.4	11.9*
1981	122.55	6.63	5.4	7.8	13.2	16.0
1990	330.22	12.10	3.7	6.9	10.6	?

[a]Column (2) expressed as a percent of column (1).

[b]Compound average annual growth rates for the associated dividend figures in column (2), 1926–29, 1929–37, etc.

[c]Column (3) plus column (4).

[d]Compound average annual financial return (price appreciation plus dividends associated with the S&P index) from the end of the year in question to the end of the next year of peak prosperity.

*Acutal return in the following period was less than the projected return. For these three cases there was both an increase in the dividend yield in the following period and a slump in the dividend growth rate.

Source of basic data: Standard & Poor's *Security Price Index Record.*

TABLE 1.05

Compound Average Growth Rates for GNP in Current Dollars and the Dividends Associated with the S&P Composite Stock Price Index in Percent for the Decades 1889–1989

Decade	Nominal GNP	Dividends
1889–1899	3.4	−.5
1899–1909	6.7	7.7*
1909–1919	9.7	1.8
1919–1929	2.1	6.9*
1929–1939	−1.3	−4.4
1939–1949	8.5	6.3
1949–1959	9.2	4.8
1959–1969	6.9	5.6
1969–1979	10.0	6.0
1979–1989	7.6	6.9

*Cases where the dividend growth rate exceeded the average growth rate for nominal GNP.

Source of basic data: *Historical Statistics of the U.S.: Colonial Times to 1970*, Appendix to the *Economic Report of the President*, and Standard & Poor's *Security Price Index Record.*

TABLE 1.06

The Financial Returns Associated with the S&P Stock Price Index during Presidential Election and Post-Election Years, 1928–1989

Election Year	The Financial Returns for the S&P Index	
	Election Year (1)	Post-Election Year (2)
1928	41.9	−7.9
1932	−9.0	53.0
1936	33.3	−33.9
1940	−9.9	−11.2
1944	19.3	35.7
1948	5.4	17.8
1952	17.7	−1.2
1956	6.4	−10.4
1960	.3	26.6
1964	16.3	12.3
1968	10.8	−8.3
1972	18.7	−14.5
1976	23.6	−7.2
1980	31.5	−4.8
1984	6.0	31.3
1988	16.3	31.0

Source of basic data: Standard & Poor's *Security Price Index Record.*

TABLE 1.11

Business Cycle Expansions and Contractions, 1854–1991

Business Cycle Reference Dates		Duration in Months	
Trough	Peak	Contraction Previous Peak to Trough	Expansion Trough to Peak
Dec. 1854	June 1857	—	30
Dec. 1858	Oct. 1860	18	22
June 1861	Apr. 1865	8	46*
Dec. 1867	June 1869	32	18
Dec. 1870	Oct. 1873	18	34
Mar. 1879	Mar. 1882	65	36
May 1885	Mar. 1887	38	22
Apr. 1888	July 1890	13	27
May 1891	Jan. 1893	10	20
June 1894	Dec. 1895	17	18

TABLE 1.11 (concluded)

Business Cycle Reference Dates		Duration in Months	
Trough	Peak	Contraction Previous Peak to Trough	Expansion Trough to Peak
June 1897	June 1899	18	24
Dec. 1900	Sep. 1902	18	21
Aug. 1904	May 1907	23	33
June 1908	Jan. 1910	13	19
Jan. 1912	Jan. 1913	24	12
Dec. 1914	Aug. 1918	23	44*
Mar. 1919	Jan. 1920	7	10
July 1921	May 1923	18	22
July 1924	Oct. 1926	14	27
Nov. 1927	Aug. 1929	13	21
Mar. 1933	May 1937	43	50
June 1938	Feb. 1945	13	80*
Oct. 1945	Nov. 1948	8	37
Oct. 1949	July 1953	11	45*
May 1954	Aug. 1957	10	39
Apr. 1958	Apr. 1960	8	24
Feb. 1961	Dec. 1969	10	106*
Nov. 1970	Nov. 1973	11	36
Mar. 1975	Jan. 1980	16	58
July 1980	July 1981	6	12
Nov. 1982	July 1990	16	92*
Apr. 1991p		9	
Average, peacetime cycles			
1854–1982 (25 cycles)		19	27
1854–1919 (14 cycles)		22	24
1919–1945 (5 cycles)		20	26
1945–1982 (6 cycles)		11	34

*Business expansions which may have been prolonged or shortened by wars (Civil War, World Wars I and II, Korean War, Vietnam War, and Operation Desert Storm).
p equals a preliminary estimate.

Source: National Bureau of Economic Research, Inc.

TABLE 1.12

Differences in the Peak and Trough Months for Industrial Production, BEA's Coincident Index, Personal Income in 1982 Dollars, and the NBER Official Turning Points[a]

Peak Months				Trough Months		
Industrial Production	Coincident Index	Personal Income	NBER Peak	Industrial Production	Coincident Index	NBER Trough
July 48 (4)	Oct. 48 (1)	Oct. 48 (1)	Nov. 48	Oct. 49 (0)	Oct. 49 (0)	Oct. 49
July 53 (0)	July 53 (0)	Oct. 53 (−3)	July 53	Apr. 54 (1)	May 54 (0)	May 54
Mar. 57 (5)	Feb. 57 (6)	Aug. 57 (0)	Aug. 57	Apr. 58 (0)	Apr. 58 (0)	Apr. 58
Jan. 60 (3)	Jan. 60 (3)	June 60 (−2)	Apr. 60	Feb. 61 (0)	Feb. 61 (0)	Feb. 61
Oct. 69 (2)	Oct. 69 (2)	Sep. 70 (−9)	Dec. 69	Nov. 70 (0)	Nov. 70 (0)	Nov. 70
Nov. 73 (0)	Nov. 73 (0)	Nov. 73 (0)	Nov. 73	Mar. 75 (0)	Mar. 75 (0)	Mar. 75
May 79 (8)	May 79 (8)	Jan. 80 (0)	Jan. 80	July 80 (0)	July 80 (0)	July 80
July 81 (0)	Jan. 81 (6)	Aug. 81 (−1)	July 81	Dec. 82 (−1)	Dec. 82 (−1)	Nov. 82
Sep. 90 (−2)	June 90 (1)	July 90 (0)	July 90	Mar. 91 (1)	Mar. 91 (1)	Apr. 91p

[a]The numbers in parentheses are monthly lead or lag (−) times for industrial production, the coincident index, and personal income relative to the official NBER turning points.

p equals a preliminary estimate of the author.

Source of basic data: BCI series 47, 920, and 52.

115

TABLE 1.13

Fluctuations of 2.5 Percent or More in the Commerce Department's Composite Index of 11 Leading Economic Indicators

	Dates of			Leading Indicator Values			Percent Decline L.I.		Adjusted Lead Time in Months[a]
L.I. Peak	NBER Peak	L.I. Trough	L.I. Peak	NBER Peak	L.I. Trough	L.I. Peak NBER Peak	L.I. Peak L.I. Trough		
June 48	Nov. 48	June 49	38.3	36.9	34.8	3.7	9.1	0
Jan. 51	—	Nov. 51	46.9	—	41.0	—	12.6	27*
Feb. 53	July 53	Nov. 53	44.9	43.7	41.3	2.7	8.0	-1
Dec. 55	Aug. 57	Feb. 58	51.3	48.6	46.1	5.3	10.1	4
June 59	Apr. 60	Apr. 60	55.4	53.4	53.4	3.6	3.6	1
Mar. 62	—	June 62	60.6	—	59.1	—	2.5	—
Mar. 66	—	Mar. 67	76.9	—	72.6	—	5.6	40*
Apr. 69	Dec. 69	Apr. 69	83.1	80.2	76.3	3.5	8.2	0
Mar. 73	Nov. 73	Feb. 75	97.8	97.8	78.0	.6	20.2	-3
Oct. 78	Jan. 80	May 80	107.1	101.2	93.6	5.5	12.6	6
Nov. 81	July 81	Jan. 82	104.1	102.0	97.2	2.0	6.6	-2
Feb. 84	—	Oct. 84	123.4	—	119.4	—	3.2	—
Sep. 87	—	Jan. 88	143.2	—	139.1	—	2.9	—
July 90	July 90	Jan. 91	146.2	146.2	138.7	.0	5.1	-4

[a]Months to the NBER business peak after the index of leading indicators has declined 3.3 percent from its previous cyclical peak.

*Lead times that are associated with very substantial military procurement increases during the Korean and Vietnam wars.

Source: BCI series 910.

TABLE 1.14

Declines of 4 Percent or More in BEA's Composite Index of Four Coincident Indicators.

	Date of			Coincident Index at		% Decline Peak to Trough	Months after NBER Peak to 4.7% Decline C.I.
C.I. Peak	NBER Peak	C.I. Down 4.7%	C.I. Trough	Own Peak	Own Trough		
Oct. 48	Nov. 48	Feb. 49	Oct. 49	39.4	34.7	11.9	3
July 53	July 53	Dec. 53	Aug. 54	49.5	44.8	9.5	5
Apr. 56	—	—	July 56	52.4	50.3	4.0	—*
Feb. 57	Aug. 57	Nov. 57	Apr. 58	53.4	46.6	12.7	3
June 59	—	—	Oct. 59	53.9	51.4	4.6	—*
Jan. 60	Apr. 60	Nov. 60	Feb. 61	54.7	50.8	7.1	7
Oct. 69	Dec. 69	Oct. 70	Nov. 70	85.1	79.4	6.7	10
Nov. 73	Nov. 73	Oct. 74	Mar. 75	98.3	84.4	14.1	11
May 79	Jan. 80	May 80	July 80	111.4	104.1	6.6	4
Jan. 81	July 81	Jan. 82	Dec. 82	108.5	97.0	10.6	6
June 90	July 90	Jan. 91	Mar. 91	134.9	126.0	6.6	6

*Declines in the coincident indicators that may have been caused by strikes in the steel industry.

Source: BCI series 920.

TABLE 1.15

Fluctuations in the Composite Index of Seven Lagging Indicators Amounting to 2.5 Percent or More

	Date of			Lg. Indicators at		% Decline Peak to Trough	Months after Lg.I. Down 3.7% to NBER Trough
Lg.I. Peak	Lg.I. Down 3.7%	NBER Trough	Lg.I. Trough	Own Peak	Own Trough		
Feb. 49	Sep. 49	Oct. 49	Sep. 49	35.1	33.8	3.7	1
Dec. 53	Mar. 54	May 54	Feb. 55	50.7	45.3	10.7	2
Dec. 57	Feb. 58	Apr. 58	Aug. 58	62.6	53.4	14.7	2
July 60	Oct. 60	Feb. 61	Aug. 61	66.4	61.0	8.1	4
Mar. 70	Dec. 70	Nov. 70	Feb. 72	94.2	85.0	9.8	-1
Dec. 74	Apr. 75	Mar. 75	June 76	103.5	86.2	16.7	-1
Apr. 80	July 80	July 80	Oct. 80	113.6	97.4	14.3	0
Sep. 81	Apr. 82	Nov. 82	June 83	105.7	90.1	14.8	7
Oct. 89	June 91p	Apr. 91p		120.0			-2

p equals a preliminary estimate.

Source: BCI series 930.

TABLE 1.16

Recessions in Industrial Production and Large One-Month Increases in the Commerce Department's Index of 11 Leading Economic Indicators Amounting to More than 1 Percent

Dates of			Industrial Prod.		Increase L. I. (%) (3)	Months L. I. Gain Was from	
I. P. Peak	I. P. Trough	L. I. Up 1%	Peak (1)	Trough (2)		Industrial Peak (4)	Industrial Trough (5)
July 48	Oct. 49	July 49	24.0	21.6	2.0	12	3*
July 53	Apr. 54	May 54	32.4	29.3	1.4	10	1
Mar. 57	Apr. 58	May 58	36.3	31.4	1.9	14	1
Jan. 60	Feb. 61	Mar. 61	39.6	36.2	1.5	15	1
Oct. 69	Nov. 70	Dec. 70	64.1	59.6	2.3	14	1
Nov. 73	Mar. 75	Apr. 75	75.2	64.1	3.2	17	1
May 79	July 80	June 80	86.2	81.2	1.4	13	1*
July 81	Dec. 82	Feb. 82	87.1	79.3	1.8	7	10*
Sep. 90	Mar. 91	Feb. 91	110.6	105.0	1.1	5	1*

*Cases where the big jump in the index of leading economic indicators occurred before the trough in industrial production in column (2).

Source: BCI series 47 and 910.

TABLE 1.17

Using the Commerce Department's Index of 11 Leading Economic Indicators to Identify Poor Growth Years for the U.S. Economy

	% Change in Leading Indicators			Following Year Growth Rate	
Year	Dec.–Dec. (1)	June–Dec. (2)	Sept.–Dec. (3)	Real GNP (4)	S&P Fin. Return (5)
1948	−4.2	−5.2	−2.2	.0*	17.8$
1949	7.2	11.8	4.0	8.5	30.5@
1950	17.7	7.3	.4	10.3	23.4@
1951	−10.0	−4.0	−.2	3.9	17.7$
1952	8.0	4.0	−.9	4.0	−1.2
1953	−7.0	−5.5	−1.0	−1.3*	51.2$
1954	14.5	8.7	5.6	5.6	31.0@
1955	8.2	2.0	.6	2.1	6.4
1956	−1.8	1.0	.4	1.7	−10.4
1957	−7.5	−4.9	−2.7	−.8*	42.4$
1958	13.5	9.1	2.7	5.8	11.8@
1959	4.3	−.4	.7	2.2	.3
1960	−2.7	.4	−.6	2.6	26.6$
1961	11.5	4.4	3.3	5.3	−8.8
1962	3.0	4.4	2.8	4.1	22.5
1963	6.3	2.2	1.2	5.3	16.3

TABLE 1.17 (concluded)

Year	% Change in Leading Indicators			Following Year Growth Rate	
	Dec.–Dec. (1)	June–Dec. (2)	Sept.–Dec. (3)	Real GNP (4)	S&P Fin. Return (5)
1964	8.5	4.4	1.6	5.8	12.3
1965	6.2	4.3	3.1	5.8	−10.0
1966	−3.7	−3.4	−1.6	2.9*	23.7$
1967	7.3	4.8	1.8	4.1	10.8
1968	5.4	3.9	2.6	2.4	−8.3
1969	−2.6	−2.6	−2.1	−.3*	3.5$
1970	−1.9	2.3	2.6	2.8	14.1$
1971	10.5	4.4	3.7	5.0	18.7@
1972	11.3	5.9	2.4	5.2	−14.5
1973	−1.0	−1.7	−1.2	−.5*	−26.0
1974	−17.4	−13.2	−7.3	−1.3*	36.9$
1975	14.5	7.5	2.7	4.9	23.6@
1976	9.1	2.8	1.1	4.7	−7.2
1977	4.4	1.8	1.2	5.3	6.4
1978	2.2	.9	−.7	2.5	18.4
1979	−4.6	−3.8	−2.3	−.2*	31.5$
1980	2.2	8.3	1.7	1.9	−4.8
1981	−4.9	−4.8	−2.2	−2.5*	20.4$
1982	7.1	6.0	4.1	3.6	22.3@
1983	16.6	4.4	2.1	6.8	6.0@
1984	−1.5	−1.2	−.2	3.4	31.1
1985	6.1	3.1	1.4	2.7	18.5
1986	7.4	3.8	3.2	3.4	5.7
1987	1.8	−.8	−2.6	4.5	16.3$
1988	3.9	.7	1.0	2.5	31.2
1989	.2	.8	.3	1.0	−3.1
1990	−4.1	−4.7	−2.7	*	?$

*A poor growth rate for real GNP is predicted if the index of leading indicators declines 1.0 percent or more on a Dec.–Dec. basis, on a June–Dec. basis, and on a Sept.–Dec. basis.

$Financial returns following years when the index of leading economic indicators declined by at least 1.9 percent on either a Dec.-to-Dec. basis, a June-to-Dec. basis, or on a Sept.-to-Dec. basis.

@Financial returns following years when the index of leading economic indicators increased at least 13 percent on a Dec.-to-Dec. basis or increased at least 3.5 percent on a yearly, six-month, and three-month basis.

Source of basic data: BCI series 910 and 50 and Standard & Poor's *Security Price Index Record*.

TABLE 1.18
Using Year-to-Year Increases of 5 Percent or More in the Price of U.S. Crude Oil and Annual Declines of 1 Percent or More for BEA's Revised Index of 11 Leading Economic Indicators to Forecast Poor Growth Years for the U.S. Economy

	Growth Rates for				
Year	Crude Oil Price[a]	Index of Leading Indicators[b]	The Real Money Supply[c]	Treasury Bill Rate[d]	Following Year Real GNP[e]
1948	34.7	−4.2	−4.0	21.1	.0*
1953	5.9	−7.0	.5	−23.5	−1.3*
1957	10.8	−7.5	−3.6	−4.0	−.8*
1969	5.1	−2.6	−2.6	30.4	−.3*
1971	6.6	10.5	3.0	−17.3	5.0
1973	14.7	−1.0	−3.0	45.5	−.5*
1974	76.6	−17.4	−7.0	−2.4	−1.3*
1975	11.6	14.5	−2.0	−23.4	4.9
1976	6.8	9.1	1.6	−20.9	4.7
1978	5.0	2.2	−.7	50.5	2.5
1979	40.4	−4.6	−4.8	32.3	−.2*
1980	70.8	2.2	−5.1	29.7	1.9
1981	47.2	−4.9	−2.2	−30.2	−2.5*
1987	23.2	1.8	−.9	6.0	4.4
1989	26.1	.2	−3.9	−5.6	1.0
1990	26.3	−4.1	−2.0	−17.5	?*

[a]The year-to-year growth rate for U.S. crude oil prices at the well head.

[b]The December-to-December growth rate for the U.S. Commerce Department's revised index of 11 leading economic indicators.

[c]The December-to-December growth rate for the money supply M1 expressed in 1982 dollars.

[d]The December-to-December growth rate for the yield on new issues of 91-day Treasury bills.

[e]The following year-to-year growth rate for real GNP expressed in 1982 dollars.

*The growth rates for real GNP following increases in the price of crude oil of 5 percent or more and a decline in the index of leading economic indicators amounting to 1 percent or more.

Source: *Monthly Energy Review* and BCI series 910, 105, 114, and 50.

TABLE 1.20

The Recession of 1990–1991 and Fluctuations in the Average Weekly Hours of Production Workers in Manufacturing of 1.1 Hours or More

	Date of			Weekly Hours Worked			Decline in Hours Worked		Adjusted Lead Time in Months[a]
W.H. Peak	NBER Peak	W.H. Trough	W.H. Peak	NBER Peak	W.H. Trough	W.H. Peak – NBER Peak	W.H. Peak – W.H. Trough	
Apr. 48	Nov. 48	Apr. 49	40.4	39.7	38.8	.7	1.6	–4
Apr. 51	July 53	Apr. 54	41.2	40.6	39.4	.6	1.8	15*
Nov. 55	Aug. 57	Apr. 58	41.0	39.8	38.6	1.2	2.4	3
May 59	Apr. 60	Dec. 60	40.6	39.7	38.4	.9	2.2	–5
Feb. 66	Dec. 69	Sep. 70	41.6	40.5	39.3	1.1	2.3	34*
Apr. 73	Nov. 73	Mar. 75	40.9	40.7	38.8	.2	2.1	–5
Apr. 78	Jan. 80	July 80	40.8	40.0	39.1	.8	1.7	9
Dec. 80	July 81	Jan. 82	40.3	39.9	38.0	.4	2.3	–6
Recession of 1990–91								
Nov. 88	July 90	Apr. 91	41.2	40.9	40.2	.3	1.0	No signal

[a]Months to the NBER business peak after a 1.1 hour decline in the average weekly hours of production workers.

*Lead times that are associated with a substantial military procurement increase during the Korean and Vietnam wars.

Source of basic data: BCI series 1.

TABLE 1.21
Civilian Employment by Major Industry in the United States, Selected Years, 1947–1990

Year	Total Employment	Agriculture	Mining	Construction	Manufacturing	Government	Other Services
				Thousands of Persons			
1947	57,038	7,890	955	2,009	15,545	5,474	25,165
1960	65,778	5,458	712	2,926	16,796	8,358	31,533
1970	78,678	3,463	623	3,588	19,367	12,554	39,083
1980	99,303	3,364	1,027	4,346	20,285	16,241	54,040
1990	117,914	3,186	735	5,204	19,063	18,291	71,435
				% of Total Employment			
1947	—	13.8	1.8	3.5	27.2	9.6	44.1
1960	—	8.3	1.1	4.5	25.5	12.7	47.6
1970	—	4.4	.8	4.6	24.6	16.0	49.6
1980	—	3.4	1.0	4.4	20.4	16.4	54.4
1990	—	2.7	.6	4.4	16.2	15.5	60.6

Source of basic data: *Economic Report of the President*, February 1991.

TABLE 1.22
Fluctuations in the Number of Employees on Nonagricultural Payrolls Amounting to 1.4 Percent or More

Date of			Number of Employees (Thousands)		Percent Decline	Duration in Months		
Peak	Trough	Recovery	Peak	Trough		Trough to Peak	Peak to Trough	Trough to Recovery
Sep. 48	Oct. 49	July 50	45,167	42,823	5.19	—	13	9
Jun. 53	Aug. 54	May 55	50,386	48,644	3.46	44	14	9
Mar. 57	May 58	Apr. 59	53,052	50,760	4.32	31	14	11
Apr. 60	Feb. 61	Nov. 61	54,561	53,373	2.18	23	10	9
Mar. 70	Nov. 70	Sep. 71	71,363	70,264	1.54	109	8	10
Oct. 74	Apr. 75	Feb. 76	78,599	76,333	2.88	47	6	10
Mar. 80	July 80	Feb. 81	90,970	89,670	1.43	59	4	7
July 81	Dec. 82	Nov. 83	91,467	88,644	3.09	12	17	11
Jun. 90			110,435			90		
Average values for the periods:								
1948–61					3.79	33	13	9.5
1962–90					2.24	63	9	9.5

Source of basic data: BCI series 41.

123

TABLE 1.23

Cyclical Declines in Employees in Nonagricultural Goods Producing Industries and Changes in Civilian and Other Types of Employment

Date	Thousands of Persons Employed in the			% Change in Employment in the		
	Civilian Sector	Goods Production	Other Industries	Civilian Sector	Goods Production	Other Industries
Sep. 48	58,513	18,915	39,598			
Feb. 50	57,751	17,119	40,632	−1.3	−9.5	2.6
Apr. 53	61,444	21,304	40,140			
Aug. 54	59,853	19,418	40,435	−2.6	−8.9	.7
Dec. 56	63,910	21,292	42,618			
May 58	62,874	19,165	43,709	−1.6	−10.0	2.6
Feb. 60	65,620	20,903	44,717			
Feb. 61	65,588	19,559	46,029	−.0	−6.4	2.4
July 69	77,959	24,497	53,462			
Nov. 70	78,650	22,702	55,948	.9	−7.3	4.6
Dec. 73	86,401	25,268	61,133			
July 75	85,894	22,251	63,643	−.6	−11.9	4.1
July 79	99,006	26,619	72,387			
July 80	98,796	25,035	73,761	−.2	−6.0	1.9
July 81	100,693	25,699	74,994			
Mar. 83	99,179	22,797	76,382	−1.5	−11.3	1.8
Jan. 89	116,708	25,406	91,302			
Apr. 91	117,398	23,793	93,605	.6	−6.3	2.5

Source of basic data: BCI series 442 and 40.

TABLE 1.24

The Duration of Employment Recessions in Months Ranked in Order on the Basis of the Steepest Monthly Decline Percentage in Nonagricultural Payroll Employment during the First Three Months of the Recession

Date of Employment Peak	Worst Monthly % Change in Employment	Duration of Recession (months)
Mar. 80	−.53	4
Oct. 74	−.48	6
Apr. 60	−.45	10
Mar. 70	−.40	8
June 53	−.22	14
Sep. 48	−.18	13
June 90	−.15	?
July 81	−.10	17
Mar. 57	−.07	14

The correlation between the worst monthly percentage change in employment and the duration of the recession is .93.

Source of basic data: BCI series 41.

TABLE 1.25

The Duration of Employment Recessions in Months Ranked in Order of the Monthly Lead Time for Industrial Production

Date of Peak for		Monthly Lead Time Industrial Production	Duration of Recession (months)
Industrial Production	Payroll Employment		
Nov. 73	Oct. 74	11	6
May 79	Mar. 80	10	4
Oct. 69	Mar. 70	5	8
Jan. 60	Apr. 60	3	10
July 48	Sep. 48	2	13
Mar. 57	Mar. 57	0	14
July 81	July 81	0	17
July 53	June 53	−1	14
Sep. 90	June 90	−3	?

The correlation coefficient for the industrial production lead time and the duration of employment recessions is −.93.

Source of basic data: BCI series 47 and 41.

TABLE 1.26

Employment Declines and Some Alternative Ways to Date Business Peaks and Measure the Duration of Economic Recessions

Date of				Duration of Recession in Months				
Coin. Ind. Peak[a]	Indust. Prod. Peak[b]	NBER Bus. Peak[c]	Empl. Ind. Peak[d]	Coin. Ind.[a]	Indust. Prod.[b]	NBER Ind.[c]	Empl. Ind.[d]	CPI Inflation Rate[e] (%)
Oct. 48	July 48	Nov. 48	Sep. 48	12	15	11	13	−2.1
July 53	July 53	July 53	Jun. 53	10	9	10	14	−.7
Feb. 57	Mar. 57	Aug. 57	Mar. 57	14	13	8	14	1.8
Jan. 60	Jan. 60	Apr. 60	Apr. 60	13	13	10	10	.7
Oct. 69	Oct. 69	Dec. 69	Mar. 70	13	13	11	8	5.6
Nov. 73	Nov. 73	Nov. 73	Oct. 74	16	16	16	6	12.3
May 79	May 79	Jan. 80	Mar. 80	14	14	6	4	8.9
Jan. 81	July 81	July 81	July 81	23	17	16	17	3.8
June 90	Sep. 90	July 90	June 90	9	6	9p	?	?
Average values				13.8	12.9	10.8	10.8	

[a]The U.S. Commerce Department's composite index of four coincident indicators.

[b]Federal Reserve's index of industrial production, 1987 = 100.

[c]Dates and duration of business recessions identified by the National Bureau of Economic Research.

[d]U.S. Labor Department's estimate of the number of employees on nonagricultural payrolls.

[e]December-to-December percentage change in the CPI inflation rate in the year after the NBER peak in business activity.

p equals a preliminary estimate.

Source of basic data: BCI series 920, 47, 41, and 320.

TABLE 1.27
Fluctuations in the Civilian Unemployment Rate of .6 Percentage Points or More and U.S. Business Cycles

Unemployment Trough	Unemployment up .6% Points	Unemployment Peak	Business Peak	Unemployment Rate at		Monthly Lead Time	
				Trough (1)	Peak (2)	Total (3)	Adjusted[a] (4)
Jan. 1948	Mar. 1948	Oct. 1949	Nov. 1948	3.4	7.9	10	8
June 1953	Oct. 1953	Sep. 1954	July 1953	2.5	6.1	1	-3
Mar. 1957	June 1957	July 1958	Aug. 1957	3.7	7.5	5	1
June 1959	Oct. 1959	Nov. 1959	—	5.0	5.8	10	6
Feb. 1960	Mar. 1960	May 1961	Apr. 1960	4.8	7.1	2	1
May 1969	Feb. 1970	Aug. 1971	Dec. 1969	3.4	6.1	7	-2
Oct. 1973	Feb. 1974	May 1975	Nov. 1973	4.6	9.0	1	-3
May 1979	Jan. 1980	July 1980	Jan. 1980	5.6	7.8	8	0
July 1981	Oct. 1981	Dec. 1982	July 1981	7.2	10.8	0	-3
Mar. 1989	Sep. 1990		July 1990	5.1		16	-2

[a]Months to the next business peak after the civilian unemployment rate has reversed itself on the upside by at least .6 percentage points after experiencing a trough.

Source of data: BCI series 43.

TABLE 1.28

Following Year Percentage Changes in the S&P Composite Stock Price Index One Month after Cumulative Increases in the Unemployment Rate of from .9 to 1.8 Percentage Points, 1947–1990

Month Containing		Buy Months and the Following Year Percentage Change in S&P Index When Stock Is Purchased at the End of the Month after a Cumulative Increase in the Unemployment Rate of			
Unemployment Trough	S&P Index Trough	.9% Points	1.2% Points	1.5% Points	1.8% Points
Jan. 48	Jun. 49	Feb. 49 17.8	Mar. 49 14.8	Apr. 49 22.6	May 49 32.3*
Jun. 53	Sep. 53	Dec. 53 45.0*	Jan. 54 40.5	Jan. 54 40.5	Jan. 54 40.5
Mar. 57	Oct. 57	Dec. 57 38.1*	Dec. 57 38.1	Jan. 58 32.9	Feb. 58 35.7
Feb. 60	Oct. 60	Nov. 60 28.4*	Nov. 60 28.4	Jan. 61 11.4	Jan. 61 11.4
May 69	May 70	Apr. 70 27.5	May 70 30.5*	Jul. 70 22.5	Oct. 70 13.2
Oct. 73	Oct. 74	Aug. 74 20.4	Oct. 74 20.5	Dec. 74 31.6*	Dec. 74 31.6
May 79	Mar. 80	May 80 19.2*	May 80 19.2	Jun. 80 14.9	Jun. 80 14.9
Jul. 81	Aug. 82	Dec. 81 14.8	Jan. 82 20.7	Mar. 82 36.6	Apr. 82 41.2*
Mar. 89	Oct. 90	Jan. 91	Mar. 91	Apr. 91	Jun. 91
Average gain 1947–88		26.4	26.6	26.6	27.6

*The highest following year gain for the S&P index for the four cumulative increases in the unemployment rate considered in this table.

Source of basic data: BCI series 43 and Standard & Poor's *Security Price Index Record*.

TABLE 1.29

Recessionary Increases in Average Weekly Initial Claims for Unemployment Insurance of 150,000 or More

Low Claim Month	Claims up 150,000	High Claim Month	NBER Peak Month	Average Weekly Claims		Increase in Claims Low to High Month	Months after NBER Peak[a]
				Low Month	High Month		
Jan. 48	Mar. 49	Oct. 49	Nov. 48	166	386	220	4
Sep. 52	Feb. 54	Sep. 54	July 53	168	322	154	7
Sep. 55	Dec. 57	Apr. 58	Aug. 57	204	438	234	4
Apr. 59	Feb. 61	Feb. 61	Apr. 60	244	429	185	10
Jan. 69	Oct. 70	Oct. 70	Dec. 69	179	329	150	10
Feb. 73	Sep. 74	Mar. 75	Nov. 73	223	536	313	10
Sep. 78	Apr. 80	May 80	Jan. 80	321	616	295	3
July 81	Dec. 81	Sep. 82	July 81	395	653	258	5
Oct. 88	Nov. 90	Mar. 91	July 90	290	512	222	4

[a]Months after the NBER peak to a cumulative increase in average weekly unemployment claims of 150,000 or more.

Source of data: BCI series 5.

127

TABLE 1.30
Recessionary Declines in Real GNP and the Associated Percentage Changes in Some of Its Components, Billions of 1982 Dollars

| Year and Qtr. | Real GNP | Consumption Expenditures | | |
		Durable Goods	Non. D. Goods	Services
48-4	1,125.5	62.9	340.5	284.9
49-4	1,103.3	71.2	344.5	285.2
% Change	− 2.0	13.2	1.2	.1
53-2	1,444.9	79.3	389.4	335.0
54-2	1,401.2	79.6	389.0	345.6
% Change	− 3.0	.4	−.1	3.2
57-3	1,561.5	91.0	438.6	393.1
58-1	1,506.1	86.2	432.3	398.0
% Change	− 3.5	−5.3	− 1.4	1.2
60-1	1,671.6	96.9	460.7	439.6
60-4	1,654.1	96.4	463.6	447.9
% Change	− 1.0	−.5	.6	1.8
69-3	2,433.2	167.6	617.6	674.7
70-2	2,406.5	165.6	629.6	692.8
% Change	− 1.1	−1.2	1.9	2.7
73-4	2,762.8	213.8	679.4	793.5
75-1	2,642.7	193.5	666.9	816.7
% Change	− 4.3	−9.5	− 1.8	2.9
80-1	3,233.4	260.6	767.9	986.9
80-2	3,157.0	231.9	760.9	981.3
% Change	− 2.4	−11.0	− .9	− .6
81-3	3,264.6	255.5	764.7	1,011.4
82-3	3,154.5	251.8	772.8	1,027.2
% Change	− 3.4	−1.4	1.1	1.6
90-3	4,170.0	429.5	916.4	1,350.8
91-1	4,124.1	402.9	897.1	1,363.7
% Change	− 1.1	−6.2	− 2.1	1.0

[a]Gross private domestic investment.

Source of basic data: *Survey of Current Business.*

| GPDI[a] | Government Purch. | | Exports | Imports |
	Fed.	State & Local		
206.0	118.6	96.6	63.0	47.1
163.4	117.2	111.2	57.0	46.3
−20.7	−1.2	15.1	−9.5	−1.7
225.1	299.3	120.9	67.2	71.2
206.4	247.5	131.5	71.8	70.2
−8.3	−17.3	8.8	6.8	−1.4
249.2	224.5	157.6	94.6	87.0
210.9	220.9	165.7	82.3	90.1
−15.4	−1.6	5.1	−13.0	3.6
288.7	217.0	178.2	95.0	104.3
233.6	223.2	186.9	100.5	97.9
−19.1	2.9	4.9	5.8	−6.1
419.5	294.2	296.2	170.3	206.9
376.4	268.9	300.8	181.2	208.9
−10.3	−8.6	1.6	6.4	1.0
534.2	223.9	340.3	254.1	276.5
370.6	226.3	351.1	260.0	242.6
−30.6	1.1	3.2	2.3	−12.3
556.7	243.3	374.5	398.9	355.4
499.2	251.6	373.5	393.1	334.5
−10.3	3.4	−.3	−1.5	−5.9
560.7	262.7	367.5	391.1	349.0
448.6	273.8	368.6	359.5	347.8
−20.0	4.2	.3	−8.1	−.3
697.0	346.0	476.7	630.5	677.0
623.7	349.5	480.1	648.0	641.0
−10.5	1.0	.7	2.8	−5.3

TABLE 1.31

Stock Returns and the Shifting Propensity to Spend out of Previous Income When the Government Expenditure Multiplier Is Assumed to Be Equal to Two and the Basic Data Are in Billions of Current Dollars, Selected Years

Year	Gross Private Domestic Investment (1)	Government Deficit (2)	Government Purchases (3)	Net Exports (4)	Actual GNP (5)	Shifting Propensity to Spend[a] (6)	Following Financial Return S&P Index (7)
1929	16.7	−1.0	8.9	1.1	103.9	63.0	−23.9
1930	10.6	.3	9.5	1.0	91.1	56.9	−41.7
1932	1.1	1.8*	8.3	.4	58.5	60.0	53.0
1934	3.5	2.4	10.2	.6	65.6	81.1	46.3
1937	12.1	−.3	13.2	.4	91.3	64.7	30.0
1938	6.7	1.8*	13.6	1.3	85.4	60.6	− .8
1941	18.3	3.8	25.0	1.5	125.5	58.4	19.2
1942	10.3	31.4	59.9	.2	159.0	37.4	25.7**
1944	7.7	51.8	97.1	−1.7	211.4	25.3	35.7**
1947	35.0	−14.4	26.4	11.9	235.2	66.5	5.4
1948	47.1	−8.4	32.6	7.0	261.6	66.9	17.8
1949	36.5	3.4*	39.0	6.5	260.4	52.9	30.5
1950	55.1	−8.0	38.8	2.2	288.3	55.7	23.4
1951	60.5	−6.1	60.4	4.5	333.4	53.3	17.7
1952	53.5	3.8	75.8	3.2	351.6	48.5	−1.2**
1953	54.9	7.0	82.8	1.3	371.6	48.6	51.2**
1954	54.1	7.1*	76.0	2.6	372.5	48.1	31.0**
1955	69.7	−3.1	75.3	3.0	405.9	51.4	6.4
1956	72.7	−5.2	79.7	5.3	428.2	50.0	−10.4
1957	71.1	− .9	87.3	7.3	451.0	50.2	42.4
1958	63.6	12.6*	95.4	3.3	456.8	48.4	11.8**
1959	80.2	1.6	97.9	1.5	495.8	51.3	.3
1960	78.2	−3.1	100.6	5.9	515.3	51.5	26.6
1961	77.1	4.3*	108.4	7.2	533.8	50.4	−8.8
1962	87.6	3.8	118.2	6.9	574.6	50.7	22.5
1963	93.1	−.7	123.8	8.2	606.9	50.4	16.3
1964	99.6	2.3	130.0	10.9	649.8	50.6	12.3
1965	116.2	− .5	138.6	9.7	705.1	50.0	−10.0
1966	128.6	1.3	158.6	7.5	772.0	49.3	23.7**
1967	125.7	14.2	179.7	7.4	816.4	47.1	10.8**
1968	137.0	6.0	197.7	5.5	892.7	50.2	−8.3
1969	153.2	−9.9	207.3	5.6	963.9	50.9	3.5
1970	148.8	10.6*	218.2	8.5	1015.5	49.9	14.1**
1971	172.5	19.5	232.4	6.3	1102.7	49.2	18.7**
1972	202.0	3.4	250.0	3.2	1212.8	50.1	−14.5
1973	238.8	−7.9	266.5	16.8	1359.3	50.0	−26.0
1974	240.8	4.3	299.1	16.3	1472.8	49.4	36.9**
1975	219.6	64.9*	335.0	31.3	1598.4	49.4	23.6**
1976	277.7	38.4	356.9	18.8	1782.8	50.9	−7.2
1977	344.1	19.1	387.3	1.9	1990.5	50.2	6.4
1978	416.8	.4	425.2	4.1	2249.7	49.6	18.4**
1979	454.8	−11.5	467.8	18.8	2508.2	49.9	31.5**
1980	437.0	34.5*	530.3	32.1	2732.0	50.3	−4.8
1981	515.5	29.7	588.1	33.9	3052.6	50.1	20.4
1982	447.3	110.8*	641.7	26.3	3166.0	48.9	22.3**
1983	502.3	128.6	675.0	−6.1	3405.7	50.6	6.0
1984	664.8	105.0	735.9	−58.9	3772.2	48.8	31.1**
1985	643.1	131.8	820.8	−78.0	4014.9	49.2	18.5**

TABLE 1.31 (concluded)

Year	Gross Private Domestic Investment (1)	Government Deficit (2)	Government Purchases (3)	Net Exports (4)	Actual GNP (5)	Shifting Propensity to Spend[a] (6)	Following Financial Return S&P Index (7)
1986	659.4	144.1	872.2	−97.4	4231.6	49.7	5.7**
1987	699.5	107.1	921.4	−114.7	4515.6	52.0	16.3
1988	747.1	95.3	962.5	−74.1	4873.7	53.0	31.2
1989	771.2	87.8	1025.6	−46.1	5200.8	53.1	−3.1
1990	741.0	130.6	1098.1	−31.2	5465.1	53.6	?

[a]The shifting propensity to spend out of the previous year's income is equal to column (5) minus two times column (1) minus the sum of columns (2), (3), and (4) when this Keynesian-type residual is expressed as a percent of GNP in the preceding year.

*The government deficit in the national income and product accounts in those years containing a recessionary trough in economic activity.

**Financial returns following a shifting propensity to spend in column (6) that is less than 50 percent.

Source of basic data: Economic Report of the President and Standard & Poor's Security Price Index Record.

TABLE 1.32
Stock Returns and the Accelerator Relationship between the Year-to-Year Growth Rates for Real GNP and Gross Private Fixed Domestic Investment in 1982 Dollars

Year	Real GNP (1)	Actual Investment (2)	Predicted Investment[a] (3)	Actual minus Predicted Investment (4)	Following Year S&P Financial Return (5)
1946	−19.0	76.9	−63.0	139.9*	5.5**
1947	−2.8	19.1	−14.4	33.5*	5.4**
1948	3.9	9.6	5.7	3.9*	17.8
1949	.0T	−9.0#	−6.0	−3.0	30.5
1950	8.5	18.2	19.5	−1.3	23.4
1951	10.3	−3.1#	24.9	−28.0	17.7
1952	3.9	−1.2#	5.7	−6.9	−1.2
1953	4.0	5.9	6.0	−.1	51.2
1954	−1.3T	1.6	−9.9	11.5*	31.0**
1955	5.6	12.1	10.8	1.3	6.4
1956	2.1X	.6#	.3	.3	−10.4
1957	1.7X	−1.8#	−.9	−.9	42.4
1958	−.8T	−6.5#	−8.4	1.9	11.8**
1959	5.8	12.9	11.4	1.5	.3
1960	2.2X	−.4#	.6	−1.0	26.6
1961	2.6T	−.4#	1.8	−2.2	−8.8
1962	5.3	8.2	9.9	−1.7	22.5

TABLE 1.32 (concluded)

Year	Real GNP (1)	Actual Investment (2)	Predicted Investment[a] (3)	Actual minus Predicted Investment (4)	Following Year S&P Financial Return (5)
1963	4.1	6.6	6.3	.3	16.3
1964	5.3	6.8	9.9	−3.1	12.3
1965	5.8	10.2	11.4	−1.2	−10.0
1966	5.8	3.5#	11.4	−7.9	23.7
1967	2.9	−2.3#	2.7	−6.0	10.8
1968	4.1	7.3	6.3	1.0	−8.3
1969	2.4X	3.9	1.2	2.7*	3.5
1970	−.3T	−3.1#	−6.9	3.8*	14.1**
1971	2.8	7.1	2.4	4.7*	18.7
1972	5.0	11.0	9.0	2.0	−14.5
1973	5.2	8.4	9.6	−1.2	−26.0
1974	−.5	−6.8#	−7.5	.7	36.9**
1975	−1.3T	−11.6#	−9.9	−1.7	23.6**
1976	4.9	8.9	8.7	.2	−7.2
1977	4.7	14.1	8.1	6.0*	6.4
1978	5.3	9.8	9.9	−.1	18.4
1979	2.5X	3.7	1.5	2.2*	31.5
1980	−.2T	−7.8#	−6.6	−1.2	−4.8
1981	1.9X	1.1#	−.3	1.4	20.4
1982	−2.5T	−9.6#	−13.5	3.9*	22.3**
1983	3.6	8.2	4.8	3.4*	6.0
1984	6.8	16.8	14.4	2.4*	31.1
1985	3.4	5.3	4.2	1.1	18.5
1986	2.7	1.0#	1.8	−1.1	5.7
1987	3.4	1.9#	4.2	−2.3	16.3
1988	4.5	5.6	7.5	−1.9	31.2
1989	2.5X	1.6#	1.5	.1	−3.1
1990	1.0X	−.1	−3.0	2.9*	?

[a]The predicted growth rate for fixed investment is equal to three times the growth rate for real GNP in column (1) minus 6 percentage points.

T denotes years containing a trough in business activity.

X denotes years when the growth rate for real GNP was positive but less than 2.6 percent. All of these years contained a recessionary peak in business activity or were followed by a recession.

# denotes years when the growth of real fixed investment was less than the growth rate for real GNP in column (1).

* denotes years when the difference between the actual and the predicted growth rate for fixed investment was equal to 2.2 percentage points or more. Since 1946 these years have so far been followed by a positive financial return for the S&P index.

** denotes financial returns following a year-to-year decline in real GNP in column (1) of minus .3 percentage points or more.

Source of basic data: *Economic Report of the President* and Standard & Poor's *Security Price Index Record*.

TABLE 1.33
Recessionary Declines in Personal Income less Transfer Payments in Billions of 1982 Dollars and the Associated Percentage Changes in Personal Income with Transfer Payments

Dates of		Personal Income Less Transfer Payments at		% Decline Peak to Trough	
Peak	Trough	Peak	Trough	P. I. less Trans. Payments	P. I with Trans. Payments
Oct. 48	July 49	788.4	744.5	5.6	4.4
Oct. 53	Apr. 54	959.6	934.2	2.5	2.2
Aug. 57	Apr. 58	1,085.9	1,059.7	2.4	1.1
Jun. 60	Dec. 60	1,161.6	1,145.6	1.4	.8
Dec. 69	Feb. 70	1,737.7	1,729.8	.5	
Sep. 70	Oct. 70	1,749.8	1,732.9	1.0	.7
Nov. 73	Feb. 75	2,000.0	1,873.1	6.3	3.6
Mar. 79	July 80	2,263.7	2,204.6	2.6	.4
Aug. 81	Sep. 82	2,296.3	2,244.9	2.2	1.0
July 90	Feb. 91	2,919.6	2,837.0	2.8	1.8

Source of data: BCI series 51 and 52.

TABLE 1.34
Cumulative Declines in U.S. Industrial Production Amounting to 2 Percent or More

Date of				Indust. Production at		% Decline Peak to Trough	Months after NBER Peak to 2.0% Decline I.P.
I.P. Peak	NBER Peak	I.P. down 2%	I.P. Trough	Own Peak	Own Trough		
July 48	Nov. 48	Dec. 48	Oct. 49	24.0	21.6	10.0	1
Apr. 51	—	July 51	Aug. 51	28.5	27.5	3.5	—
Mar. 52	—	June 52	July 52	28.6	27.4	4.2*	—
July 53	July 53	Sep. 53	Apr. 54	32.4	29.3	9.6	2
Apr. 56	—	July 56	July 56	35.1	33.4	4.8*	—
Mar. 57	Aug. 57	Oct. 57	Apr. 58	36.3	31.4	13.5	2
June 59	—	July 59	Oct. 59	38.6	36.1	6.5*	—
Jan. 60	Apr. 60	Apr. 60	Feb. 61	39.6	36.2	8.6	0
Oct. 69	Dec. 69	Jan. 70	Nov. 70	64.1	59.6	7.0	1
Nov. 73	Nov. 73	Jan. 74	Mar. 75	75.2	64.1	14.8	2
May 79	Jan. 80	Apr. 80	July 80	86.2	81.2	5.8	3
July 81	July 81	Nov. 81	Dec. 82	87.1	79.3	9.0	4
Sep. 90	July 90	Nov. 90	Mar. 91	110.6	105.0	5.1	4

*Declines in industrial production that were associated with nationwide steel strikes.

Source of basic data: BCI series 47.

TABLE 1.35
The Financial Returns for the S&P Composite Stock Price Index Following Years When the Index of Industrial Production for Durable Goods Declined by 2 Percent or More on a December-to-December Basis

Year	% Change in Industrial Production (1)	Following Year Financial Return S&P Index (2)
1949	−9.0	30.5
1953	−6.7	51.2
1957	−11.7	42.2
1960	−11.4	26.6
1970	−7.9	14.1
1974	−9.4	36.9
1975	−2.4	23.6
1981	−5.5	20.4
1982	−8.6	22.3
1990	−2.6	?

Source of basic data: BCI series 73 & Standard & Poor's *Security Price Index Record.*

TABLE 1.36
One-Year Price Appreciation Associated with a Strategy of Purchasing the S&P Composite Stock Price Index One Month after a Recessionary Decline of 6 Percent or More in Total Wages and Salaries in Mining, Manufacturing, and Construction in 1982 Dollars

Purchase Date	Value of the S&P Index		% Change S&P Index
	Purchase Date	One Year Later	
June 30, 49	14.16	17.69	24.9
Feb. 26, 54	26.15	36.76	40.6
Jan. 31, 58	41.70	55.42	32.9
Jan. 31, 61	61.78	68.84	11.4
Oct. 30, 70	83.25	94.23	13.2
Dec. 31, 74	68.56	90.19	31.5
Apr. 30, 80	106.29	132.81	25.0
June 30, 82	109.61	168.11	53.4
Sep. 28, 90	306.05		?
Average price appreciation			29.1

Source of basic data: BCI series 53 and Standard & Poor's *Security Price Index Record.*

TABLE 1.40
Fluctuations of 7 Percentage Points or More in the University of Michigan Index of Consumer Expectations and the Associated Percentage Changes in the S&P Composite Stock Price Index

Date of		Consumer Exp. Index		Value of S&P Index at		Peak to Trough Change	
C.E. Peak	C.E. Trough	Own Peak	Own Trough	C.E. Peak	C.E. Trough	C.E. (points)	S&P Index (%)
Feb. 53	Nov. 53	95.5	83.9	25.86	24.50	−11.6	−5.3
Nov. 56	May 58	105.2	82.9	45.76	43.70	−22.3	−4.5*
Feb. 60	Nov. 60	104.6	93.4	55.78	55.47	−11.2	−.6
Feb. 62	Aug. 62	103.4	93.4	70.22	58.52	−10.0	−16.7
Nov. 65	Aug. 68	107.3	89.6	92.15	98.11	−17.7	6.5
Feb. 69	May 70	98.0	71.2	101.46	76.06	−26.8	−25.0*
Aug. 72	Feb. 74	91.3	49.4	111.01	93.45	−41.9	−15.8*
May 74	Feb. 75	63.9	50.0	89.67	83.78	−13.9	−6.6
Nov. 76	Dec. 78	85.9	53.8	101.19	96.11	−32.1	−5.0*
Feb. 79	July 79	62.2	44.2	98.23	102.71	−18.0	4.6
Feb. 80	Mar. 80	54.9	44.3	115.34	107.69	−10.6	−6.6
Nov. 80	Dec. 80	76.2	59.7	135.65	133.48	−16.5	−1.6
May 81	Mar. 82	72.9	53.1	131.73	110.84	−19.8	−15.9*
May 83	Sep. 83	93.4	85.8	164.10	167.16	−7.6	1.9
Mar. 84	Oct. 85	97.7	80.8	157.44	186.18	−16.9	18.3
June 86	Nov. 87	90.3	72.7	245.30	245.01	−17.6	−.1
Jan. 89	Aug. 89	89.9	80.3	285.41	346.61	−9.6	21.4
Sep. 89	Oct. 90	88.6	50.9	347.33	307.12	−37.7	−11.6*
Mar. 91		84.5		372.28			

*Changes in the S&P index that are associated with a decline in the consumer expectations index of 19 percentage points or more.

Source of basic data: BCI series 83 and 19.

TABLE 1.41
Using Some Consumer-Oriented Leading Indicators to Discriminate between Poor and More Satisfactory Growth Rates for Real GNP

	November-to-November % Change in			Following Year Growth Rate	
Year	Unemployment Claims (1)	Housing Starts (2)	Consumer Sentiment (3)	Real GNP (4)	S&P Financial Return (5)
1948	22.7*	−23.2*	—	.0**	17.8$
1949	63.0*	49.2	—	8.5	30.5$@
1950	−41.9	−12.6	—	10.3#	23.4
1951	5.0	−15.2	—	3.9#	17.7
1952	−19.5	11.4	—	4.0	−1.2
1953	76.3*	−6.2	−6.3*	−1.3**	51.2$

TABLE 1.41 (concluded)

| | November-to-November % Change in | | | Following Year Growth Rate | |
| | Unemployment Claims | Housing Starts | Consumer Sentiment | Real GNP | S&P Financial Return |
Year	(1)	(2)	(3)	(4)	(5)
1954	−7.4	25.1	7.7	5.6	31.0[a]
1955	−22.1	−17.1	14.6	2.1[#]	6.4
1956	3.7	−15.5	.5	1.7[#]	−10.4
1957	43.5*	−4.1	−16.5*	−.8**	42.4[$]
1958	−2.8	37.1	8.5	5.8	11.8[a]
1959	12.9	−11.1	3.3	2.2[#]	.3
1960	9.7	−12.0	−3.9	2.6[#]	26.6
1961	−20.8	11.2	4.8	5.3	−8.8
1962	−2.0	17.1	.6	4.1	22.5
1963	−7.7	.0	2.0	5.3	16.3
1964	−5.1	−8.4	2.6	5.8	12.3
1965	−19.1	−1.7	3.5	5.8	−10.0
1966	−1.9	−34.2*	−14.2*	2.9**	23.7
1967	.5	60.0	5.2	4.1	10.8[a]
1968	−9.1	6.0	−.9	2.4	−8.3
1969	11.1	−24.6*	−13.5*	−.3**	3.5
1970	52.6*	34.0	−5.4	2.8	14.1[$(a]
1971	−12.1	32.5	9.0	5.0	18.7[a]
1972	−14.8	11.0	10.5	5.2	−14.5
1973	4.1	−28.8*	−16.6*	−.5**	−26.0
1974	88.4*	−40.5*	−22.2*	−1.3**	36.9[$]
1975	−16.9	32.6	29.1	4.9	23.6[a]
1976	−.8	20.7	14.1	4.7	−7.2
1977	−11.0	24.4	−3.4	5.3	6.4
1978	−2.0	2.5	−9.7*	2.5	18.4
1979	23.5*	−27.2*	−15.6*	−.2**	31.5[$]
1980	.5	−.9	21.2	1.9	−4.8
1981	27.7*	−44.6*	−18.2*	−2.5**	20.4[$]
1982	14.3	63.9	15.4	3.6	22.3[a]
1983	−38.2	30.1	26.4	6.8	6.0[a]
1984	4.2	−5.4	5.0	3.4	31.1
1985	−6.6	.5	−5.0	2.7	18.5
1986	−7.8	−4.0	.6	3.4	5.7
1987	−4.3	1.9	−9.1*	4.5	16.6
1988	−1.0	−5.5	11.9	2.5	31.2
1989	15.5	−14.4	−2.3	1.0[#]	−3.1
1990	33.8*	−16.1	−27.4*	[#]**	?[$]

*A poor growth rate for real GNP is predicted if unemployment claims increase by 22 percent or more, if housing starts decline by 23 percent or more, or if the index of consumer sentiment declines by 6 percent or more.

**Following year growth rates for real GNP when at least two of the three indicators are predicting a poor growth rate for real GNP.

[#]Since 1952 there has been a high incidence of slow and below-average growth rates for real GNP that can be identified by a decline in housing starts of 10 percent or more.

[$] Financial returns following years when the unemployment claims in column (1) increased by 16 percent or more.

[a] Financial returns following years when housing starts in column (2) increased 25 percent or more.

Source of basic data: BCI series 5, 28, 58, and 50 and Standard & Poor's *Security Price Index Record*.

TABLE 1.50
Cyclical Peaks in the Index of New Private Housing Units Authorized by Local Building Permits (1967 = 100) and Recessionary Peaks in Business Activity

Peak Months for		Housing Permit Index			Lead Time in Months	
Housing Permits	Economic Activity	Permit Peak	Economic Peak	% Decline	Unadjusted	Adjusted[a]
Oct. 1947	Nov. 1948	118.2	86.2	27.1	13	1
July 1950	July 1953	182.8	100.0	45.3	36	28
Feb. 1955	Aug. 1957	151.0	92.1	39.0	30	11
Nov. 1958	Apr. 1960	134.1	95.6	28.7	17	5
Feb. 1969	Dec. 1969	131.0	101.3	22.7	10	0
Dec. 1972	Nov. 1973	208.5	120.8	42.1	11	0
Jun. 1978	Jan. 1980	160.2	103.4	35.5	19	1
Sep. 1980	July 1981	119.9	75.5	37.0	10	1
Feb. 1984	July 1990	158.5	86.6	45.4	77	3

[a]Months to the next economic peak after the building permit index has been down 20 percent for two months in a row if the permit peak was less than 150 and down 35 percent for two months in a row if the permit peak was over 150.

Source of basic data: BCI series 29.

TABLE 1.51
Cyclical Fluctuations in the Number of New Private Housing Units Started

Date of Housing		Thousands of Units Started at			% Decline to		
Peak	Trough	Housing Peak (1)	Business Peak (2)	Housing Trough (3)	Business Peak (4)	Housing Trough (5)	Adjusted Lead Time in Months[a]
1889	1891	342	—	298	—	12	
1892	1896	381	—	257	—	32	
1897	1900	292	—	189	—	35	
1905	1910	507	—	387	—	24	
1916	1918	437	—	118	—	73	
1925	1933	937	—	93	—	90	
1941	1944	619	—	193	—	78	
Oct. 1947	Feb. 1949	1,571	1,196	1,137	24	28	2
Aug. 1950	July 1951	2,121	1,346	1,257	37	41	23
Dec. 1954	Feb. 1958	1,807	1,193	1,107	34	39	13
Feb. 1959	Dec. 1960	1,667	1,289	1,063	23	36	0
Feb. 1964	Oct. 1966	1,820	—	843	—	54	43
Jan. 1969	Jan. 1970	1,769	1,327	1,085	25	39	0
Jan. 1972	Feb. 1975	2,494	1,724	904	31	64	−9
Apr. 1978	May 1980	2,197	1,341	927	39	58	−1
Jan. 1981	Nov. 1981	1,547	1,041	837	33	46	4
Feb. 1984	Jan. 1991	2,260	1,155	847	49	63	3

[a]Months to the NBER business peak after the number of new private housing units started has declined to 1,350 thousand units for two months in a row.

Source of basic data: BCI series 28.

TABLE 1.60
Investment in Business Inventories at Post-World War II Peaks and Troughs and Real GNP in Billions of 1982 Dollars at Annualized Rates of Change

Contraction Dates for Real GNP		Inventory Sales Ratio[a]	Change in Business Inventories				Peak to Trough Decline In	
Peak Quarter	Trough Quarter	Peak Quarter (1)	Quarter before Peak (2)	Peak Quarter (3)	Trough Quarter (4)	Quarter after Trough (5)	Inventory Investment[b] (6)	Real GNP (7)
1948–4	1949–4	1.48	15.9	11.8	−16.5	11.0	28.3	22.2
1953–2	1954–2	1.55	8.4	10.7	−7.7	−5.8	18.4	43.7
1957–3	1958–1	1.54	6.1	7.3	−15.2	−12.8	22.5	55.4
1960–1	1960–4	1.49	19.3	26.7	−13.9	−7.1	40.6	17.5
1969–3	1970–2	1.55	22.9	29.2	10.0	16.1	19.2	26.7
1973–4	1975–1	1.49	30.1	56.3	−21.8	−30.3	86.6	120.1
1980–1	1980–2	1.60	−7.6	4.1	2.3	−29.5	33.6	76.4
1981–3	1982–3	1.65	21.8	35.7	−9.4	−59.3	95.0	110.1
1990–3	1991–1	1.44	9.5	4.7	−25.0	−21.2	29.7	45.9

[a]The ratio of manufacturing and trade inventories to sales in 1982 dollars.
[b]Column (3) minus the smaller of column (4) or (5).

Source of basic data: BCI series 30, 77, and 50.

TABLE 1.61

The Duration of Recessions in GNP Expressed in 1982 Dollars Ranked in Order of the Four-Quarter Change in Business Inventories Ending in the First Quarter after a Peak in Real GNP, 1948–1990

Date of Real GNP Peak	Four-Quarter Change in Business Inventory (billions of 1982 $)	Duration of Recession (quarters)	Does the Recession Have Double Bottom?
1990–3	−14.4	2	No
1980–1	9.7	1	No
1957–3	12.1	2	No
1953–2	37.4	4	No
1948–4	40.1	4	Yes
1960–1	57.8	3	Yes
1981–3	95.4	4	Yes
1969–3	100.6	5	Yes
1973–4	161.3	5	Yes

Source of basic data: BCI series 30.

TABLE 1.70

Fluctuations in the Average Monthly Values of the S&P Composite Stock Price Amounting to 10 Percent or More

Date of Cycle		Index Value		Months Duration		% Change	
Peak	Trough	Peak (1)	Trough (2)	Rise (3)	Decline (4)	Rise (5)	Decline (6)
Apr. 1872	Nov. 1873	5.18	4.01	15	19	16.7	22.0
Feb. 1874	June 1877	4.80	2.73	3	40	18.8	43.1*
June 1881	Jan. 1885	6.58	4.24	48	43	141.0	35.6*
May 1887	June 1888	5.90	5.01	28	13	39.2	15.1
May 1890	Dec. 1890	5.62	4.60	23	7	12.2	18.1
Aug. 1892	Aug. 1893	5.62	4.08	20	12	22.2	27.4*
Sep. 1895	Aug. 1896	4.82	3.81	25	11	18.1	21.0
Apr. 1899	Sep. 1900	6.48	5.80	32	17	70.1	10.5
Sep. 1902	Oct. 1903	8.85	6.26	24	13	52.6	29.3*
Sep. 1906	Nov. 1907	10.03	6.25	35	14	60.2	37.7*
Dec. 1909	July 1910	10.30	8.64	25	7	64.8	16.1
June 1911	Sep. 1911	9.67	8.67	11	3	11.9	10.3
Sep. 1912	Dec. 1914	9.86	7.35	12	27	13.7	25.5
Nov. 1916	Dec. 1917	10.21	6.80	23	13#	38.9	33.4*
July 1919	Aug. 1921	9.51	6.45	19	25	39.9	32.2*
Mar. 1923	Oct. 1923	9.43	8.03	19	7	46.2	14.8
Sep. 1929	Nov. 1929	31.30	20.58	71	2	289.8	34.2*
Apr. 1930	Dec. 1930	25.46	15.51	5	8	23.7	39.1*
Mar. 1931	June 1932	17.53	4.77	3	15	13.0	72.8*
Sep. 1932	Mar. 1933	8.26	6.23	3	6	73.2	24.6
July 1933	Oct. 1933	11.23	9.55	4	3#	80.3	15.0

TABLE 1.70 (concluded)

Date of Cycle		Index Value		Months Duration		% Change	
Peak	Trough	Peak (1)	Trough (2)	Rise (3)	Decline (4)	Rise (5)	Decline (6)
Feb. 1934	Mar. 1935	11.32	8.41	4	13*	18.5	25.7
Feb. 1937	Apr. 1938	18.11	9.89	23	14	115.3	45.4*
Nov. 1938	Apr. 1939	13.07	10.83	7	5#	32.2	17.1
Oct. 1939	June 1940	12.90	9.67	6	8#	19.1	25.0
Nov. 1940	Apr. 1942	10.98	7.84	5	17#	13.5	28.6*
May 1946	May 1947	18.70	14.34	49	12#	138.5	23.3
July 1947	Feb. 1948	15.77	14.10	2	7#	10.0	10.6
June 1948	June 1949	16.82	13.97	4	12	19.3	16.9
Jan. 1953	Sep. 1953	26.18	23.27	42	8	87.4	11.1
July 1956	Feb. 1957	48.78	43.47	34	7#	109.6	10.9
July 1957	Dec. 1957	48.51	40.33	5	5	11.6	16.9
July 1959	Oct. 1960	59.74	53.73	19	15	48.1	10.1
Dec. 1961	June 1962	71.74	55.63	14	6#	33.5	22.5
Jan. 1966	Oct. 1966	93.32	77.13	43	9#	67.8	17.3
Dec. 1968	June 1970	106.48	75.59	26	18	38.1	29.0*
Jan. 1973	Dec. 1974	118.42	67.07	31	23	56.7	43.4*
Sep. 1976	Mar. 1978	105.45	88.82	21	18#	57.2	15.8
Feb. 1980	Apr. 1980	115.34	102.97	23	2	29.9	10.7
Nov. 1980	July 1982	135.65	109.38	7	20	31.7	19.4
Aug. 1987	Dec. 1987	329.36	240.96	61	4#	201.1	26.8
June 1990	Oct. 1990	360.39	307.12	30	4	49.6	14.8

#Stock market declines in the midst of prosperity that were not associated with economic recessions.
*Bear markets of greater magnitude than the 26.8 percent decline experienced during the crash of 1987.

Source of basic data: BCI series 19 and Standard & Poor's Trade and Securities Statistics, *Security Price Index Record*.

TABLE 1.71
Stock Market Crashes Amounting to 10 Percent or More for the Average Monthly Values of the S&P Composite Stock Price Index in the Post-1947 Period and Related Information

Date of Crash		Dividend Yield at Peak[a] (1)	12-Month % Change T-Bill Rate at Peak[b] (2)	24-Month % Change S&P Index at Peak (3)	% Decline in S&P Index Peak-Trough (4)
Peak	Trough				
Jan. 1953	Sep. 1953*	5.45	20.7	23.4	11.1
Feb. 1980	Apr. 1980*	5.24	38.2	29.6	10.7
June 1948	June 1949*	5.02	163.2	−9.5	16.9
Nov. 1980	July 1982*	4.63	17.0	43.2	19.4
July 1957	Dec. 1957*	3.95	35.6	13.6	16.9
July 1956	Feb. 1957	3.89	43.8	61.9	10.9
Sep. 1976	Mar. 1978	3.71	−20.4	54.8	15.8
June 1990	Oct. 1990*	3.37	−5.8	33.1	14.8

TABLE 1.71 (concluded)

Date of Crash		Dividend Yield at Peak[a] (1)	12-Month % Change T-Bill Rate at Peak[b] (2)	24-Month % Change S&P Index at Peak (3)	% Decline in S&P Index Peak-Trough (4)
Peak	Trough				
July 1959	Oct. 1960*	3.11	237.5	23.1	10.1
Jan. 1966	Oct. 1966	3.02	20.1	22.1	17.3
Dec. 1968	June 1970*	2.93	18.2	30.9	29.0
Dec. 1961	June 1962	2.85	15.4	21.5	22.5
Aug. 1987	Dec. 1987	2.69	7.7	74.9	26.8
Jan. 1973	Dec. 1974*	2.69	56.2	26.7	43.4

[a]Aggregate cash dividends associated with the S&P index (based on latest known annual rate) divided by the aggregate market value based on Wednesday closing prices. The monthly data for the peak month are averages of the weekly figures.
[b]Percentage change in the average monthly yield on new three-month Treasury bills, calculated on a bank discount basis.
*Stock market crashes that were associated with economic recessions.

Source of basic data: BCI series 19 and 114 and Standard & Poor's *Security Price Index Record.*

TABLE 1.72
End of the Decade Values for the S&P Composite Stock Price Index and Associated Dividend Yields, 1879–1989

Year	December Dividend Yield for the S&P Index (1)	Average December Value for the S&P Index (2)	% Change in S&P Index (3)
1879	4.26	4.92	—
1889	4.03	5.32	8.1
1899	3.46	6.02	13.2
1909	4.17	10.30	71.1
1919	5.26	8.92	−13.4
1929	4.48	21.40	139.9*
1939	4.54	12.37	−42.2
1949	6.75	16.54	33.7
1959	3.18	59.06	257.1*
1969	3.52	91.11	54.3
1979	5.53	107.78	18.3
1989	3.33	348.57	223.4*

*Decade gains in the S&P index following a closing yield of 5 percent or more in the preceding decade.

Source of basic data: Standard & Poor's *Security Price Index Record.*

TABLE 1.73
Duration and Amplitude of Monthly Average Stock Market Fluctuations
Amounting to 5.5 Percent or More

Date of Cycle		S&P Stock Index		Months Duration		% Change in Index	
Peak	Trough	Peak (1)	Trough (2)	Rise (3)	Decline (4)	Rise (5)	Decline (6)
May 1946	Nov. 1946	18.70	14.69	30	6	65.0	21.4
Feb. 1947	May 1947	15.80	14.34	3	3	7.6	9.2
July 1947	Feb. 1948	15.77	14.10	2	7	10.0	10.6
June 1948	June 1949	16.82	13.97	4	12	19.3	16.9*
June 1950	July 1950	18.74	17.38	12	1	34.1**	7.3
Jan. 1953	Sep. 1953	26.18	23.27	30	8	50.6	11.1*
July 1956	Feb. 1957	48.78	43.47	34	7	109.6**	10.9
July 1957	Dec. 1957	48.51	40.33	5	5	11.6	16.9*
July 1959	Oct. 1960	59.74	53.73	19	15	48.1**	10.1*
Dec. 1961	June 1962	71.74	55.63	14	6	33.5**	22.5
Jan. 1966	Oct. 1966	93.32	77.13	43	9	67.8	17.3
Sep. 1967	Mar. 1968	95.81	89.09	11	6	24.2	7.0
Dec. 1968	June 1970	106.48	75.59	9	18	19.5	29.0*
Apr. 1971	Nov. 1971	103.04	92.78	10	7	36.3**	10.0
Jan. 1973	Aug. 1973	118.42	103.80	14	7	27.6	12.3
Oct. 1973	Dec. 1974	109.84	67.07	2	14	5.8	38.9*
July 1975	Sep. 1975	92.49	84.67	7	2	37.9**	8.5
Sep. 1976	Mar. 1978	105.45	88.82	12	18	24.5	15.8
Aug. 1978	Nov. 1978	103.92	94.71	5	3	17.0	8.9
Feb. 1980	Apr. 1980	115.34	102.97	15	2	21.8	10.7*
Nov. 1980	July 1982	135.65	109.38	7	20	31.7**	19.4*
Oct. 1983	July 1984	167.65	151.08	15	9	53.5**	9.9
Aug. 1987	Dec. 1987	329.36	240.96	37	4	118.0	26.8
June 1990	Oct. 1990	360.39	307.12	30	4	49.6	14.8*

*Stock market declines that were associated with economic recessions.
**Rises following economic recessions.

Source of basic data: BCI series 19.

TABLE 1.74

Stock Market Declines Associated with Business Peaks in the Post-World War II Period

Date of			Closing Values for the S&P Index			% Decline
Market Peak	Business Peak	Market Low	Market Peak	Business Peak	Market Low	Bus. Peak Mkt. Low
6/15/48	11/30/48	6/13/49	17.06	14.75	13.55	8.1
1/05/53	7/31/53	9/14/53	26.66	24.75	22.71	8.2
8/02/56	8/30/57	10/22/57	49.74	45.22	38.98	13.8
8/03/59	4/29/60	10/25/60	60.71	54.37	52.30	3.8
11/29/68	12/31/69	5/26/70	108.37	92.06	69.29	24.7
1/11/73	11/30/73	10/03/74	120.24	95.96	62.28	35.1
2/13/80*	1/31/80	3/27/80	118.44*	114.16	98.22	14.0
11/28/80	7/31/81	8/12/82	140.52	130.92	102.42	21.8
07/16/90	7/31/90	10/11/90	368.95	356.15	295.46	17.0

*Only case where the stock market peak occurred after the business peak.

Source of basic data: Standard & Poor's *Security Price Index Record.*

TABLE 1.75

Some Monthly Lead Times for Stock Prices at Business Peaks and Troughs

Date of NBER Business		Unadjusted Lead Times		Adjusted Lead Times at	
Peak	Trough	Months to Peak	Months to Trough	Business Peak[a]	Business Trough[b]
Nov. 48	Oct. 49	30	4	27	3
July 53	May 54	6	8*	3	5
Aug. 57	Apr. 58	13	4	0	−1
Apr. 60	Feb. 61	9	4	2	2
Dec. 69	Nov. 70	12	5*	6	2
Nov. 73	Mar. 75	10	3	8	2
Jan. 80	July 80	−1	3	−2	1
July 81	Nov. 82	8	4	−2	2
July 90	Apr. 91p	1	6*	−1	4

[a]Months to the business peak after the monthly average value for the S&P composite stock price index has declined 5 percent or more from its preceding cyclical high and maintained that degree of downness until after the next cyclical trough in the S&P index.

[b]Months to business trough after the monthly average value for the S&P index has increased the 5.5 percent needed to offset abortive rallies in the midst of an economic recession.

*Lead times that may have been influenced by major military operations.

p equals a preliminary estimate.

Source of basic data: BCI series 19.

TABLE 1.76

Using Stock Prices and Other Cyclical Indicators to Discriminate between Poor and More Satisfactory Growth Rates for Real GNP

Year	Nov. Decline Ratio Building Permits[a] (1)	December Down Ratios for[b]				Following Year Growth Rate for Real GNP (6)
		Help Wanted Advertising to Persons Unemployed (2)	M1 1982 Dollars (3)	Stock Prices (4)	Inverted Treasury Bill Rate (5)	
1948	.788*	.618*	.909*	.903*	.330*	.0**
1949	1.646	.949	1.005	1.027	.945	8.5
1950	.871	.941	.972	.994	.759	10.3
1951	.735*	.933	.968*	.997	.601	3.9
1952	1.289	1.044	.996	1.034	.488	4.0
1953	.854*	.349*	.996	.948*	.638	−1.3**
1954	1.358	1.090	1.005	1.046	.556	5.6
1955	.791*	1.028	.999	1.009	.254*	2.1#
1956	.872	.881*	.982	.952	.201*	1.7#
1957	.944	.475*	.948*	.827*	.210*	−.8**
1958	1.515	1.063	1.007	1.019	.313*	5.8#
1959	.751*	.935	.978	.989	.193*	2.2#
1960	.915	.538*	.970	.951	.388*	2.6#
1961	1.176	1.010	1.003	1.009	.866	5.3
1962	1.073	.908	1.000	.873*	.794	4.1
1963	1.058	.971	.995	1.016	.645	5.3
1964	.924	.973	1.002	.983	.588	5.8
1965	1.042	1.035	1.001	.995	.521	5.8
1966	.563*	.936	.984	.872*	.453	2.9
1967	1.707	.895	1.002	.995	.453	4.1
1968	1.107	.985	1.004	1.010	.383*	2.4#
1969	.829*	.873*	.969*	.856*	.294*	−.3**
1970	1.261	.965	.999	1.068	1.088	2.8
1971	1.383	.994	.998	.962	.826	5.0
1972	1.057	1.104	1.010	1.021	.628	5.2
1973	.627*	.879*	.964*	.800*	.432*	−.5**
1974	.559*	.413*	.894*	.566*	.443*	−1.3**
1975	1.416	1.006	.978	.959	.944	4.9
1976	1.381	1.002	.993	.992	1.106	4.7
1977	1.157	1.100	.999	.890*	.718	5.3
1978	.950	.956	.989	.911	.477	2.5
1979	.771*	.889*	.942*	.992	.360*	−.2**

TABLE 1.76 (*concluded*)

Year	Nov. Decline Ratio Building Permits[a] (1)	December Down Ratios for[b]				Following Year Growth Rate for Real GNP (6)
		Help Wanted Advertising to Persons Unemployed (2)	M1 1982 Dollars (3)	Stock Prices (4)	Inverted Treasury Bill Rate (5)	
1980	1.083	1.000	.978	.984	.519	1.9
1981	.541*	.687*	.957*	.913*	.744	−2.5**
1982	1.644	1.032	1.011	1.009	1.004	3.6
1983	1.356	1.058	1.002	.980	.872	6.8
1984	.973	1.017	1.005	.981	.957	3.4
1985	1.030	.979	1.008	1.050	.992	2.7
1986	.972	.986	1.024	1.013	.944	3.4
1987	.887	.971	.986	.732*	.893	4.5
1988	1.040	.995	.992	.840*	.640	2.5
1989	.889	.923	.957*	1.003	.678	1.0
1990	.664*	.571*	.930*	.912*	.761	?**

[a]The November building permit index divided by the building permit index for the preceding November.

[b]The down ratio is the December value of the index expressed as a proportion of its previous cyclical high.

*A poor growth year is predicted by a decline ratio of. 854 or less for building permits; a down ratio of .890 or less for the ratio of help wanted advertising in newspapers to persons unemployed; a down ratio of .969 or less for M1; a down ratio of .950 or less for stock prices; and a down ratio of .450 or less for the inverted yield on new 91-day Treasury bills.

**Those years where three or more of the ratios are predicting a poor growth rate in the following year.

#Mostly slow and below-average growth years that are identified by a December down ratio of .450 or less for the inverted yield on new 91-day Treasury bills.

Source of basic data: BCI series 29, 60, 105, 19, 114, and 50.

TABLE 1.77

Using Monetary and Fiscal Policy Variables to Help Identify Years with Positive Financial Returns for the S&P Composite Stock Price Index

Year	Budget Surplus % GNP (1)	Federal Purchases % GNP (2)	1st Diff. Fed. Pur. % GNP (3)	Dec.–Dec. Growth Real M1 (4)	1st Diff. Growth Real M1 (5)	Financial Return S&P Index (6)
1942	−20.8*	32.7	19.2	21.4**	13.7	19.2[(a]
1943	−24.2*	42.2	9.5	23.7**	2.3	25.7[#(a]
1944	−25.8*	42.3	.1	12.0**	−11.7	19.3[(a]
1945T	−19.7	35.1	−7.2	10.0**	−2.0	35.7
1946	1.6	9.0	−26.1	−14.9	−24.9	−7.8
1947	5.7	5.8	−3.2	−8.4	6.5	5.5
1948	3.2*	6.6	.8	−4.0	4.4	5.4[#]
1949T	−1.0*	8.1	1.5	1.6**	5.6	17.8[#(a]
1950	3.2	6.6	−1.5	−1.3	−2.9	30.5[#(a]
1951	1.9*	11.6	5.0	−.3	1.0	23.4
1952	−1.1*	15.0	3.4	2.9**	3.4	17.7[(a]
1953	−1.9	15.6	.6	.5	−2.4	−1.2[(a]
1954T	−1.6	13.0	−2.6	3.2**	2.7	51.2[(a]
1955	1.1	11.1	−1.9	1.7**	−1.5	31.0
1956	1.4	10.8	−.3	1.5	−3.2	6.4
1957	.5	11.2	.4	−3.6	−2.1	−10.4
1958T	−2.3*	11.9	.7	2.0**	5.6	42.4
1959	−.2	11.0	−.9	.2	−1.8	11.8[#(a]
1960	.6	10.6	−.4	−.9	−1.1	.3
1961T	−.7*	10.9	.3	2.7**	3.6	26.6
1962	−.7	11.2	.3	.6	−2.1	−8.8
1963	.1	10.8	−.4	2.0**	1.4	22.5
1964	−.5	10.2	−.6	3.4**	1.4	16.3
1965	.1	9.7	−.5	2.7**	−.7	12.3
1966	−.2	10.4	.7	−.8	−3.5	−10.0
1967	−1.6*	11.4	1.0	3.3**	4.1	23.7[(a]
1968	−.7	11.2	−.2	2.9**	−.4	10.8[#(a]
1969	−.9	10.4	−.8	−2.6	−5.5	−8.3
1970T	−1.2	9.7	−.7	−.2	2.4	3.5
1971	−2.0	9.1	−.6	3.0**	3.2	14.1
1972	−1.4	8.7	−.4	5.6**	2.6	18.7
1973	−.4	7.8	−.9	−3.0	−8.6	−14.5
1974	−.8	7.9	.1	−7.0	−4.0	−26.0
1975T	−4.3*	8.1	.2	−2.0	5.0	36.9

TABLE 1.77 (concluded)

Year	Budget Surplus % GNP (1)	Federal Purchases % GNP (2)	1st Diff. Fed. Pur. % GNP (3)	Dec.–Dec. Growth Real M1 (4)	1st Diff. Growth Real M1 (5)	Financial Return S&P Index (6)
1976	−3.0	7.6	−.5	1.6**	3.6	23.6#
1977	−2.3	7.6	.0	1.2	−.4	−7.2
1978	−1.3	7.2	−.4	−.7	−1.9	6.4
1979	−.6	7.1	−.1	−4.8	−4.1	18.4
1980T	−2.2*	7.6	.5	−5.1	−.3	31.5
1981	−2.1	7.9	.3	−2.2	2.9	−4.8
1982T	−4.6*	8.6	.7	4.5**	6.7	20.4
1983	−5.2	8.3	−.3	5.6**	1.1	22.3#(a
1984	−4.5	8.2	−.1	1.6**	−4.0	6.0
1985	−4.9	8.8	.6	8.2**	6.6	31.1
1986	−4.9	8.7	−.1	15.8**	7.6	18.5#(a
1987	−3.5	8.4	−.3	−.9	−16.7	5.7#
1988	−2.9	7.8	−.6	.5	1.4	16.3
1989	−2.6	7.7	−.1	−3.9	−4.4	31.2
1990	−3.0	7.8	.1	−2.3	1.6	−3.1

T equals a year containing a recessionary trough in economic activity.

*Years when the federal budget surplus or deficit (−) in the National Income and Product Accounts expressed as a percent of nominal GNP deteriorated by at least one full percentage point. In these years the financial returns in column (6) have always been positive.

**Years when the growth of the real money supply was equal to 1.6 percent or more. In these years the financial returns in column (6) have always been positive.

#Financial returns following years when the first differences in the December-to-December growth rates for the real money supply in column (5) are equal to four percentage points or more.

(a Financial returns following years when the first differences in the share of federal purchases of goods and services in column (3) are equal to .6 percentage points or more.

Source of basic data: *Economic Report of the President*, BCI series 105, and Standard & Poor's *Security Price Index Record*.

TABLE 1.80
Fluctuations in the Conventional Money Supply (M1) in Billions of 1982 Dollars Amounting to 3 Percent or More

M1 Peak	Business Peak	M1 Trough	Peak (1)	Trough (2)	% Decline (3)	Unadjusted[a] (4)	Adjusted[b] (5)
			Value of M1 at			Lead Time in Months	
Jan. 1947	Nov. 1948	Aug. 1948*	480.9	433.4	9.9	22	20
May 1950	July 1953	Feb. 1951*	451.3	427.2	5.3	38	31
Jan. 1956	Aug. 1957	Mar. 1958	476.3	447.3	6.1	19	12
July 1959	Apr. 1960	June 1960	469.2	454.7	3.1	9	6
Jan. 1969	Dec. 1969	July 1970	538.5	516.4	4.1	11	5
Jan. 1973	Nov. 1973	Dec. 1975	569.5	499.3	12.3	10	7
Jan. 1978	Jan. 1980	May 1980	515.2	449.6	12.7	24	11
Sep. 1980	July 1981	June 1982	470.8	443.4	5.8	10	7
May 1987	July 1990	Jan. 1991	637.9	591.8	7.2	38	20

[a]Months from the peak in M1 to the business peak.
[b]Months to the business peak after M1 has declined 1.5 percent.
*Cases where the trough in the real money supply occurred before the following peak in business activity.

Source of basic data: BCI series 105.

TABLE 1.81
Fluctuations in the Money Supply M2 in Billions of 1982 Dollars Amounting to 1.5 Percent or More

M2 Peak	M2 Down 1.5%	Business Peak	M2 Trough	Own Peak	Down 1.5%	Business Peak	Own Trough	Adjusted Lead Time in Months[a]
				M2 in Billions of Dollars at				
Mar. 48	May 48	Nov. 48	July 48	835.7	816.1	812.8	804.3	6
Apr. 50	Sep. 50	July 53	Mar. 51	841.2	828.2	851.3	791.0	34
Jan. 56	Jan. 58	Aug. 57	Jan. 58	916.9	897.0	904.8	897.0	-5
Jan. 69	Aug. 69	Dec. 69	Apr. 70	1,543.1	1,515.9	1,507.9	1,481.2	4
Jan. 73	Aug. 73	Nov. 73	Jan. 75	1,841.2	1,810.5	1,795.2	1,683.4	3
Jan. 78	Feb. 79	Jan. 80	May 80	1,994.3	1,955.4	1,865.5	1,808.5	11
Sep. 80	Jan. 81	July 81	Sep. 81	1,846.1	1,813.6	1,811.1	1,810.4	6
May 88	Mar. 89	July 90	Jan. 91	2,472.3	2,432.5	2,437.4	2,384.4	16

[a]Months to the business peak after real M2 has declined by at least 1.5 percent from its own peak.

Source of basic data: BCI series 106.

TABLE 1.82

Money and the Bond Market: The Inventory Theoretic Approach

Year	Average Yield Aaa Corporate Bonds (1)	Dec.-Dec. Growth of M1 (2)	Average Growth of		% Changes in Moody's Aaa Corp. Bond Yields	
			CPI (3)	Real GNP (4)	Predicted[a] (5)	Actual (6)
1969	7.03	3.3	5.5	2.4	6.8	13.8
1970	8.04	5.1	5.7	−.3	.9	14.4
1971	7.39	6.5	4.4	2.8	−1.4	−8.1
1972	7.21	9.2	3.2	5.0	−7.0	−2.4
1973	7.44	5.5	6.2	5.2	6.6	3.2
1974	8.57	4.3	11.0	−.5	12.9	15.8
1975	8.83	4.8	9.1	−1.3	7.3	3.0
1976	8.43	6.6	5.8	4.9	3.3	−4.5
1977	8.02	8.2	6.5	4.7	1.5	−4.9
1978	8.73	8.2	7.6	5.3	4.1	8.9
1979	9.63	7.6	11.3	2.5	9.9	10.3
1980	11.94	6.8	13.5	−.2	13.2	24.0
1981	14.17	6.5	10.3	1.9	9.5	18.7
1982	13.79	8.5	6.2	−2.5	−7.1	−2.7
1983	12.04	9.6	3.2	3.6	−9.2	−12.7
1984	12.71	5.7	4.3	6.8	4.0	5.6
1985	11.37	12.4	3.6	3.4	−14.2	−10.5
1986	9.02	17.0	1.9	2.7	−27.5	−20.7
1987	9.38	3.6	3.6	3.4	3.4	4.0
1988	9.71	5.1	4.1	4.5	2.5	3.5
1989	9.26	.9	4.8	2.5	10.3	−4.6
1990	9.32	3.9	5.4	1.0	4.0	.6

[a]The predicted change is equal to two times the inflation rate in column (3) plus the growth of real GNP in column (4) minus two times the growth of M1 in column (2).

Source of basic data: *Economic Report of the President.*

TABLE 1.83

Cyclical Increases in the Average Discount Rate on New Issues of 91-Day Treasury Bills Amounting to 70 Percent or More

	Date of				Average Discount Rate			Adjusted Lead Time in Months[a]
Low Yield	Yield Up 70%	Business Peak	High Yield	Low Yield	Yield Up 70%	Yield at Bus. Peak	High Yield	
June 47	Aug. 47	Nov. 48	June 49	.38	.74	1.14	1.16	15
July 49	Dec. 51	July 53	June 53	.98	1.73	2.10	2.23	19
June 54	Dec. 54	Aug. 57	Oct. 57	.65	1.17	3.40	3.59	32*
June 58	Aug. 58	Apr. 60	Dec. 59	.88	1.69	3.24	4.57	20
July 61	Dec. 64	Dec. 69	Jan. 70	2.27	3.86	7.72	7.91	60*
Mar. 71	Mar. 73	Nov. 73	Aug. 74	3.32	6.05	7.87	8.74	8
Dec. 76	Sep. 78	Jan. 80	Mar. 80	4.35	7.84	12.04	15.53	16
June 80	Nov. 80	July 81	Dec. 80	7.00	13.89	14.70	15.66	8
Oct. 86	Mar. 89	July 90	Mar. 89	5.18	8.83	7.66	8.83	16

[a]Months to the business peak after the discount rate has increased at least 70 percent from its cyclical low.
*Lead times that may have been prolonged by the Korean and Vietnam wars.

Source of basic data: BCI series 114.

TABLE 1.84

Cyclical Increases in the Yield on New Issues of High-Grade Long-Term Corporate Bonds Amounting to 25 Percent or More

	Date of				Average Yield		Low to High % Increase in Yield	Adjusted Lead Time in Months[a]
Low Yield	Yield Up 25%	High Yield	Business Peak	Low Yield	Yield Up 25%	High Yield		
Apr. 47	Dec. 48	Dec. 48	Nov. 48	2.43	3.15	3.15	29.6	−1
Sep. 49	June 51	June 53	July 53	2.40	3.24	3.82	59.2	25
Mar. 54	Apr. 56	June 57	Aug. 57	2.74	3.55	4.81	75.5	16
June 58	Sep. 58	Oct. 59	Apr. 60	3.61	4.56	5.37	48.8	19
Jan. 63	Mar. 66	June 70	Dec. 69	4.22	5.33	9.70	129.9	43
Jan. 72	May 74	Sep. 74	Nov. 73	7.36	9.36	10.44	41.8	−6
Dec. 76	Oct. 79	Mar. 80	Jan. 80	7.90	11.17	14.08	78.2	3
June 80	Nov. 80	Sep. 81	July 81	11.12	14.10	16.97	52.6	8
Feb. 87	Oct. 87	Oct. 87	July 90	8.58	10.80	10.80	25.9	33

[a]Months to the business peak after the yield on new issues of high-grade corporate bonds has increased 25 percent from its cyclical low.

Source of basic data: BCI series 116.

TABLE 1.85
Average Return on Investment and the Time Required for an Investment of $2,000 per Year to Grow to $1 Million

Average Interest Rate (%)	Time Required(years)
0	500
3	94
8	49
9	45
10	42
11	39
12	37
13	35
14	33
15	31

TABLE 1.86
Months When the Average Yield on 3-Year Treasury Securities Was at Least 4.5 Percent Greater than the Average Yield on 10-Year Securities: Months Containing Business Peaks and Months When the S&P Stock Price Index Registered a Cyclical Low, 1955–1991

Month and Year	Treasury Bond Yields for Maturities of		Col. (1) Divided by Col. (2) (3)	S&P Index Values at		
	3 Years (1)	10 Years (2)		Monthly High (4)	Monthly Low (5)	Monthly Close (6)
Dec. 1956	3.76	3.59	1.047	47.04	45.84	46.67
Aug. 1957P	4.02	3.93	1.023	47.79	43.89	45.22
Oct. 1957	4.09	3.97	1.030	43.14	39.98L	41.06
July 1959	4.60	4.40	1.045	60.62	58.91	60.51
Sep. 1959	4.97	4.68	1.062	58.92	55.14	56.88
Oct. 1959	4.78	4.53	1.055	57.52	56.00	57.52
Nov. 1959	4.85	4.53	1.071	58.28	56.22	58.28
Dec. 1959	5.12	4.69	1.092	59.89	58.60	59.89
Jan. 1960	4.99	4.72	1.057	60.39	55.61	55.61
Feb. 1960	4.73	4.49	1.053	56.82	54.73	56.12
Apr. 1960P	4.27	4.28	.998	56.59	54.37	54.37
Oct. 1960	3.53	3.89	.907	54.86	52.30L	53.39

TABLE 1.86 (concluded)

Month and Year	Treasury Bond Yields for Maturities of 3 Years (1)	Treasury Bond Yields for Maturities of 10 Years (2)	Col. (1) Divided by Col. (2) (3)	S&P Index Values at Monthly High (4)	S&P Index Values at Monthly Low (5)	S&P Index Values at Monthly Close (6)
Jan. 1966	4.90	4.61	1.063	93.95	92.18	92.88
June 1966	5.05	4.81	1.050	87.07	84.74	84.74
July 1966	5.26	5.02	1.048	87.61	83.60	83.60
Aug. 1966	5.68	5.22	1.088	84.00	74.53	77.10
Sep. 1966	5.79	5.18	1.118	80.08	76.05	76.56
Oct. 1966	5.48	5.01	1.094	80.24	73.20L	80.20
Nov. 1966	5.53	5.16	1.072	82.37	79.67	80.45
Dec. 1966	5.19	4.84	1.072	83.00	80.08	80.33
July 1969	7.31	6.72	1.088	99.61	89.48	91.83
Aug. 1969	7.29	6.69	1.090	95.92	92.63	95.51
Sep. 1969	7.77	7.16	1.085	95.63	92.70	93.12
Oct. 1969	7.57	7.10	1.066	98.12	92.52	97.24
Nov. 1969	7.65	7.14	1.071	98.33	92.94	93.81
Dec. 1969P	8.10	7.65	1.059	93.22	89.20	92.06
Jan. 1970	8.24	7.79	1.058	93.46	85.02	85.02
Feb. 1970	7.79	7.24	1.076	89.50	85.75	89.50
May 1970	7.94	7.91	1.004	81.44	69.29L	76.55
July 1973	7.54	7.13	1.058	109.85	101.28	108.22
Aug. 1973	7.89	7.40	1.066	106.83	100.53	104.25
Nov. 1973P	7.00	6.73	1.040	107.69	95.70	95.96
Apr. 1974	8.05	7.51	1.072	94.78	89.57	90.31
May 1974	8.27	7.58	1.091	92.96	86.89	87.28
June 1974	8.15	7.54	1.081	93.10	86.00	86.00
July 1974	8.41	7.81	1.077	86.02	79.31	79.31
Aug. 1974	8.66	8.04	1.077	82.65	69.99	72.15
Sep. 1974	8.41	8.04	1.046	71.42	63.54	63.54
Oct. 1974	8.00	7.90	1.013	74.31	62.28L	73.90
Oct. 1979	10.95	10.30	1.063	111.27	100.00	101.82
Nov. 1979	11.18	10.65	1.050	106.81	99.87	106.16
Jan. 1980P	10.88	10.80	1.007	115.20	105.22	114.16
Mar. 1980	14.05	12.75	1.102	112.78	98.22L	102.09
Apr. 1980	12.02	11.47	1.048	106.29	99.80	106.29
Nov. 1980	13.31	12.68	1.050	140.52	128.91	140.52
Dec. 1980	13.65	12.84	1.063	137.21	127.36	135.76
May 1981	15.08	14.10	1.070	133.77	129.71	132.59
June 1981	14.29	13.47	1.061	133.75	130.62	131.21
July 1981P	15.15	14.28	1.061	130.92	127.13	130.92
Aug. 1981	16.00	14.94	1.071	133.85	122.79	122.79
Sep. 1981	16.22	15.32	1.059	123.49	112.77	116.18
Aug. 1982	12.62	13.06	.966	119.51	102.42L	119.51

P equals a month containing a business peak.
L equals a month containing a major bear market low.

Source: *Federal Reserve Bulletin* and Standard & Poor's *Security Price Index Record.*

TABLE 1.87
Months When the Average Prime Rate Charged by Banks Increased by 9.6 Percent or More; Months Containing Business Peaks; and Months When the S&P Stock Price Index Registered a Cyclical Low, 1948–1991

Month and Year	Average Prime Rate (1)	% Change in Prime (2)	Monthly Value of S&P Index at		
			High (3)	Low (4)	Close (5)
Aug. 1948	2.00	14.3	16.15	15.67	15.97*
Nov. 1948P	2.00	.0	16.70	14.70	14.75
Jun. 1949	2.00	.0	14.16	13.55L	14.16
Aug. 1957P	4.42	10.5	47.79	43.89	45.22
Oct. 1957	4.50	.0	43.14	38.98L	41.06
Sep. 1959	5.00	11.1	58.92	55.14	56.88*
Apr. 1960P	5.00	.0	56.59	54.37	54.37
Oct. 1960	4.50	.0	54.86	52.30L	53.39
Jun. 1969	8.23	9.7	102.94	96.23	97.71
Dec. 1969P	8.50	.0	93.22	89.20	92.06
May 1970	8.00	.0	81.44	69.29L	76.55
July 1973	8.30	10.8	109.85	101.28	108.22
Aug. 1973	9.23	11.2	106.83	100.53	104.25*
Nov. 1973P	9.75	−1.9	107.69	95.70	95.96
Apr. 1974	10.02	13.5	94.78	89.57	90.31
May 1974	11.25	12.3	92.96	86.89	87.28
Oct. 1974	11.68	−2.7	74.31	62.28L	73.90
Nov. 1978	10.94	10.1	96.85	92.49	94.70
Oct. 1979	14.39	11.6	111.27	100.00	101.82*
Jan. 1980P	15.25	−.3	115.20	105.22	114.16
Mar. 1980	18.31	17.1	112.78	98.22L	102.09
Sep. 1980	12.23	10.0	130.40	123.31	125.46
Oct. 1980	13.79	12.8	133.70	126.29	127.47*
Nov. 1980	16.06	16.5	140.52	128.91	140.52
Dec. 1980	20.35	26.7	137.21	127.36	135.76
May 1981	19.61	14.3	133.77	129.71	132.59
July 1981P	20.39	1.8	130.92	127.13	130.92
Aug. 1982	14.39	−11.5	119.51	102.42L	119.51

P equals a month containing a business peak.

L equals a month containing a major bear market low.

*Closing price associated with the first one-month increase in the prime rate of 11 percent or more in a business expansion. The S&P index could have always been repurchased at a discount of 3.5 percent or more during the following bear market.

Source of data: BCI series 109 and Standard & Poor's *Security Price Index Record*.

TABLE 1.88

The Fed's Recessionary Reaction Function: Some Basic Data Pertaining to the Civilian Unemployment Rate, the Discount Rate on New Issues of 91-Day Treasury Bills, and the 12-Month CPI Inflation Rate at Payroll Employment Peaks and Troughs, 1947–1990

| Date of Employment | | Duration (months) | Unemployment Rate at Peak (%) | T-Bill Rate at | | CPI Inflation Rate | | Average Real T-Bill Rate |
Peak	Trough			Peak	Trough	Peak[a]	Trough[b]	Peak-Trough[c]
Sep. 48	Oct. 49	13	3.8	1.09	1.04	6.5	3.5	.68
June 53	Aug. 54	14	2.5	2.23	.89	1.0	-.5	.51
Mar. 57	May 58	14	3.7	3.14	1.05	3.6	.4	-.71
Apr. 60	Feb. 61	10	5.2	3.24	2.41	2.0	.9	1.06
Mar. 70	Nov. 70	8	4.4	6.71	5.29	6.0	3.3	.53
Oct. 74	Apr. 75	6	6.0	7.24	5.69	12.0	6.0	-5.00
Mar. 80	July 80	4	6.3	15.53	8.13	14.7	10.8	-4.59
July 81	Dec. 82	17	7.2	14.70	8.01	10.7	3.8	4.18
June 90			5.3	7.74		4.7		1.14p

[a]12-month inflation rate at the employment peak.

[b]12-month inflation rate one year after the employment trough.

[c]Average value for the decline months obtained by subtracting the 12-month CPI inflation rate from the T-bill rate each month.

p equals a preliminary rate for the 10 months ending April 1991.

Source of basic data: BCI series 41, 43, 114, and 320.

TABLE 1.89
The Interest Rate Reaction of the Federal Reserve and the Saving Behavior of Consumers in Response to Changes in Unemployment and the Consumer Price Index

Year	December Unemployment Rate (%) (1)	Dec.–Dec. CPI Inflation Rate (%) (2)	Dec. T-Bill Rate (%) (3)	Change in T-Bill Rate[a] (4)	4th-Quarter Personal Saving Rate[b] (%) (5)
1950	4.3	5.9	1.4*	.3(+)	6.7(+)
1951	3.1	6.0	1.7*	.3(+)	7.9(+)
1952	2.7	.8	2.1	.4	6.7(+)ER
1953	4.5	.7	1.6	−.5(−)	7.6(−)ER
1954	5.0	−.7	1.2	−.4(−)	6.1(−)
1955	4.2	.4	2.6	1.4(+)	6.2(+)
1956	4.2	3.0	3.2	.6(+)	7.6(+)
1957	5.2	2.9	3.1	−.1(−)	6.9(−)
1958	6.2	1.8	2.8	−.3(−)	8.0(−)ER
1959	5.3	1.7	4.6	1.8	6.0(+)ER
1960	6.6	1.4	2.3	−2.3(−)	5.4(−)
1961	6.0	.7	2.6	.3	7.0(+)
1962	5.5	1.3	2.9	.3(+)	5.8(+)ER
1963	5.5	1.6	3.5	.6(+)	6.3(+)
1964	5.0	1.0	3.9	.4	7.5(+)
1965	4.0	1.9	4.4	.5(+)	7.0(+)ER
1966	3.8	3.5	5.0	.6(+)	7.4(+)
1967	3.8	3.0	5.0	.0	8.2
1968	3.4	4.7	5.9	.9(+)	6.4(+)ER
1969	3.5	6.2	7.7	1.8(+)	7.2(+)
1970	6.1	5.6	4.9*	−2.8(−)	8.5(−)ER
1971	6.0	3.3	4.0	−.9	7.9(−)
1972	5.2	3.4	5.1	1.1	8.4(+)
1973	4.9	8.7	7.4*	2.3*(+)	10.6(+)
1974	7.2	12.3	7.2*	−.2(−)(+)	9.7(−)
1975	8.2	6.9	5.5*	−1.7(−)	8.7(−)
1976	7.8	4.9	4.4*	−1.1	6.9(−)
1977	6.4	6.7	6.1*	1.7(+)	6.7(+)ER
1978	6.0	9.0	9.1	3.0(+)	7.1(+)
1979	6.0	13.3	12.1*	3.0(+)	6.2(+)ER
1980	7.2	12.5	15.7	3.6(−)	7.5(+)
1981	8.5	8.9	10.9	−4.8(−)	7.8(−)ER
1982	10.8	3.8	8.0	−2.9(−)	6.2(−)
1983	8.3	3.8	9.0	1.0	5.8(+)ER
1984	7.3	3.9	8.2	−.8	5.8(−)ER
1985	7.0	3.8	7.1	−1.1	3.9(−)
1986	6.6	1.1	5.5	−1.6	3.3(−)
1987	5.7	4.4	5.8	.3(+)	3.9(+)
1988	5.3	4.4	8.1	2.3	4.1(+)
1989	5.3	4.6	7.6	−.5	4.6(−)ER
1990	6.1	6.1	6.8	−.8(+)(−)	4.2(−)

*Years when the December yield on 91-day Treasury bills was less than the Dec.–Dec. inflation rate for the consumer price index in column (2).

[a]An increase in the T-bill rate (+) is expected when there is an increase in the CPI inflation rate of .3 percentage points or more in column (2) and a decrease in the T-bill rate (−) is expected when the unemployment rate in column (1) increases by .1 percentage points or more.

[b]An increase in the personal saving rate (+) is expected when the change in the T-bill rate in column (4) is positive and a decrease in the saving rate (−) is expected when the change in the T-bill rate is negative. ER identifies those years when these expectations were not satisfied.

Source of basic data: BCI series 43, 320, 114, and 293.

TABLE 1.90

Checking Up on the Health of the U.S. Economy: Some Adjusted Monthly Lead Times for Recessionary Indicators at Business Peaks

Business Peak	$T\text{-}B^a$	$P\text{-}R^b$	$I\text{-}Y^c$	$M1^d$	$R\text{-}B^e$	$S\text{-}P^f$	$L\text{-}I^g$	$C\text{-}U^h$	$I\text{-}P^i$	$U\text{-}C^j$	$C\text{-}I^k$
Nov. 48	15**	3	NS	20	1*	27	0	8	−1	−4	−3
July 53	19**	NS	NS	31	28	3	−1*	−3	−2	−7	−5
Aug. 57	32	0	8	12	11**	0	4*	1	−2	−4	−3
Apr. 60	20	7**	9	6	5	2*	1	1	0	−10	−7
Dec. 69	60	6**	5	5*	0	6	0	−2	−1	−10	−10
Nov. 73	8	4	4*	7**	0	8	−3	−3	−2	−10	−11
Jan. 80	16	14	3*	11**	1	−2	6	0	−3	−3	−4
July 81	8	10	8**	7	1*	−2	−2	−3	−4	−5	−6
July 90	16	NS	NS	20	3**	−1	−4	−2*	−4	−4	−6

aMonths to the business peak after the discount rate on new issues of 91-day Treasury bills in Table 1.83 has increased at least 70 percent from its cyclical low.

bMonths to the business peak after the first monthly increase in the average prime rate charged by banks of 9.6 percent or more in Table 1.87.

cMonths to the business peak after the first month when the average yield on 3-year Treasury securities was at least 4.5 percent greater than the average yield on 10-year Treasury securities (ignoring all those cases of a highly inverted yield curve which occurred during the Vietnam War build-up year of 1966) in Table 1.86.

dMonths to the business peak after M1 in billions of 1982 dollars in Table 1.80 has declined 1.5 percent.

eMonths to the business peak after the building permit index in Table 1.50 has been down 20 percent for two months in a row if the permit peak was less than 150 and down 35 percent for two months in a row if the permit peak was over 150.

fMonths to the business peak after the monthly average value for the S&P composite stock price index in Table 1.75 has declined 5 percent or more from its preceding cyclical high and maintained that degree of downness until after the next cyclical trough in the S&P index.

gMonths to the business peak after the index of leading indicators in Table 1.13 has declined 3.3 percent from its previous cyclical peak.

hMonths to the business peak after the civilian unemployment rate in Table 1.27 has reversed itself on the upside by at least .6 percentage points after experiencing a trough.

iMonths to the business peak after U.S. industrial production in Table 1.34 has declined 2.0 percent or more from its cyclical peak.

jMonths to the business peak after the average weekly unemployment claims in Table 1.29 have increased 150 thousand or more from their cyclical low.

kMonths to the business peak after the composite index of four coincident indicators in Table 1.14 has declined 4.7 percent or more.

NS means that no recessionary signal can be derived from the data.

*Adjusted lead time associated with the fifth signal to be derived from the 11 indicators in this table.

TABLE 1.91
A Summary Table for Forecasting Poor Growth Years for the U.S. Economy

Year	Index of Leading Indicators[a] (1)	Crude Oil Price Shocks[b] (2)	Unempl. Claims, Housing Starts, Consumer Sent.[c] (3)	Stock Prices and Other Indicators[d] (4)	Indicator Sum[e] (5)	Following Year Growth Rate Real GNP (6)
1948	3	2	2	5	12	.0*
1953	3	2	2	3	10	−1.3*
1957	3	2	2	4	11	−.8*
1966	3	1	2	2	8	2.9
1969	3	2	2	5	12	−.3*
1973	3	2	2	5	12	−.5*
1974	3	2	3	5	13	−1.3*
1979	3	2	3	4	12	−.2*
1981	3	2	3	4	12	−2.5*
1990	3	2	2	4	11	?*

[a]From Table 1.17. A poor growth year is predicted if the index of leading indicators declines 1.0 percent or more on a Dec.–Dec. basis, on a June–Dec. basis, and on a Sept.–Dec. basis.

[b]From Table 1.18. A poor growth year is predicted if the price of U.S. crude oil at the well head (first purchase price) has increased 5 percent or more on a year-to-year basis and the index of leading economic indicators has declined one percent or more on a Dec.–Dec. basis.

[c]From Table 1.41. A poor growth year is predicted if unemployment claims increased 22 percent on a Nov.–Nov. basis, if housing starts declined by 23 percent, or if consumer sentiment declined by 6 percent or more.

[d]From Table 1.76. A poor growth year is predicted by a Nov.–Nov. decline ratio of .854 for residential building permits; a Dec. down ratio of .890 or less for the ratio of help wanted advertising in newspapers to persons unemployed; a down ratio of .969 or less for M1; a down ratio of .950 or less for stock prices; and a down ratio of .450 or less for the inverted yield on new 91-day Treasury bills.

[e]The sum of the number of indicators in columns (1) through (4) which are pointing in the direction of a poor growth year.

*Those years when 10 or more of the indicators in columns (1) through (4) are pointing in the direction of a poor growth year.

TABLE 1.92
Employment Recessions: Some Monthly Duration Indicators

Date of Employment Peak	Duration of Recession (months)	Predicted Duration of Recession in Months[a]		
		Industrial Production[b]	Employment Decline[c]	Real Return on T-Bills[d]
Sep. 48	13	12(1)*	14(−1)	12(1)
June 53	14	15(−1)	13(1)*	12(2)
Mar. 57	14	14(0)*	16(−2)	10(4)
Apr. 60	10	11(−1)*	7(3)	13(−3)
Mar. 70	8	10(−2)*	9(−1)	12(−4)
Oct. 74	6	4(2)	7(−1)	5(1)*
Mar. 80	4	5(−1)	6(−2)*	6(−2)
July 81	17	14(3)	15(2)*	16(1)
June 90	?	16(?)	15(?)*	13(?)p

[a]The figures in parentheses are the error terms obtained by subtracting the predicted duration of the recession in months from the actual duration in months.

[b]From Table 1.25. The predicted duration of the recession is equal to 14.17 months minus 91 percent of the monthly lead time for industrial production at its peak relative to the peak in payroll employment.

[c]From Table 1.24. The predicted duration of the recession is equal to 17.73 months minus 23 times the steepest monthly decline percentage in nonagricultural payroll employment during the first three months of the recession.

[d]From Table 1.88. The predicted duration of the recession is equal to 11.26 months plus 123 percent of the average real (inflation adjusted) return on three-month Treasury bills during the employment recession.

*The median forecast for the three duration indicators.

p equals a preliminary estimate based on the average real return on Treasury bills for the 10 months ending April 1991.

TABLE 1.93
Using Peaks in Industrial Production and the Average Yield on New Three-Month Treasury Bills to Help Explain the Duration of Recessions in Payroll Employment, 1947–1991

Date of Employment Peak	Lead Time (months)		Real Return on T-Bills[a] (%) (3)	Duration of Recession (months)	
	Industrial Production (1)	T-Bill Yield (2)		Actual (4)	Predicted[b] (5)
Sep. 48	2	−4	.68	13	13
June 53	−1	0	.51	14	13
Mar. 57	0	−7	−.71	14	14
Apr. 60	3	4	1.06	10	10
Mar. 70	5	2	.53	8	10
Oct. 74	11	2	−5.00	6	4
Mar. 80	10	0	−4.59	4	5
July 81	0	−1	4.18	17	15
June 90p	−3	15	1.14	10	10

[a]Average (T-bill yield minus the 12-month CPI inflation rate) from the peak in payroll employment to the trough in payroll employment.

[b]The predicted duration of the employment recession is equal to 12.6 months minus half of the monthly lead time for industrial production in column (1), minus 30 percent of the monthly lead time for the T-bill yield in column (2) plus 60 percent of the inflation adjusted return on T-bills during the employment recession in column (3).

p equals a preliminary estimate. The actual duration of the employment recession for 1990–91 might turn out to be longer.

Source of basic data: *Survey of Current Business*, BCI series 41, 47, 114, and 320.

TABLE 1.94
Some Recovery Indicators for the Recessionary Troughs Dated by the National Bureau of Economic Research

	Lead Time (months) to NBER Trough for				
Trough Date	Coincident Indicators[a]	Industrial Production[b]	Spec. Diff. Index[c]	Lead. Diff. Index[d]	Coin. Diff. Index[e]
Oct. 49	1	1*	2	2	1
May 54	−5	−1*	0	2	−4
Apr. 58	−2	−2*	−1	−2	−2
Feb. 61	−2	−2*	0	−1	−3
Nov. 70	−2	−2*	4	−2	−1
Mar. 75	−4	9	−1*	−2	9
July 80	−2	−2*	−1	−1	−2
Nov. 82	−5	−5	0*	1	0
Apr. 91p	−1	−1*	−1		

[a]Recovery from a recession is indicated by two consecutive monthly increases in the Commerce Department's composite index of four coincident indicators (BCI series 920).

[b]Recovery from a recession is indicated by two consecutive monthly increases in the Federal Reserve's index of industrial production (BCI series 47).

[c]Recovery from a recession is indicated by nine or more monthly increases in the following seven indicators over a two-month period: average weekly hours in manufacturing (BCI series 1), stock prices (BCI series 19), index of new private housing units authorized by local building permits (BCI series 29), employees on nonagricultural payrolls (BCI series 41), industrial production (BCI series 47), personal income less transfer payments in billions of 1982 dollars (BCI series 51), and the money supply M2 in billions of 1982 dollars (BCI series 106).

[d]Recovery from a recession is indicated by two consecutive monthly values for the one-month span diffusion index for the Commerce Department's index of leading economic indicators amounting to 70 percent or more (BCI series 950).

[e]Recovery from a recession is indicated by two not necessarily consecutive monthly values for the one-month span diffusion index for the Commerce Department's coincident indicator index amounting to 75 percent or more (BCI series 951).

p represents a preliminary estimate.

*The median lead time for the index of coincident indicators, industrial production, and the three diffusion indexes.

TABLE 1.95
Some Alternative Ways to Forecast the Year-to-Year Growth Rate for Real GNP

| Year | Forecasted Growth Rates for Real GNP for Following Year[a] | | | | Following Year Growth Rate Real GNP[f] |
	Two-Quarter Growth Rate[b]	Real M2[c]	Leading Indicators[d]	Blue Chip Consensus[e]	
1976	3.4(1.5)*	3.4(1.5)	3.3(1.6)	5.1(−.2)	4.9
1977	4.6(−.7)	4.1(−.2)	4.5(−.6)*	4.3(−.4)	3.9
1978	4.3(−2.0)	3.4(−1.1)*	3.4(−1.1)	2.5(−.2)	2.3
1979	2.3(−2.4)	1.5(−1.6)*	1.3(−1.4)	−.3(.2)	−.1
1980	3.7(−1.8)*	3.1(−1.2)	5.0(−3.1)	1.0(.9)	1.9
1981	−2.0(.2)*	−1.4(−.4)	−2.3(.5)	.0(−1.8)	−1.8
1982	−.9(4.2)	.0(3.3)*	.0(3.3)	2.5(.8)	3.3
1983	6.0(.8)	5.0(1.8)	5.5(1.3)*	5.2(1.6)	6.8
1984	2.7(−.4)*	2.7(−.4)	1.9(.4)	3.7(−1.4)	2.3
1985	2.7(−.2)*	2.5(.0)	2.9(−.4)	3.1(−.6)	2.5
1986	2.2(.7)	2.5(.4)*	2.7(.2)	2.3(.6)	2.9
1987	4.2(−.4)	3.4(.4)*	3.4(.4)	2.2(1.6)	3.8
1988	2.2(.7)	1.7(1.2)	1.8(1.1)*	2.7(.2)	2.9
1989	1.7(−.8)*	1.9(−1.0)	1.6(−.7)	1.6(−.7)	.9
1990	−.4	−.6*	−1.1		?

TABLE 1.95 (concluded)

	Forecasted Growth Rates for Real GNP for Following Year[a]				Following Year Growth Rate Real GNP[f]
Year	Two-Quarter Growth Rate[b]	Real M2[c]	Leading Indicators[d]	Blue Chip Consensus[e]	
	Mean Absolute Forecasting Errors				
1976–82	1.83	1.33	1.66	.64	
1983–89	.57	.74	.64	.96	

[a]The figures in parentheses are the actual following year growth rates minus the predicted growth rates for real GNP.
[b]The preliminary annualized two-quarter growth rate for real GNP from the second quarter of the year to the fourth quarter of the year published in the following January issue of the *Survey of Current Business*.
[c]Eighty percent of the preliminary annualized two-quarter growth rate for real GNP plus 20 percent of the preliminary June-to-December growth rate for M2 in constant dollars.
[d]Eighty percent of the preliminary annualized two-quarter growth rate for real GNP plus 20 percent of the preliminary June-to-December growth rate for the composite index of leading economic indicators.
[e]The median forecast from the *Blue Chip Economic Indicators* newsletter survey conducted in early February of the following year.
[f]The actual preliminary year-to-year growth rates for real GNP published in the following January issue of the *Survey of Current Business*.

TABLE 1.96
A Summary Table for Forecasting Slow Growth Years for the U.S. Economy

Year	T-Bill Rate[a]	Housing Starts[b]	Real M1[c]	Unused Labor[d]	Inflation Acceleration[e]	Following Year % Change Real GNP
1955	.254	-17.1	-1.5	4.7	.7	2.1*
1956	.201	-15.5	-3.6	6.2	1.6	1.7*
1957	.210					-.8*
1958	.313					5.8
1959	.193	-11.1	.2	6.6		2.2*
1960	.388	-12.0	-.9		.9	2.6*
1965						5.8
1966		-34.2	-.8	6.0	1.5	2.9*
1967				6.3		4.1
1968	.383			6.5		2.4*
1969	.294	-24.6	-2.6	3.2	1.1	-.3*
1970			-.2	5.4		2.8*
1972					.7	5.2
1973	.432	-28.8	-3.0		2.6	-.5*
1974	.443	-40.5	-7.0	3.7	2.9	-1.3*
1975			-2.0			4.9
1978			-.7		1.4	2.5*
1979	.360	-27.6	-4.8	4.3	1.6	-.2*
1980			-5.1	6.8		1.9*
1981		-44.6	-2.2			-2.5*

TABLE 1.96 (concluded)

Year	T-Bill Rate[a]	Housing Starts[b]	Real M1[c]	Unused Labor[d]	Inflation Acceleration[e]	Following Year % Change Real GNP
1985					.8	2.7
1987			−.9			4.5
1988			.5		1.5	2.5*
1989		−14.4	−3.9	4.6		1.0*
1990		−16.1	−2.0	4.7	.7	?*

[a]A slow growth year is predicted by a December down ratio of .450 or less for the inverted Treasury bill rate in column (5) of Table 1.76.
[b]A slow growth year is predicted by a Nov.–Nov. decline in housing starts of 10 percent or more in column (2) of Table 1.41.
[c]A slow growth year is predicted by an increase in real M1 of one-half percent or less in column (4) of Table 1.77.
[d]A slow growth year is predicted by an increase of 6.8 percent or less in the index of labor's unused capacity in column (3) of Table 2.03.
[e]A slow growth year is predicted by an acceleration of .7 percentage points or more in the producer price index for finished goods in column (3) of Table 2.01.
*Growth rates for real GNP when two or more of the indicators are pointing in the direction of a slow following year growth rate for real GNP in 1982 dollars.

164

TABLE 1.97

Using the Diffusion Index for the 11 Leading Economic Indicators (percent rising over a six-month span) to Help Delineate Unhealthy Expansion Periods for the U.S. Economy: All Months When the Noncentered Diffusion Index Values Were Less than 30 in the Midst of Business Expansions

Date	Diffusion Index Value	Interim High Value for the Diff. Index[a]	Months to the Next Business Peak
Sep. 48	22.2	33.2	2
Nov. 48	11.1	.0	0
July 51	25.0	20.0	24
Aug. 51	20.0	30.0	23
Oct. 51	20.0	20.0	21
Nov. 51	20.0	20.0	20
Dec. 51	20.0	100.0	19
June 53	27.3	18.2	1
July 53	18.2	18.2	0
May 56	18.2	27.3	15
June 56	27.3	27.3	14
July 56	27.3	36.4	13
Sep. 56	13.6	18.2	11
Oct. 56	18.2	63.6*	10
Feb. 57	27.3	36.4	6
Apr. 57	9.1	9.1	4
May 57	9.1	9.1	3
June 57	9.1	18.2	2
July 57	18.2	18.2	1
Aug. 57	18.2	18.2	0
Sep. 59	22.7	18.2	7
Oct. 59	18.2	9.1	6
Nov. 59	9.1	27.3	5
Dec. 59	27.3	27.3	4
Jan. 60	27.3	45.5	3
Mar. 60	18.2	54.5	1
May 62	22.7	27.3	91
June 62	27.3	36.4	90
Aug. 62	22.7	31.8	88
Oct. 62	18.2	90.9	86
Aug. 66	18.2	13.6	40
Sep. 66	13.6	.0	39
Oct. 66	.0	.0	38
Nov. 66	.0	9.1	37
Dec. 66	9.1	90.9	36
June 69	27.3	27.3	6
July 69	27.3	18.2	5
Aug. 69	18.2	27.3	4
Sep. 69	27.3	18.2	3
Oct. 69	18.2	.0	2
Nov. 69	.0	.0	1
Dec. 69	.0	9.1	0

TABLE 1.97 (*concluded*)

Date	Diffusion Index Value	Interim High Value for the Diff. Index[a]	Months to the Next Business Peak
Sep. 73	27.3	40.9	2
May 79	18.2	27.3	8
June 79	27.3	36.4	7
Aug. 79	27.3	9.1	5
Sep. 79	9.1	27.3	4
Oct. 79	27.3	18.2	3
Nov. 79	18.2	31.8	2
Jan. 80	18.2	36.4	0
June 81	27.3	18.2	1
July 81	18.2	63.6*	0
July 84	18.2	36.4	72
Sep. 84	27.3	36.4	70
Nov. 84	27.3	27.3	68
Dec. 84	27.3	100.0	67
June 89	13.6	18.2	13
July 89	18.2	54.5	12
Feb. 90	27.3	63.6*	5

[a]The next value for the diffusion index if it is less than 30 or the highest interim value before the next diffusion value under 30.

*The highest interim value observed for those diffusion values under 30 which have occurred within one year of a recessionary peak in`business activity.

Source: BCI series 950.

TABLE 2.00
Exceptionally Slow Growth Rates for Real GNP That Were under 2.5 Percent in 1982 Dollars and the Financial Returns Associated with the S&P Index, 1929–1990

Year	GNP Growth Rate (1)	Financial Return S&P Index (2)
1956	2.1GR	6.4
1957	1.7GR	−10.4P
1960	2.2	.3P
1969	2.4GR	−8.3P
1981	1.9GR	−4.8P
1990	1.0GR	−3.1P

GR signifies a year containing at least one quarter in the midst of a business expansion when the growth rate for real GNP was less than .3 percent.

P signifies a year containing a recessionary peak in business activity.

Source of basic data: BCI series 50 and Standard & Poor's *Security Price Index Record*.

TABLE 2.01

Using Acceleration in the Producer Price Index for Finished Goods to Forecast Slow Growth Years for Real GNP in 1982 Dollars

Year	% Change in Finished Goods		Column (1) minus Col. (2) (3)	Following Year % Change Real GNP (4)
	Dec.–Dec. (1)	Year–Year (2)		
1955	1.0	.3	.7	2.1*
1956	4.2	2.6	1.6	1.7*
1957	3.4	3.8	−.4	−.8
1958	.3	2.2	−1.9	5.8
1959	−.3	−.3	.0	2.2
1960	1.8	.9	.9	2.6*
1961	−.6	.0	−.6	5.3
1962	.3	.3	.0	4.1
1963	−.3	−.3	.0	5.3
1964	.6	.3	.3	5.8
1965	3.3	1.8	1.5	5.8*
1966	2.0	3.2	−1.2	2.9
1967	1.7	1.1	.6	4.1
1968	3.1	2.8	.3	2.4
1969	4.9	3.8	1.1	−.3*
1970	2.1	3.4	−1.3	2.8
1971	3.3	3.1	.2	5.0
1972	3.9	3.2	.7	5.2*
1973	11.7	9.1	2.6	−.5*
1974	18.3	15.4	2.9	−1.3*
1975	6.6	10.6	−4.0	4.9
1976	3.8	4.5	−.7	4.7
1977	6.7	6.4	.3	5.3
1978	9.3	7.9	1.4	2.5*
1979	12.8	11.2	1.6	−.2*
1980	11.8	13.4	−1.6	1.9
1981	7.1	9.2	−2.1	−2.5
1982	3.6	4.1	−.5	3.6
1983	.6	1.6	−1.0	6.8
1984	1.7	2.1	−.4	3.4
1985	1.8	1.0	.8	2.7*
1986	−2.3	−1.4	−.9	3.4
1987	2.2	2.1	.1	4.5
1988	4.0	2.5	1.5	2.5*
1989	4.9	5.2	−.3	1.0
1990p	5.6	4.9	.7	?*

*Growth rates for real GNP following Dec.–Dec. increases in the producer price index for finished goods which were .7 or more percentage points greater than the year–year growth rates for the producer price index for finished goods.

Source of basic data: BCI series 50 and 336.

TABLE 2.02

Using the December–December Growth Rates for Currency and the CPI to Help Identify Slow Growth Rates for Real GNP in 1982 Dollars in the Following Year

Year	December–December Growth Rates (%) Currency (1)	CPI (2)	Growth of Real Currency[a] (%) (3)	Following Year % Change Real GNP (4)
1959	1.0	1.7	−.7	2.2*
1960	− .3	1.4	−1.7	2.6*
1961	2.1	.7	1.4	5.3
1962	3.4	1.3	2.1	4.1
1963	6.3	1.6	4.7	5.3
1964	5.3	1.0	4.3	5.8
1965	6.2	1.9	4.3	5.8
1966	5.6	3.5	2.1	2.9
1967	5.3	3.0	2.3	4.1
1968	7.5	4.7	2.8	2.4
1969	6.3	6.2	.1	− .3*
1970	6.3	5.6	.7	2.8*
1971	7.0	3.3	3.7	5.0
1972	8.3	3.4	4.9	5.2
1973	8.0	8.7	−.7	− .5*
1974	10.2	12.3	−2.1	− 1.3*
1975	8.7	6.9	1.8	4.9
1976	9.2	4.9	4.3	4.7
1977	9.9	6.7	3.2	5.3
1978	10.0	9.0	1.0	2.5*
1979	9.2	13.3	−4.1	− .2*
1980	9.8	12.5	−2.7	1.9*
1981	6.3	8.9	−2.6	−2.5*
1982	8.1	3.8	4.3	3.6
1983	10.3	3.8	6.5	6.8
1984	6.7	3.9	2.8	3.4
1985	7.6	3.8	3.8	2.7
1986	7.6	1.1	6.5	3.4
1987	8.9	4.4	4.5	4.5
1988	7.7	4.4	3.3	2.5
1989	4.8	4.6	.2	1.0*
1990	10.8	6.1	4.7	?

[a]Column (1) minus column (2).

*Growth rates for real GNP following increases in real currency in column (3) of 1 percent or less.

Source of basic data: BCI series 320 and *SCB* monetary statistics.

TABLE 2.03
Using the Civilian Unemployment Rate and the Growth of Output per Hour in the Nonfarm Business Sector to Identify Slow Growth Rates for Real GNP in the Following Year

Year	Civilian Unemployment Rate (%) (1)	Growth of Labor Productivity (%) (2)	An Index of Labor's Unused Capacity[a] (3)	Following Year Growth Rate for Real GNP (%) (4)
1955	4.4	3.0	7.4	2.1
1956	4.1	.6	4.7	1.7*
1957	4.3	1.9	6.2	−.8*
1958	6.8	2.3	9.1	5.8
1959	5.5	3.2	8.7	2.2
1960	5.5	1.1	6.6	2.6*
1961	6.7	3.2	9.9	5.3
1962	5.5	3.3	8.8	4.1
1963	5.7	3.6	9.3	5.3
1964	5.2	3.9	9.1	5.8
1965	4.5	2.6	7.1	5.8
1966	3.8	2.2	6.0	2.9*
1967	3.8	2.5	6.3	4.1*
1968	3.6	2.9	6.5	2.4*
1969	3.5	−.3	3.2	−.3*
1970	4.9	.5	5.4	2.8*
1971	5.9	3.0	8.9	5.0
1972	5.6	3.0	8.6	5.2
1973	4.9	2.2	7.1	−.5
1974	5.6	−1.9	3.7	−1.3*
1975	8.5	1.9	10.4	4.9
1976	7.7	2.7	10.4	4.7
1977	7.1	1.7	8.8	5.3
1978	6.1	.9	7.0	2.5
1979	5.8	−1.5	4.3	−.2*
1980	7.1	−.3	6.8	1.9*
1981	7.6	1.0	8.6	−2.5
1982	9.7	−.9	8.8	3.6
1983	9.6	2.9	12.5	6.8
1984	7.5	2.1	9.6	3.4
1985	7.2	1.3	8.5	2.7
1986	7.0	2.0	9.0	3.4
1987	6.2	1.0	7.2	4.5
1988	5.5	2.5	8.0	2.5
1989	5.3	−.7	4.6	1.0*
1990	5.5	−.8	4.7	?*

[a]Column (1) plus column (2).
*Years when the index of labor's unused capacity in column (3) was less than 6.9 percent.

Source of basic data: BCI series 43 and 358.

TABLE 2.04
Real GNP and the Labor Force, Selected Years and Growth Rates, 1949–1989

Years	Real GNP (billions of 1982 $) (1)	Real GNP per Worker (1982 $) (2)	Civilian Population 16 and Over (millions) (3)	Civilian Labor Force Participation Rates (%)			Civilian Employment Rate (%) (7)
				Total (4)	Males (5)	Females (6)	
1949	1,109.0	19,236	104.0	58.9	86.4	33.1	94.1
1959	1,629.1	25,207	115.3	59.3	83.7	37.1	94.5
1969	2,423.3	31,107	134.3	60.1	79.8	42.7	96.5
1979	3,192.4	32,303	164.9	63.7	77.8	50.9	94.2
1989	4,117.7	35,091	186.4	66.5	76.4	57.4	94.7
			Growth Rates[a]				
1949–59	3.9	2.8	1.0	.1	—	—	.0
1959–69	4.0	2.1	1.6	.1	—	—	.2
1969–79	2.8	.4	2.1	.6	—	—	-.3
1979–89	2.6	.8	1.2	.4	—	—	.1

[a]The GNP growth rate in column (1) is approximately equal to the sum of the growth rates in columns (2), (3), (4), and (7).

Source of basic data: *Economic Report of the President.*

TABLE 2.05

Using the Year-to-Year Growth Rates for Real GNP and the Civilian Population 16 and Over to Explain Changes in the Civilian Unemployment Rate, 1967–1990

Year	Growth Rates for GNP 1982 Dollars (1)	Growth Rates for Civilian Population 16 and Over (2)	Civilian Unemployment Rate (3)	Change in the Unemployment Rate Actual (4)	Change in the Unemployment Rate Predicted (5)	Actual minus the Predicted Change[b] (6)
1967	2.9	1.4	3.8	.0	−.2	.2
1968	4.1	1.7	3.6	−.2	−.4	.2
1969	2.4	1.7	3.5	−.1	.2	−.3P
1970	−.3	2.0	4.9	1.4	1.5	−.1
1971	2.8	2.3	5.9	1.0	.5	.5*
1972	5.0	2.8	5.6	−.3	−.0	−.3
1973	5.2	2.1	4.9	−.7	−.6	−.1P
1974	−.5	2.1	5.6	.7	1.7	−1.0
1975	−1.3	2.0	8.5	2.9	1.9	1.0*
1976	4.9	2.0	7.7	−.8	−.6	−.2
1977	4.7	1.8	7.1	−.6	−.6	.0
1978	5.3	1.8	6.1	−1.0	−.9	−.1
1979	2.5	1.8	5.8	−.3	.3	−.6P
1980	−.2	1.7	7.1	1.3	1.3	
1981	1.9	1.4	7.6	.5	.2	
1982	−2.5	1.3	9.7	2.1	1.9	
1983	3.6	1.1	9.6	−.1	−.7	.6*
1984	6.8	1.2	7.5	−2.1	−1.9	−.2
1985	3.4	1.0	7.2	−.3	−.7	.4
1986	2.7	1.3	7.0	−.2	−.2	.0
1987	3.4	1.2	6.2	−.8	−.5	−.3
1988	4.5	1.0	5.5	−.7	−1.1	.4
1989	2.5	1.0	5.3	−.2	−.3	.1
1990	1.0	.9	5.5	.2	.2	.0

[a]The predicted change in the unemployment rate is equal to minus 40 percent of the growth rate for real GNP in column (1) plus 70 percent of the population growth rate in column (2).

[b]Column (4) minus column (5).

P represents peak years preceding a negative growth rate for real GNP in column (1). All of these error terms are zero or negative except for the short-lived recovery year of 1981.

*Years following a transition from positive to negative growth rates for real GNP in column (1). All of these error terms are positive.

Source of basic data: *Economic Report of the President.*

TABLE 2.06
Annualized Estimates of the Natural Growth Rate for the U.S. Economy Based on Okun's Law

Year	Civilian Unemployment Rate (%) (1)	Change in Unemployment Rate (%) (2)	Actual Growth of Real GNP (%) (3)	The Natural Growth Rate	
				Yearly Estimate[a] (%) (4)	Median Rate[b] (%) (5)
1961	6.7	1.2	2.6	5.6	4.1
1962	5.5	−1.2	5.3	2.3	4.0
1963	5.7	.2	4.1	4.6	4.0
1964	5.2	−.5	5.3	4.1	4.0
1965	4.5	−.7	5.8	4.0	4.0
1966	3.8	−.7	5.8	4.0	4.0
1967	3.8	.0	2.9	2.9	3.6
1968	3.6	−.2	4.1	3.6	3.6
1969	3.5	−.1	2.4	2.2	3.6
1970	4.9	1.4	−.3	3.2	3.4
1971	5.9	1.0	2.8	5.3	3.4
1972	5.6	−.3	5.0	4.2	3.4
1973	4.9	−.7	5.2	3.4	3.4
1974	5.6	.7	−.5	1.3	3.4
1975	8.5	2.9	−1.3	5.9	3.2
1976	7.7	−.8	4.9	2.9	2.9
1977	7.1	−.6	4.7	3.2	2.9
1978	6.1	−1.0	5.3	2.8	3.0
1979	5.8	−.3	2.5	1.7	2.9
1980	7.1	1.3	−.2	3.0	3.0
1981	7.6	.5	1.9	3.1	2.8
1982	9.7	2.1	−2.5	2.7	2.7
1983	9.6	−.1	3.6	3.4	2.7
1984	7.5	−2.1	6.8	1.6	2.6
1985	7.2	−.3	3.4	2.6	2.6
1986	7.0	−.2	2.7	2.2	2.2
1987	6.2	−.8	3.4	1.4	2.0
1988	5.5	−.7	4.5	2.7	?
1989	5.3	−.2	2.5	2.0	?
1990	5.5	.2	1.0	1.5	?

[a]The yearly estimate of the natural growth rate for real GNP is equal to 2.5 times the change in the unemployment rate in column (2) plus the actual growth rate for real GNP in column (3).

[b]The median of the current yearly estimate in column (4), the three preceding yearly estimates and the following three yearly estimates.

Source of basic data: BCI series 43 and 50.

TABLE 2.10
Major Fluctuations in the Inflation Adjusted Average Monthly Values for the S&P Composite Stock Price Index since January 1966

Month and Year	S&P Index (1941 − 43 = 10) (1)	Consumer Price Index (1982 − 84 = 100) (2)	S&P Index in 1982–84 Dollars[a] (3)
Jan. 1966	93.32	31.8	293.5
Oct. 1966	77.13	32.9	234.4
Dec. 1968	106.48	35.5	299.9P
June 1970	75.59	38.8	194.8
Jan. 1973	118.42	42.6	278.0
Dec. 1974	67.07	51.9	129.2
Nov. 1980	135.65	85.5	158.7
July 1982	109.38	97.5	112.2
Aug. 1987	329.36	114.4	287.9
Dec. 1987	240.96	115.4	208.8
June 1990	360.39	129.9	277.4
Oct. 1990	307.12	133.5	230.1
Apr. 1991	379.68	135.2	280.8

[a]Column (1) divided by column (2).
P equals a historic peak in the inflation adjusted value of the S&P stock price index.

Source of basic data: BCI series 19 and 320.

TABLE 2.11
Annual Price Appreciation for Gold and the Financial Returns Associated with the S&P Index, 1970–1990

Year	Closing Price for Gold (1)	% Change Price of Gold (2)	Financial Return S&P Index (3)
1970	$37.80	6.4	3.5
1971	44.00	16.4	14.1
1972	65.40	48.6	18.7
1973	112.75	72.4	−14.5
1974	186.75	65.6	−26.0
1975	140.75	−24.6	36.9*
1976	135.25	−3.9	23.6*
1977	165.45	22.3	−7.2
1978	226.30	36.8	6.4
1979	512.40	126.4	18.4
1980	589.75	15.1	31.5*
1981	397.50	−32.6	−4.8*
1982	460.50	15.8	20.4*
1983	382.25	−17.0	22.3*
1984	308.25	−19.4	6.0*

TABLE 2.11 (*concluded*)

Year	Closing Price for Gold (1)	% Change Price of Gold (2)	Financial Return S&P Index (3)
1985	330.00	7.1	31.1*
1986	396.50	20.2	18.5
1987	486.37	22.7	5.7
1988	412.00	−15.3	16.3*
1989	403.50	−2.1	31.2*
1990	384.60	−4.7	−3.1*

*Years when the financial return for the S&P index exceeded the annual percentage change in the price per troy once for Engelhard industrial bullion.

Source of basic data: *The Wall Street Journal* and Standard & Poor's *Security Price Index Record.*

TABLE 2.12
Some Inflation Indicators and the Financial Returns Associated with the S&P Composite Stock Price Index

Year	Average First Purchase Price U.S. Crude Oil ($) (1)	% Change Implicit Price Deflator for Real GNP (2)	Financial Return S&P Index (3)
1942	1.19	6.6	19.2**
1943	1.20	2.6*	25.7**
1944	1.21	1.4*	19.3**
1945	1.22	2.9	35.7**
1946	1.41	22.9	−7.8
1947	1.93	13.9*	5.5
1948	2.60	7.0*	5.4
1949	2.54*	−.5*	17.8**
1950	2.51*	2.0	30.5**
1951	2.53	4.8	23.4**
1952	2.53*	1.5*	17.7**
1953	2.68	1.6	−1.2
1954	2.77	1.6	51.2**
1955	2.77*	3.2	31.0**
1956	2.79	3.4	6.4**
1957	3.09	3.6	−10.4
1958	3.01*	2.1*	42.4**
1959	2.90*	2.4	11.8**

TABLE 2.12 (concluded)

Year	Average First Purchase Price U.S. Crude Oil ($) (1)	% Change Implicit Price Deflator for Real GNP (2)	Financial Return S&P Index (3)
1960	2.88*	1.6*	.3
1961	2.89	1.0*	26.6**
1962	2.90	2.2	−8.8
1963	2.89*	1.6*	22.5**
1964	2.88*	1.5*	16.3**
1965	2.86*	2.7	12.3**
1966	2.88	3.6	−10.0
1967	2.92	2.6*	23.7**
1968	2.94	5.0	10.8**
1969	3.09	5.6	−8.3
1970	3.18	5.5*	3.5
1971	3.39	5.7	14.1**
1972	3.39*	4.7*	18.7**
1973	3.89	6.5	−14.5
1974	6.87	9.1	−26.0
1975	7.67	9.8	36.9**
1976	8.19	6.4*	23.6**
1977	8.57	6.7	−7.2
1978	9.00	7.3	6.4
1979	12.64	8.9	18.4**
1980	21.59	9.0	31.5**
1981	31.77	9.7	−4.8
1982	28.52*	6.4*	20.4**
1983	26.19*	3.9*	22.3**
1984	25.88*	3.7*	6.0**
1985	24.09*	3.0*	31.1**
1986	12.51*	2.6*	18.5**
1987	15.40	3.2	5.7**
1988	12.58*	3.3	16.3**
1989	15.86	4.1	31.2**
1990	20.03	4.1	−3.1

*A positive financial return for the S&P index is indicated by a decline or no change in the average price of crude oil or by a decline in the inflation rate for the implicit price deflator for real GNP. The financial returns for the S&P index have been positive in these years.

**Years when the financial return exceeded the inflation for the implicit price deflator in column (2).

Source of basic data: *Monthly Energy Review,* BCI series 310 and Standard & Poor's *Security Price Index Record.*

TABLE 2.13

Consensus Forecasts and Error Terms for the Year-to-Year Inflation Rates for the Implicit Price Deflator for Real GNP Compiled by Blue Chip Economic Indicators and Simpler Forecasts Which Assume that There Will Be No Change in the Inflation Rate, 1977–1990[a]

Year	Blue Chip Consensus Forecasts		4th-Quarter Projection[c] (3)	Actual Inflation Rate[d] (4)
	January Survey[b] (1)	February Survey[b] (2)		
1977	5.3(.2)B	5.4(.1)B	4.7(.8)	5.5(.3)
1978	6.1(1.3)B	6.0(1.4)B	5.8(1.6)	7.4(1.9)
1979	7.8(1.1)	7.9(1.0)	8.2(.7)	8.9(1.5)
1980	9.1(−.1)	9.2(−.2)	8.9(.1)	9.0(.1)
1981	9.6(−.5)B	9.8(−.7)	9.8(−.7)	9.1(.1)
1982	7.7(−1.7)B	7.6(−1.6)B	8.6(−2.6)	6.0(−3.1)
1983	5.1(−.9)	4.9(−.7)	4.5(−.3)	4.2(−1.8)
1984	4.7(−.9)	4.5(−.7)	4.0(−.2)	3.8(−.4)
1985	4.1(−.8)	3.7(−.4)	3.5(−.2)	3.3(−.5)
1986	3.5(−.8)	3.4(−.7)	3.1(−.4)	2.7(−.6)
1987	3.2(−.2)B	3.0(.0)B	2.2(.8)	3.0(.3)
1988	3.6(−.2)	3.4(.0)B	3.3(.1)	3.4(.4)
1989	4.3(−.2)	4.5(−.4)	4.1(.0)	4.1(.7)
1990	4.0(.1)B	4.0(.1)B	3.8(.3)	4.1(.0)

Average Absolute Forecasting Errors, 1977–90

.643	.571	.629	.836

[a]The figures in parentheses are the actual minus predicted forecasting error terms expressed in percentage points.

[b]The January and February surveys are conducted very early in the month.

[c]The preliminary fourth-quarter-to-fourth-quarter growth rate for the implicit price deflator for the preceding year which is published in the January issue of the *Survey of Current Business*.

[d]The preliminary year-to-year growth rate for the implicit price deflator which is published in the *Survey of Current Business* in January of the following year. The figures in parentheses are first differences in these preliminary inflation rates.

B represents years when the forecasting error for the Blue Chip Consensus was smaller than the forecasting error for the fourth-quarter projection in column (3).

TABLE 2.14
Some Alternative Ways to Forecast the Year-to-Year Inflation Rate for the Implicit Price Deflator for Real GNP

Year	T-Bill Rate (1)	M1 (2)	Hourly Earnings (3)	CPI (4)	4th Q IPD (5)	Following Inflation Rate[b] (6)
	Forecasted Inflation Rate for the Following Year[a]					
1968	5.9(−1.2)*	6.5(−1.8)	7.3(−2.6)	4.7(.0)	3.9(.8)	4.7(.9)
1969	7.7(−2.4)	2.5(2.8)	6.5(−1.2)	6.1(−.8)*	5.1(.2)	5.3(.6)
1970	4.9(−.2)	5.4(−.7)*	5.8(−1.1)	5.5(−.8)	5.3(−.6)	4.7(−.6)
1971	4.0(−1.0)*	6.2(−3.2)	6.1(−3.1)	3.4(−.4)	3.3(−.3)	3.0(−1.7)
1972	5.1(.2)*	8.2(−2.9)	6.0(−.7)	3.4(1.9)	3.0(2.3)	5.3(2.3)
1973	7.4(2.8)	5.7(4.5)	7.2(3.0)*	8.8(1.4)	7.0(3.2)	10.2(4.9)
1974	7.2(1.5)	4.5(4.2)	8.7(.0)*	12.2(−3.5)	11.8(−3.1)	8.7(−1.5)
1975	5.5(−.3)	4.2(1.0)	6.6(−1.4)	7.0(−1.8)	6.4(−1.2)*	5.2(−3.5)
1976	4.4(1.1)	5.8(−.3)	7.0(−1.5)	4.8(.7)*	4.7(.8)	5.5(.3)
1977	6.1(1.3)	7.4(.0)	7.8(−.4)	6.8(.6)*	5.8(1.6)	7.4(1.9)
1978	9.1(−.2)	6.7(2.2)	9.1(−.2)	9.0(−.1)*	8.2(.7)	8.9(1.5)
1979	12.1(−3.1)	5.7(3.3)	7.9(1.1)	13.3(−4.3)	8.9(.1)*	9.0(.1)
1980	15.7(−6.6)	6.5(2.6)	8.6(.5)	12.4(−3.3)	9.8(−.7)*	9.1(.1)
1981	10.9(−4.9)	6.3(−.3)	7.4(−1.4)	8.9(−2.9)	8.6(−2.6)*	6.0(−3.1)
1982	8.0(−3.8)	8.5(−4.3)	5.0(−.8)*	3.9(.3)	4.5(−.3)	4.2(−1.8)
1983	9.0(−5.2)	9.0(−5.2)	4.5(−.7)*	3.8(.0)	4.0(−.2)	3.8(−.4)
1984	8.2(−4.9)	5.5(−2.2)	3.7(−.4)	4.0(−.7)*	3.5(−.2)	3.3(−.5)
1985	7.1(−4.4)	11.9(−9.2)	3.3(−.6)	3.8(−1.1)*	3.1(−.4)	2.7(−.6)
1986	5.5(−2.5)	16.6(−13.6)	1.6(1.4)	1.1(1.9)	2.2(.8)*	3.0(.3)
1987	5.8(−2.4)	3.1(.3)	2.9(.5)	4.4(−1.0)	3.3(.1)*	3.4(.4)
1988	8.1(−4.0)	4.9(−.8)	3.7(.4)	4.4(−.3)*	4.1(.0)	4.1(.7)
1989	7.6(−3.5)	.9(3.2)	4.1(.0)*	4.6(−.5)	3.8(.3)	4.1(1.0)
1990	6.8	3.9	3.7	6.1	4.0( )*	?

Average Absolute Forecasting Errors, 1968–88

2.57	3.11	1.10	1.32	.96	1.32

[a]The forecasted inflation rates for the following year are equal to the average December yield on new 3-month Treasury bills in column (1); the preliminary Dec.–Dec. growth rates for M1 in column (2); the preliminary Dec.–Dec. growth rates for total private nonagricultural average hourly earnings in column (3); the Dec.–Dec. growth rate for the all item CPI in column (4); and the preliminary fourth-quarter-to-fourth-quarter growth rates for the implicit price deflator for real GNP in column (5). These estimates are obtained from the following January issue of the *Survey of Current Business*. The figures in parentheses are error terms based on the actual following year inflation rate in column (6) minus the forecasted rate.

[b]The preliminary inflation rate for the following year. The figures in parentheses are first differences in these inflation rates.

*Identifies the median forecasted inflation rate in columns (1) through (5).

TABLE 2.15
Using December–December and Year-to-Year Percentage Changes in the Consumer Price Index to Forecast Good Years to Have Been in the Stock Market, 1942–1990

Year	CPI Growth Rate		Column (1) minus Column (2) (3)	Following Year Financial Return S&P Index* (4)
	December-to-December (1)	Year-to-Year (2)		
1942	9.0	10.9	−1.9	25.7
1943	3.0	6.1	−3.1	19.3
1947	8.8	14.4	−5.6	5.4
1948	3.0	9.1	−5.1	17.8
1951	6.0	7.9	−1.9	17.7
1954	−.7	.7	−1.4	31.0
1975	6.9	9.1	−2.2	23.6
1981	8.9	10.3	−1.4	20.4
1982	3.8	6.2	−2.4	22.3

*A positive financial return is predicted by a negative first difference in column (3) of 1.4 percentage points or more.

Source of basic data: BCI series 320 and Standard & Poor's *Security Price Index Record*.

TABLE 2.16

Annual December-to-December Consumer Price Inflation and the Financial Returns from Holding Corporate Bonds and Stocks

Year	CPI Inflation Rate (%) (1)	Inflation Rate First Differences (%) (2)	Financial Returns	
			Corporate Bonds (%) (3)	S&P Index (4)
1955	.4	1.1	.5*	31.0
1956	3.0	2.6	−6.8*	6.4
1957	2.9	−.1	8.7	−10.4
1958	1.8	−1.1	−2.2	42.4
1959	1.7	−.1	−1.0	11.8
1960	1.4	−.3	9.1	.3
1961	.7	−.7	4.8	26.6
1962	1.3	.6	7.9	−8.8
1963	1.6	.3	2.2	22.5
1964	1.0	−.6	4.8	16.3
1965	1.9	.9	−.4*	12.3
1966	3.5	1.6	.2*	−10.0
1967	3.0	−.5	−4.9	23.7
1968	4.7	1.7	2.6*	10.8
1969	6.2	1.5	−8.1*	−8.3
1970	5.6	−.6	18.4	3.5
1971	3.3	−2.3	11.0	14.1
1972	3.4	.1	7.3	18.7
1973	8.7	5.3	1.1*	−14.5
1974	12.3	3.6	−3.0*	−26.0
1975	6.9	−5.4	14.6	36.9
1976	4.9	−2.0	18.6	23.6
1977	6.7	1.8	1.7*	−7.2
1978	9.0	2.3	−.1*	6.4
1979	13.3	4.3	−4.2*	18.4
1980	12.5	−.8	−2.6	31.5
1981	8.9	−3.6	−1.0	−4.8
1982	3.8	−5.1	48.5	20.4
1983	3.8	.0	1.1	22.3
1984	3.9	.1	16.4	6.0
1985	3.8	−.1	30.9	31.1
1986	1.1	−2.7	19.9	18.5
1987	4.4	3.3	−.3*	5.7
1988	4.4	.0	10.7	16.3
1989	4.6	.2	16.2	31.2
1990	6.1	1.5	6.8*	−3.1

*Identifies bond returns during years when the price acceleration for the CPI was over .7 percentage points.

Sources: Ibbotson and Sinquefield, Standard & Poor's, Salomon Brothers, and Johnson's Charts.

179

TABLE 2.17
Some Consumer Price Inflation Indicators

Year	Capacity Utilization Rate for December (%) (1)	Vendor Performance for December (2)	Dec.–Dec. T-Bill Rate Change (3)	6-Mo. CPI Inflation Rate Change (4)	Relative Inflation for Food (5)	Following Year CPI Inflation Change (6)
1954	81.8	50	-.5	-.99	-1.1	1.1
1955	89.0*	56*	1.4*	.37*	-1.3	2.6**
1956	86.8*	36	.7	.36*	.2	-.1
1957	77.5	25	-.1	-.86	-.2	-1.1
1958	79.0	52	-.3	-1.76	.4	-.1
1959	83.6	50	1.8*	.11	-2.3	-.3
1960	74.3	38	-2.3	-.12	1.6*	-.7
1961	81.6	53	.4	.45*	-1.6	.6
1962	81.7	48	.2	-.12	.3	.3
1963	84.0	46	.7	.10	.3	-.6
1964	88.0*	66*	.3	.32*	.2	.9**
1965	90.5*	72*	.5	-.44	1.5*	1.6**
1966	90.0*	57*	.6	-.24	.5	-.5
1967	87.6*	48	.0	.78*	-1.8	1.7
1968	87.3*	56*	.9*	-.05	-.4	1.5**
1969	84.2	64*	1.8*	-.18	1.1	-.6
1970	76.8	36	-2.9	-.60	-3.3	-2.3
1971	78.9	51	-.8	-.70	.9	.1
1972	86.0*	77*	1.0*	.30*	1.3*	5.3**

	(1)	(2)	(3)	(4)	(5)	
1973	85.7*	88*	2.3*	.60*	11.3*	3.6**
1974	75.7	22	-.2	-.27	.0	-5.4
1975	74.8	39	-1.7	.20*	-.5	-2.0
1976	79.4	45	-1.2	.19*	-4.2	1.8
1977	82.5	56*	1.7*	-1.94	1.2*	2.3**
1978	86.5*	68*	3.1*	-1.05	2.8*	4.3**
1979	82.9	49	3.0*	-.61	-3.1	-.8
1980	79.6	47	3.6*	-3.34	-2.2	-3.6
1981	73.8	30	-4.7	-1.21	-4.6	-5.1
1982	68.0	38	-2.9	-2.61	-.8	.0
1983	77.6	67*	1.0*	-.14	-1.2	.1
1984	80.4	45	-.8	-.83	-.2	-.1
1985	80.1	46	-1.1	-.58	-1.1	-2.7
1986	80.2	56*	-1.6	.83*	2.7*	3.3**
1987	82.6	71*	.3	-1.08	-.9	.0
1988	84.4	53	2.3*	-.13	.6	.2
1989	83.7	42	-.4	-1.38	1.0	1.5
1990	80.4	47	-1.1	-.01	-.8	?

*Rapid acceleration in the December-to-December CPI inflation rate of .9 percentage points or more in the following year is indicated by a December capacity utilization rate for manufacturing of 85 percent or more; a vendors performance rating (percent of companies receiving slower deliveries) over 55 percent; a first difference in the average December yield on new three-month Treasury bills of .9 percentage points or more; acceleration in the half-year inflation rate for the CPI of .18 percentage points or more; and an annual December-to-December inflation rate for the food component of the consumer price index that is 1.2 percentage points greater than the annual inflation rate for the all item CPI.

**Those years when three or more of the inflation indicators in columns (1) through (5) are predicting a rapid acceleration in the consumer price index in the following year.

Source of basic data: BCI series 82, 32, 114, 320, and the *Economic Report of the President*.

TABLE 2.18
Using Changes in Short-Term Interest Rates to Predict Good Years to Own Stock

Year	December–December % Change Average Yield New 3-Month T-Bills (1)	Following Year Financial Return S&P Stock Index (%) (3)
1948	21.1	17.8
1949	−4.3	30.5*
1950	24.5	23.4
1951	26.3	17.7
1952	23.1	−1.2
1953	−23.5	51.2**
1954	−28.2	31.0**
1955	118.8	6.4
1956	26.2	−10.4
1957	−4.0	42.4*
1958	−9.4	11.8*
1959	62.6	.3
1960	−50.3	26.6**
1961	15.4	−8.8
1962	9.2	22.5*
1963	23.1	16.3
1964	9.7	12.3*
1965	13.0	−10.0
1966	14.9	23.7
1967	.0	10.8*
1968	18.2	−8.3
1969	30.4	3.5
1970	−37.0	14.1**
1971	−17.3	18.7**
1972	25.9	−14.5
1973	45.5	−26.0
1974	−2.4	36.9*
1975	−23.4	23.6**
1976	−20.9	−7.2**
1977	39.3	6.4
1978	50.5	18.4
1979	32.3	31.5
1980	29.7	−4.8
1981	−30.2	20.4**
1982	−26.7	22.3**
1983	11.9	6.0
1984	−8.9	31.1*
1985	−13.4	18.5**

TABLE 2.18 (concluded)

Year	December–December % Change Average Yield New 3-Month T-Bills (1)	Following Year Financial Return S&P Stock Index (%) (3)
1986	−22.3	5.7**
1987	6.0	16.3*
1988	39.5	31.2
1989	−5.6	−3.1*
1990	−10.9	?**

*Financial return following a decline in the T-bill rate of not more than 10 percent or an increase in the T-bill rate of less than 10 percent.
**Financial return following a decline in the T-bill rate of more than 10 percent.

Source of basic data: BCI series 114 and Standard & Poor's *Security Price Index Record*.

TABLE 2.19
Purchasing the S&P Index at the End of the Month after a Cumulative Decline of 20 Percent or More in the Average Monthly Discount Rate on New Issues of 91-Day Treasury Bills

Purchase Date	T-Bill Rate (%)	Value S&P Index	% Change S&P Index Following Year
10/30/53	1.40	24.54	29.1
1/31/58	2.60	41.70	32.9
3/31/60	3.44	55.34	17.6
3/31/67	4.29	90.20	.0
9/30/70	6.27	84.21	16.6
11/30/71	4.19	93.99	24.1
1/31/75	6.49	76.98	31.0
1/30/76	4.96	100.86	1.2
5/30/80	9.15	111.24	19.2
11/30/81	11.27	126.35	9.6
8/31/82	9.01	119.51	37.6
12/31/84	8.16	167.24	26.0
12/31/90	6.81	330.22	?
Average gain			20.4

Source of basic data: BCI series 114 and Standard & Poor's *Security Price Index Record*.

TABLE 2.20
Average Annual Growth Rates for the Hourly Earnings of Production Workers on Private, Nonagricultural Payrolls and the Implicit Price Deflator for Real GNP

Year	Hourly Earnings[a] (%) (1)	IPD Real GNP (%) (2)	Actual minus the Predicted Inflation Rate[b] (3)
1954	3.3	1.6	−.4
1955	3.5	3.2	1.0#
1956	4.9	3.4	−.2
1957	5.0P	3.6	−.1
1958	4.2	2.1	−.8
1959	3.5	2.4	.2*#
1960	3.4P	1.6	−.5
1961	3.0	1.0	−.7
1962	3.4	2.2	.1
1963	2.8	1.6	.1
1964	2.8	1.5	.0
1965	3.6	2.7	.4#
1966	4.3	3.6	.6#
1967	5.0	2.6	−1.1
1968	6.1	5.0	.2
1969	6.7P	5.6	.2
1970	6.6	5.5	.2
1971	7.2	5.7	−.2
1972	6.2	4.7	−.2
1973	6.2	6.5	.3*
1974	8.0	9.1	1.1*
1975	8.4	9.8	1.4*
1976	7.2	6.4	−.8
1977	7.6	6.7	−.9
1978	8.2	7.3	−.9
1979	7.9	8.9	1.0*
1980	9.0P	9.0	.0*
1981	9.1P	9.7	.6*
1982	6.9	6.4	−.5
1983	4.6	3.9	−.7
1984	3.2	3.7	.5#
1985	3.1	3.0	−.1
1986	2.5	2.6	.1
1987	2.4	3.2	.8*
1988	3.2	3.3	.1
1989	4.1	4.1	.0

TABLE 2.20 (concluded)

Year	Hourly Earnings[a] (%) (1)	IPD Real GNP (%) (2)	Actual minus the Predicted Inflation Rate[b] (3)
1990	3.8P	4.1	.3*

[a]The earnings of production workers have been adjusted for overtime in manufacturing and for interindustry shifts for the years 1954–88 and are unadjusted earnings thereafter.

[b]The predicted inflation rate is equal to the growth of hourly earnings in column (1) minus a constant term equal to 1.3 percentage points for the years 1953–72 and zero for the years since 1972.

*Indicates years when the December-to-December percentage change in the energy component of the CPI was 2.5 percentage points or more in excess of the comparable percentage change in the all item CPI.

#Indicates years when the average annual growth rate for real GNP was in excess of 5.5 percent.

P equals a year containing an official NBER peak in business activity.

Source of basic data: *Economic Report of the President.*

TABLE 2.21
Unemployment and the December-to-December Inflation Rates for the Consumer Price Index and the Employment Cost Index for Total Compensation in Private Industry

Year	December Unemployment Rate (1)	CPI Inflation (2)	Employment Cost Inflation	
			Actual (3)	Predicted[a] (4)
1980	7.2	12.5	9.6	—
1981	8.5	8.9	9.9	8.3
1982	10.8	3.8	6.5	6.1
1983	8.3	3.8	5.7	4.2
1984	7.3	3.9	4.9	4.4
1985	7.0	3.8	3.9	3.8
1986	6.6	1.1	3.2	3.3
1987	5.7	4.4	3.3	2.8
1988	5.3	4.4	4.8	3.8
1989	5.3	4.6	4.8	5.1
1990	6.1	6.1	4.6	4.4

Average Inflation Rates 1980–90

	5.2	5.6		

[a]The predicted cost inflation is equal to four percentage points plus 20 percent of the previous year's CPI inflation plus 80 percent of the preceding year's employment cost inflation minus 70 percent of the December unemployment rate.

Source of basic data: *Economic Report of the President.*

TABLE 2.22

Year-to-Year Inflation Rates for the Consumer Price Index and Selected CPI Components

Year	All Item CPI (1)	CPI without Food, Energy, and Shelter (2)	Food (3)	Medical Care Services (4)	Shelter (5)	Motor Fuels (6)	Household Fuels and Electricity (7)
1969	5.5	4.7	5.1	8.2	8.3	3.0	1.8
1970	5.7	5.2	5.7	7.0	8.9	1.1	4.5
1971	4.4	4.9	3.1	7.4	4.2	.7	6.9
1972	3.2	2.4	4.2	3.5	4.6	1.1	4.0
1973	6.2	2.9	14.5	4.5	4.7	9.9	7.0
1974	11.0	7.7	14.3	10.4	9.6	35.3	25.1
1975	9.1	8.9	8.5	12.6	9.9	6.9	14.5
1976	5.8	7.1	3.0	10.1	5.5	4.2	9.9
1977	6.5	6.0	6.3	9.9	6.6	5.7	13.2
1978	7.6	5.6	9.9	8.5	10.2	4.2	8.2
1979	11.3	6.9	11.0	9.8	13.9	35.3	15.7
1980	13.5	8.8	8.6	11.3	17.6	38.9	22.0
1981	10.3	9.6	7.8	10.7	11.7	11.4	16.6
1982	6.2	7.7	4.1	11.8	7.1	−5.3	9.6
1983	3.2	5.2	2.1	8.7	2.3	−3.3	5.1
1984	4.3	5.0	3.8	6.0	4.9	−1.5	3.5
1985	3.6	3.8	2.3	6.1	5.6	.8	.5
1986	1.9	3.4	3.2	7.7	5.5	−21.9	−5.1
1987	3.6	3.8	4.1	6.6	4.7	4.0	−1.9
1988	4.1	4.2	4.1	6.4	4.8	.9	.7
1989	4.8	4.4	5.8	7.7	4.5	9.4	3.0
1990	5.4	4.9	5.8	9.3	5.4	14.4	3.6

Source: *Economic Report of the President.*

TABLE 2.23
Using Economic Variables to Predict the Outcome of Presidential Elections in the United States, 1920–1988

Presidential Election Year	Civilian Unemployment Rate[a] (%) (1)	CPI Inflation Rate[b] (%) (2)	Change in Misery Index[c] (3)	Real Consumption Increase[d] (%) (4)	President Elected and Political Affiliation (5)
	Cases Where the Incumbent Political Party Was Reelected				
1924	5.5	.3	−14.0	29.24	Coolidge (R)
1928	4.4	−1.2	−2.6	9.81*	Hoover (R)
1936	16.9	1.0	4.5*	20.64	Roosevelt (D)
1940	14.6	.8	−2.5	13.58	Roosevelt (D)
1944	1.2	1.6	−12.6	10.84*	Roosevelt (D)
1948	4.0	2.7	3.9*	22.38	Truman (D)
1956	4.2	2.9	3.5*	16.65	Eisenhower (R)
1964	5.0	1.2	−1.9	16.47	Johnson (D)
1972	5.2	3.4	.5	15.36	Nixon (R)
1984	7.2	4.0	−8.5	11.97	Reagan (R)
1988	5.3	4.4	−1.5	15.25	Bush (R)
	Cases Where the President Was Elected from an Opposing Party				
1920	4.0	15.8	7.6	6.69	Harding (R)

TABLE 2.23 (concluded)

Presidential Election Year	Civilian Unemployment Rate[a] (%) (1)	CPI Inflation Rate[b] (%) (2)	Change in Misery Index[c] (3)	Real Consumption Increase[d] (%) (4)	President Elected and Political Affiliation (5)
1932	23.6	−10.2*	10.2	−11.75	Roosevelt (D)
1952	2.7	.9*	−3.1*	13.14*	Eisenhower (R)
1960	6.6	1.5*	1.0	11.70	Kennedy (D)
1968	3.4	4.7	1.9	20.10*	Nixon (R)
1976	7.8	4.8	4.0	11.22	Carter (D)
1980	7.3	12.4	7.1	10.89	Reagan (R)

[a]Average rate for the years 1916–44 and the December rate for the years 1948–88.

[b]Average annual rates 1916–44 and annual rates 1948–88. An inflation rate in excess of 4.5 percent is used to predict an election turnover.

[c]The misery index is equal to the sum of the unemployment and inflation rates in columns (1) and (2). The change in the misery index is from one presidential election year to the next. An increase in the index of 1 percentage point or more is used to predict an election turnover.

[d]A four year increase in real personal consumption of 11.75 percent or less is used to predict an election turnover.

*Cases where the presidential election outcome is misclassified.

Source of basic data: BCI series 43 and 320 and John Kendrick, *Productivity Trends in the United States* (Princeton: Princeton University Press for the NBER, 1961).

TABLE 2.24

Percentage Changes in the Consumer Price Index, Hourly Earnings, the Money Supply, and the Average Price Received by U.S. Oil Producers and Farmers for Crude Oil, Wheat, and Corn during the Three Years Ending with a Condition of Double-Digit Inflation for the Consumer Price Index, 1915–1990

			Year-to-Year Inflation Rate			
Year	Crude Oil[a] (1)	Wheat[b] (2)	Corn[b] (3)	CPI (4)	Earnings[c] (5)	M1[d] (6)
1915	−21.0	−1.4	−4.5	1.2	2.7	NA
1916	71.9	49.2	68.2	7.4	12.6	17.8
1917	41.8	42.7	28.0	17.6	18.5	16.2
1940	.0	−1.3	8.8	.4	4.8	16.1
1941	11.8	38.4	21.5	5.0	10.6	17.3
1942	4.4	16.5	22.1	10.8	16.4	19.0
1945	.8	6.4	16.5	2.3	1.0	16.4
1946	15.6	27.3	22.8	8.5	5.9	7.3
1947	36.9	20.0	38.5	14.5	13.0	5.0
1972	.0	31.3	45.4	3.3	6.2	7.2
1973	14.7	124.4	62.4	6.2	6.2	7.2
1974	73.3	3.5	18.4	11.0	8.0	5.0
1977	4.6	−14.7	−6.0	6.5	7.6	7.7
1978	5.0	27.5	11.4	7.7	8.1	8.2
1979	40.4	27.3	12.0	11.3	8.0	7.7
1980	67.6	4.8	29.8	13.5	9.0	6.3
1981	49.9			10.4	9.2	7.0

[a]The average well head price received by U.S. oil producers.
[b]The corn and wheat prices are based on the seasonal average prices received by farmers.
[c]Average weekly earnings of production workers in manufacturing 1914–17, average hourly earnings of production workers in manufacturing 1939–47, and the adjusted hourly earnings of nonsupervisory production workers in private nonagricultural industries 1972–79.
[d]M1 is currently defined as currency outside banks plus demand deposits, traveler's checks, and other checkable deposits. The percentage changes are based on end of the month averages compiled by Friedman and Schwartz and the Board of Governors of the Federal Reserve System.

TABLE 2.25

The Average Cost of Imported Oil at U.S. Refineries and Its Relation to the Inflation Rate for the Consumer Price Index since the Peaking Out of U.S. Oil Production in 1970

Year	Price of Imported Oil ($ per barrel)	Inflation Rates (%) for	
		Imported Oil	CPI
1970	2.96	5.7	5.7
1971	3.17	7.1	4.4
1972	3.22	1.6	3.2
1973	4.08	26.7	6.2*
1974	12.52	206.9	11.0*
1975	13.93	11.3	9.1
1976	13.48	−3.2	5.8
1977	14.53	7.8	6.5
1978	14.57	.3	7.6
1979	21.67	48.7	11.3*
1980	33.89	56.4	13.5*
1981	37.05	9.3	10.3
1982	33.55	−9.4	6.2
1983	29.30	−12.7	3.2
1984	28.88	−1.4	4.3
1985	26.99	−6.5	3.6
1986	14.00	−48.1	1.9
1987	18.13	29.5	3.6*
1988	14.56	−19.7	4.1
1989	18.08	24.2	4.8*
1990	21.78	20.5	5.4*

*Years when the inflation rate for imported oil was at least 3 percentage points greater than the inflation rate for the CPI.

Source of basic data: *Monthly Energy Review* and *The Survey of Current Business*.

TABLE 2.26
Major Fluctuations in the Average Cost of Imported Oil at U.S. Refineries in Current and 1982–1984 Dollars

Month and Year	Price of Imported Oil ($ per barrel)	Consumer Price Index (1982–84 = 100)	Price of Imported Oil in 1982–84 Dollars
January 1977	14.11	58.5	24.12
February 1981	39.00	87.9	44.37
July 1986	10.91	109.5	9.96
August 1987	19.32	114.4	16.89
November 1988	12.66	120.3	10.52
January 1990	20.51	127.4	16.10
June 1990	14.89	129.9	11.46
October 1990	32.98	133.5	24.70

Source: *Monthly Energy Review* and *The Survey of Current Business.*

TABLE 2.30
Estimates of Conventional Oil and Gas Resources in the United States as of the End of 1986

	Oil (billions of barrels)	Natural Gas (trillions of cubic feet)
Cumulative production 12/31/86	143.0	697.5
Measured reserves	29.5	206.6
Indicated reserves	3.5	—
Inferred reserves	18. 2	98.8
Mean estimate of undiscovered recoverable resources	49.4	399.1
Total resources	243.6	1,402.0
Cumulative production 12/31/89	151.8	748.1
Remaining resources 12/31/89	91.8	653.9
Production during 1989	2.8	17.1
Life expectancy of remaining resources produced at the production rate for 1989 in years	32.8	38.2

Source of basic data: United States Department of Interior, U.S. Geological Survey Minerals Management Service, "Estimates of Undiscovered Conventional Oil and Gas Resources in the United States—A Part of the Nation's Energy Endowments" (Washington: Government Printing Office, 1989); and the *Monthly Energy Review.*

TABLE 2.31

Crude Oil Production in the United States, Selected Years (Thousands of Barrels per Day)

Year	Total Production (1)	Alaskan Production (2)	Lower 48 States Actual (3)	Lower 48 States Projected[a] (4)	Lower 48 States Actual minus Projected[b] (5)
1970	9,637	229	9,408	8,393	1,015
1971	9,463	218	9,245	8,306	939
1972	9,441	199	9,242	8,248	994
1973	9,208	198	9,010	8,103	907
1974	8,774	193	8,581	8.016	565
1975	8,375	191	8,184	7,870	314
1976	8,132	173	7,959	7,696	263
1977	8,245	464	7,781	7,550	231
1978	8,707	1,229	7,478	7,377	101
1979	8,552	1,401	7,151	7,203	− 52
1980	8,597	1,617	6,980	6,970	10
1981	8,572	1,609	6,963	6,796	167
1982	8,649	1,696	6,953	6,564	389
1983	8,688	1,714	6,974	6,360	614
1984	8,879	1,722	7,157	6,128	1,029
1985	8,971	1,825	7,146	5,858	1,288
1986	8,680	1,867	6,813	5,692	1,121
1987	8,349	1,962	6,387	5,460	927
1988	8,140	2,017	6,123	5,256	867
1989	7,613	1,874	5,739	4,995	744
1990	7,301	1,774	5,527	4,821	706
1995				3,891	
2000				2,875	

[a]Hubbert's projected production for the 48 lower states has been increased 6 percent each year to adjust for leased condensate which is included in the Department of Energy's production figures.

[b]Column (3) minus column (4).

Source of data: *Monthly Energy Review*; and Perry Renshaw, "U.S. Oil Discovery and Production: The Projections of M. King Hubbert," *Futures*, February 1980, Table 2, p. 61.

TABLE 2.32
Estimated World Crude Oil Proven Reserves, Production, and Population:
20 Leading Countries, 1989

Country	Estimated Crude Oil (millions of barrels)		Population
	Reserves 1/1/90	Production 1989	Mid-1989 (millions)
1. Saudi Arabia	254,959	1,879.0	14.7
2. Iraq	100,000	1,030.0	18.1
3. Kuwait	94,525	657.7	2.1
4. Iran	92,860	1,045.0	53.9
5. Abu Dhabi	92,205	715.0[a]	1.7[a]
6. Venezuela	58,504	687.3	18.8
7. USSR	58,400[b]	4,146.4	289.0
8. Mexico	56,365	916.5	86.7
9. USA	25,860	2,785.3	248.8
10. China	24,000	1,013.6	1,103.9
11. Libya	22,800	400.0	4.1
12. Nigeria	16,000	616.5	115.6
13. Norway	11,546	536.5	4.2
14. Algeria	9,200	401.5	24.9
15. Indonesia	8,200	501.5	184.6
16. India	7,516	245.8	835.0
17. Canada	6,133	575.2	26.3
18. Qatar	4,500	142.7	.4
19. Egypt	4,500	311.8	54.8
20. United Kingdom	4,256	652.3	57.3
Other countries	48,943	2,465.6	2,089.0
World	1,001,572	21,725.2	5,234.0

[a]Production and population figures are for the United Arab Emirates.
[b]The USSR figures are "explored reserves" which include proved, probable, and some possible.

Source: *Oil and Gas Journal*, worldwide report issue; *Monthly Energy Review*; and the *Information Please Almanac*.

TABLE 2.33

Non-OPEC Crude Oil Production (Millions of Barrels per Day)

Year	USSR	USA	China	Mexico	UK	Canada	Big Six[a]	Other	Total
1973	8.3L	9.2H	1.1L	.5L	.0L	1.8H	20.9L	3.8L	24.7L
1974	8.9	8.8	1.3	.6	.0	1.6	21.1	3.9	24.9
1975	9.5	8.4	1.5	.7	.0	1.4	21.5	4.1	25.6
1976	10.0	8.1	1.7	.8	.2	1.3	22.2	4.4	26.5
1977	10.5	8.2	1.9	1.0	.8	1.3	23.7	4.6	28.3
1978	11.0	8.7	2.1	1.2	1.1	1.3	25.3	4.8	30.1
1979	11.2	8.6	2.1	1.5	1.6	1.5	26.4	5.1	31.5
1980	11.5	8.6	2.1	1.9	1.6	1.4	27.2	5.2	32.4
1981	11.6	8.6	2.0	2.3	1.8	1.3	27.5	5.4	32.9
1982	11.6	8.6	2.0	2.7	2.1	1.3L	28.4	5.6	34.0
1983	11.7	8.7	2.1	2.7	2.3	1.4	28.8	6.2	35.1
1984	11.6	8.9	2.3	2.8	2.5	1.4	29.4	6.8	36.3
1985	11.2	9.0	2.5	2.7	2.5	1.5	29.5H	7.5	37.0
1986	11.5	8.7	2.6	2.4	2.5H	1.5	29.3	7.8	37.1
1987	11.7	8.3	2.7	2.5H	2.4	1.5	29.2	8.2	37.5
1988	11.8H	8.1	2.7	2.5	2.2	1.6	28.9	8.7	37.6H
1989	11.4	7.6	2.8	2.5	1.8	1.6	27.6	9.2	36.9
1990	10.7	7.3L	2.8H	2.5	1.8	1.5	25.2	9.7	36.4

[a]The USSR, USA, China, Mexico, United Kingdom, and Canada.
L represents the low production figure and H the high production figure for the 1973–90 period.

Source: *Monthly Energy Review.*

TABLE 2.34
OPEC Crude Oil Production (Millions of Barrels per Day)

Year	Saudi Arabia	Iran	Iraq	Kuwait	UAE	Five Gulf[a]	Other OPEC	Total OPEC
1973	7.6	5.9	2.0	3.0H	1.5	20.0	11.0H	31.0
1974	8.5	6.0H	2.0	2.5	1.6	20.7	10.0	30.7
1975	7.1	5.4	2.3	2.1	1.7	18.4	8.7	27.2
1976	8.6	5.9	2.4	2.1	1.9	21.0	9.8	30.7
1977	9.2H	5.7	2.4	2.0	2.0H	21.2H	10.1	31.3H
1978	8.3	5.2	2.6	2.1	1.8	20.1	9.8	30.0
1979	9.5	3.2	3.5H	2.5	1.8	20.5	10.5	31.0
1980	9.9	1.7	2.5	1.7	1.7	17.4	9.5	27.0
1981	9.8	1.4L	1.0L	1.1	1.5	14.8	8.0	22.8
1982	6.5	2.2	1.0	.8L	1.2	11.8	7.4	19.1
1983	5.1	2.4	1.0	1.1	1.1	10.7	7.1L	17.9
1984	4.7	2.2	1.2	1.2	1.1L	10.3	7.5	17.9
1985	3.4L	2.2	1.4	1.0	1.2	9.3L	7.3	16.6L
1986	4.9	2.0	1.7	1.4	1.3	11.3	7.4	18.7
1987	4.3	2.3	2.1	1.6	1.5	11.8	7.1	18.8
1988	5.1	2.2	2.7	1.5	1.6	13.3	7.6	20.9
1989	5.1	2.9	2.8	1.8	2.0	14.6	8.0	22.6
1990	6.5	3.1	2.0	1.2	2.1	14.9	8.8	23.7

[a]Saudi Arabia, Iran, Iraq, Kuwait, and the United Arab Emirates.
L represents the low figure and H the high figure during the 1973–90 period.

Source: *Monthly Energy Review.*

TABLE 2.35

Disposition of the World's Crude Oil Production (Thousands of Barrels per Day)

	Crude Oil Production		Net Imports USA	Apparent Consumption		% Consumed in USA
	World	USA		USA	Rest of the World	
1973	55,684	9,208H	6,025	15,233	40,451	27.4
1974	55,660	8,774	5,892	14,666	40,994	26.3
1975	52,777	8,375	5,846	14,221	38,556	26.9
1976	57,269	8,132	7,090	15,222	42,047	26.6
1977	59,589	8,245	8,565H	16,810H	42,779	28.2H
1978	60,003	8,707	8,002	16,709	43,294	27.8
1979	62,477H	8,552	7,985	16,537	45,940H	26.5
1980	59,353	8,597	6,365	14,962	44,391	25.2
1981	55,778	8,572	5,401	13,973	41,805	25.1
1982	53,184	8,649	4,298L	12,947L	40,237	24.3L
1983	52,967	8,688	4,312	13,000	39,967L	24.5
1984	54,203	8,879	4,715	13,594	40,609	25.1
1985	53,646L	8,971	4,286	13,257	40,389	24.7
1986	55,872	8,680	5,439	14,119	41,753	25.2
1987	56,306	8,349	5,914	14,263	42,043	25.3
1988	58,507	8,140	6,587	14,727	43,737	25.2
1989	59,614	7,613	7,202	14,751	44,770	24.8
1990	60,080	7,301L	7,090	14,391	45,689	24.0

L represents the low value and H the high value for the period from 1973–90.

Source: *Monthly Energy Review.*

TABLE 2.40
Using a Consensus of Monetary Indicators and the Quantity Theory of Money to Forecast Year-to-Year Percentage Changes in Nominal GNP

Year	Growth Rates and Forecasting Errors[a]			Following Year Nominal GNP
	Currency	M2	M3	
1960	−.3(3.9)	4.9(−1.3)*	5.2(−1.6)	3.6(−.3)
1961	2.1(5.5)	7.4(.2)*	8.2(−.6)	7.6(4.0)
1962	3.4(2.2)	8.1(−2.5)*	8.9(−3.3)	5.6(−2.0)
1963	6.3(.8)	8.4(−1.3)*	9.3(−2.2)	7.1(1.5)
1964	5.3(3.2)	8.0(.5)*	9.0(−.5)	8.5(1.4)
1965	6.2(3.3)	8.1(1.4)*	9.0(.5)	9.5(1.0)
1966	5.6(.2)	4.5(1.3)	4.7(1.1)*	5.8(−3.7)
1967	5.3(4.0)	9.2(.1)*	10.3(−1.0)	9.3(3.5)
1968	7.5(.5)	8.0(.0)*	8.8(−.8)	8.0(−1.3)
1969	6.3(−.9)	4.1(1.3)*	1.5(3.9)	5.4(−2.6)
1970	6.3(2.3)	6.5(2.1)*	10.1(−1.5)	8.6(3.2)
1971	7.0(3.0)	13.5(−3.5)*	14.6(−4.6)	10.0(1.4)
1972	8.1(4.0)	13.0(−.9)*	14.1(−2.0)	12.1(2.1)
1973	8.2(.1)*	6.9(1.4)	11.2(−2.9)	8.3(−3.8)
1974	10.2(−1.7)	5.5(3.0)	8.7(−.2)*	8.5(.2)
1975	8.7(2.8)	12.6(−1.1)	9.5(2.0)*	11.5(3.0)
1976	9.2(2.5)	13.7(−2.0)	11.9(−.2)*	11.7(.2)
1977	9.9(3.1)	10.6(2.4)*	12.3(.7)	13.0(1.3)
1978	9.8(1.7)*	8.0(3.5)	11.8(−.3)	11.5(−1.5)
1979	9.2(−.3)*	7.8(1.1)	9.5(−.6)	8.9(−2.6)
1980	10.0(1.7)*	8.9(2.8)	10.2(1.5)	11.7(2.8)
1981	6.3(−2.6)	10.0(−6.3)*	12.4(−8.7)	3.7(−8.0)
1982	8.1(−.5)	8.9(−1.3)*	9.3(−1.7)	7.6(3.9)
1983	10.3(.5)*	12.0(−1.2)	10.3(.5)*	10.8(3.2)
1984	6.7(−.3)	8.5(−2.1)*	10.7(−4.3)	6.4(−4.4)
1985	7.6(−2.2)*	8.4(−3.0)	7.4(−2.0)	5.4(−1.0)
1986	7.6(−.9)	9.5(−2.8)	9.1(−2.4)*	6.7(1.3)
1987	8.9(−1.0)	3.5(4.4)	5.3(2.6)*	7.9(1.2)
1988	7.7(−1.0)	5.5(1.2)	6.5(.2)*	6.7(−1.2)
1989	4.8(.2)*	4.9(.1)	3.2(1.8)	5.0(−1.7)
1990	10.8	3.2( )*	1.2	?

[a]Dec.–Dec. growth rates for currency, M2 and M3, and year-to-year growth rates for nominal GNP in the following year. The figures in parentheses are the actual following year growth rates for nominal GNP in the following year minus the predicted growth rates. The error terms in the last column assume that next year's growth rate for nominal GNP will be equal to this year's growth rate.

*The median growth rate and error term for the prediction variables in the first three columns.

Source of basic data: *Economic Report of the President.*

TABLE 2.41

Some Alternative Ways to Forecast the Preliminary Year-to-Year Growth Rates for GNP in Current Prices

	Forecasted Growth Rate for the Following Year[e]			Actual Preliminary Following Growth of Nominal GNP[d]
Year	Annualized 2-Quarter Growth of Nominal GNP[a] (1)	Dec.–Dec. Growth of Median Monetary Indicator[b] (2)	4-Quarter Growth of Consumption & Residential Construction[c] (3)	(4)
1971	6.3(3.4)	11.1(−1.4)	9.8(−.1)*	9.7(2.2)
1972	9.9(1.6)	10.7(.8)	10.3(1.2)*	11.5(1.8)
1973	9.7(−1.8)	8.6(−.7)	9.1(−1.2)*	7.9(−3.6)
1974	6.4(.1)	7.3(−.8)	6.8(−.3)*	6.5(−1.4)
1975	15.4(−3.8)	8.8(2.8)	10.2(1.4)*	11.6(5.1)
1976	8.8(2.0)	11.3(−.5)*	11.6(−.8)	10.8(−.8)
1977	10.2(1.4)*	9.8(1.8)	11.4(.2)	11.6(.8)
1978	11.8(−.5)*	8.9(2.4)	11.8(−.5)	11.3(−.3)
1979	10.8(−1.9)*	8.4(.5)	10.9(−2.0)	8.9(−2.4)
1980	13.8(−2.5)	9.6(1.7)*	9.0(2.3)	11.3(2.4)
1981	6.9(−2.8)	10.3(−6.2)	7.5(−3.4)*	4.1(−7.2)
1982	3.7(4.0)	9.7(−2.0)	7.8(−.1)*	7.7(3.6)
1983	9.8(1.0)	9.9(.9)*	10.7(.1)	10.8(3.1)
1984	5.9(−.1)	8.2(−2.4)	7.6(−1.8)*	5.8(−5.0)
1985	5.8(−.5)	7.6(−2.3)	6.3(−1.0)*	5.3(−.5)
1986	4.4(1.5)	9.0(−3.1)	6.2(−.3)*	5.9(.6)
1987	6.9(.5)	4.8(2.6)	5.3(2.1)*	7.4(1.5)
1988	6.9(.3)*	6.5(.7)	7.6(−.4)	7.2(−.2)
1989	5.2(−.2)*	4.8(.2)	6.2(−1.2)	5.0(−2.2)
1990	2.8( )	3.2( )*	5.1( )	?

[a]The preliminary growth rate for nominal GNP from the second quarter to the fourth quarter of the current year multiplied by two.

[b]The preliminary median December-to-December growth rate for currency, M2, and M3.

[c]The preliminary fourth-quarter-to-fourth-quarter growth rate for personal consumption plus residential fixed investment.

[d]The preliminary following year-to-year growth rate for nominal GNP in current prices. The figures in parentheses are first differences in these growth rates.

[e]The figures in parentheses are the error terms obtained by subtracting the growth rate in question from the actual preliminary growth rate for nominal GNP in column (4).

*The median growth rate and error term for the prediction variables in the first three columns.

Source of basic data: January issues of *The Survey of Current Business.*

TABLE 2.42
Using a Consensus Forecast of Nominal GNP and the Annualized Two-Quarter Growth Rate for the Implicit Price Deflator to Predict the Preliminary Year-to-Year Growth Rate for Real GNP

Year	Forecasted Growth Rate for Nominal GNP for the Following Year[a] (1)	Annualized Growth Rate for the Implicit Price Deflator[b] (2)	Following Year Growth Rate for Real GNP		Actual minus the Predicted Growth Rate for Real GNP[d] (5)
			Predicted[c] (3)	Actual (4)	
1971	9.8	2.0	7.8	6.5	−1.3
1972	10.3	2.6	7.7	5.9	−1.8
1973	9.1	7.3	1.8	6.2	4.4
1974	6.8	12.4	−5.6	−2.0	3.6
1975	10.2	6.7	3.5	6.2	2.7
1976	11.3	5.2	6.1	4.9	−1.2
1977	10.2	5.4	4.8	3.9	−.9
1978	11.8	7.4	4.4	2.3	−2.1
1979	10.8	8.5	2.3	−.1	−2.4
1980	9.6	9.9	−.3	1.9	2.2
1981	7.5	8.9	−1.4	−1.8	−.4
1982	7.8	4.6	3.2	3.3	.1
1983	9.9	3.7	6.2	6.8	.6
1984	7.6	3.1	4.5	2.3	−2.2
1985	6.3	3.1	3.2	2.5	−.7
1986	6.2	2.3	3.9	2.9	−1.0
1987	5.3	2.7	2.6	3.8	1.2
1988	6.9	4.6	2.3	2.9	.6
1989	5.2	3.3	1.9	.9	−1.0
1990	3.2	3.2	.0	?	

[a]The median growth rate for the prediction variables in the first three columns of Table 2.41.
[b]The preliminary growth rate for the implicit price deflator from the second quarter of the year in question to the fourth quarter multiplied by two. The data are obtained from the following January issue of *The Survey of Current Business*.
[c]Column (1) minus column (2).
[d]Column (4) minus column (3).

TABLE 2.60
December-to-December Percentage Changes in Stock Indexes for
Various Countries

Year	USA	Canada	France	Germany	Italy	Japan	UK
1954	40.7	32.1	87.4*	63.5*	29.2	−17.7	39.3
1955	30.0	22.7	−4.9	22.7	21.4	21.2	2.4
1956	2.2	5.3*	12.2*	−8.0	−1.0	35.3*	−11.7
1957	−13.1	−23.5	27.2*	8.7*	5.5*	−12.5*	−4.1*
1958	32.6	26.8	−17.8	68.4*	15.9	31.0	32.3
1959	10.3	1.3	62.8*	75.7*	62.4*	44.2*	44.1*
1960	−3.7	−1.8*	4.5*	54.0*	24.3*	25.9*	−4.7
1961	26.2	28.6*	18.1	−11.8	8.7	−11.3	−2.8
1962	−12.7	−10.2*	−2.7*	−23.2	−12.4*	6.4*	3.7*
1963	18.5	11.7	−15.8	12.1	−13.6	−8.0	19.1*
1964	13.1	21.4*	−5.8	3.7	−27.4	−3.2	−8.9
1965	9.3	3.3	−8.5	−12.3	14.5*	12.3*	4.6
1966	−11.3	−10.4*	−11.2*	−8.8*	9.3*	6.9*	−11.2*
1967	17.2	13.9	−1.1	30.2*	−6.5	−6.5	32.4*
1968	11.7	18.2*	5.8	11.8*	−1.7	29.6*	39.3*
1969	−14.4	−4.1*	27.9*	15.4*	16.8*	31.3*	−16.0
1970	−1.1	−7.0	−1.4	−28.1	−18.0	−13.3	−8.7
1971	10.1	4.5	−8.4	3.9	−18.6	27.5*	36.9*
1972	18.4	23.9*	20.5*	16.6	11.4	98.4*	15.2
1973	−19.3	−2.7*	1.5*	−19.7	13.0*	−19.4	−33.8
1974	−29.2	−29.3	−29.6	−4.5*	−25.1*	−6.9*	−53.8
1975	32.2	12.9	30.8	27.4	−15.4	12.0	140.2*
1976	17.9	6.1	−17.5	−8.7	−9.0	15.4	−5.6
1977	−10.3	4.7*	−8.3*	7.5*	−28.1	−.5*	50.0*
1978	2.4	23.6*	48.9*	7.1*	28.0*	23.1*	7.2*
1979	12.2	38.4*	18.8*	−13.5	8.2	1.6	2.0
1980	23.9	25.1*	10.7	−2.6	73.3*	7.9	23.3
1981	−7.2	−13.9	−17.3	.8*	.9*	15.7*	6.1*
1982	12.5	.2	−.4	6.7	−5.9	3.0	28.4*
1983	17.9	30.3*	92.4*	43.3*	23.6*	21.0*	18.5*
1984	.1	−6.0	−.3	4.5*	15.9*	26.0*	27.4*
1985	26.0	20.9	25.0	57.4*	118.3*	16.0	17.0
1986	19.9	5.7	57.0*	12.6	80.5*	50.6*	20.9*
1987	−3.1	3.1*	−24.2	−32.4	−29.8	17.6*	4.0*
1988	14.8	7.3	54.0*	24.7*	18.1*	26.0*	6.7
1989	26.1	17.1	21.8	25.4	6.4	24.2	28.7*
1990	−1.3	−6.9	−1.9	4.5*	−4.3	5.8*	−3.8

*Cases where another country's stock index outperformed the U.S. stock index.

Source of basic data: BCI series 19 and 742–48.

TABLE 2.70

Years Containing a Recessionary Trough in Business Activity and the Financial Returns from Holding the S&P Composite Stock Price Index

Date of Business		Financial Returns for the S&P Index[a]	
Peak	Trough	Trough Year	Following Year
Aug. 1929	Mar. 1933	53.0	−1.5
May 1937	June 1938	30.0	−.8
Feb. 1945	Oct. 1945	35.7	−7.8
Nov. 1948	Oct. 1949	17.8	30.5
July 1953	May 1954	51.2	31.0
Aug. 1957	Apr. 1958	42.4	11.8
Apr. 1960	Feb. 1961	26.6	−8.8
Dec. 1969	Nov. 1970	3.5	14.1
Nov. 1973	Mar. 1975	36.9	23.6
Jan. 1980	July 1980	31.5	−4.8
July 1981	Nov. 1982	20.5	22.3
July 1990	Apr. 1991	?	

[a]Price appreciation plus dividends expressed as a percent of price at the end of the preceding year.

Source of basic data: National Bureau of Economic Research and Standard & Poor's *Security Price Index Record*.

TABLE 2.71

The S&P 500 Stock Price Index Two Months after Two Consecutive Quarterly Declines in Real GNP and the Following Year Price Appreciation

	Value of the S&P Index at		Following Year Price Appreciation	
Purchase Date	Purchase Date (1)	One Year Later (2)	First Year (%) (3)	Second Year (%) (4)
Aug. 31, 1949	15.22	18.42	21.0	26.4
Feb. 26, 1954	26.15	36.57	39.8	23.2
May 29, 1958	44.09	58.68	33.1	−4.9
Nov. 30, 1960	55.54	71.32	28.4	−12.7
May 29, 1970	76.55	99.63	30.2	9.9
Aug. 30, 1974	72.15	86.88	20.4	18.4
May 28, 1982	111.88	164.46	47.0	−8.5
May 31, 1991	389.83			
Average return 1948–90			31.4	7.4

Source of basic data: Standard & Poor's *Security Price Index Record*.

TABLE 2.72
Using Cyclical Down Ratios for the S&P Index and the Commerce Department's Revised Index of 11 Leading Indicators to Identify Good Years to Have Been in the Stock Market

Year	December Down Ratio S&P Index[a] (1)	Percentage Change Leading Indicators Dec.–Dec. (2)	Following Year Financial Return S&P Index (3)
1948	.903	−4.2	17.8*
1949	1.027	7.2	30.5
1950	.994	17.7	23.4*
1951	.997	−10.0	17.7*
1952	1.034	8.0	−1.2
1953	.948	−7.0	51.2*
1954	1.046	14.5	31.0*
1955	1.009	8.2	6.4
1956	.952	−1.8	−10.4
1957	.827	−7.5	42.4*
1958	1.019	13.5	11.8*
1959	.989	4.3	.3
1960	.951	−2.7	26.6*
1961	1.009	11.5	−8.8
1962	.873	3.0	22.5#
1963	1.016	6.3	16.3
1964	.983	8.5	12.3#
1965	.995	6.2	−10.0
1966	.872	−3.7	23.7*
1967	.995	7.3	10.8
1968	1.010	5.4	−8.3
1969	.856	−2.6	3.5*
1970	1.068	−1.9	14.1*
1971	.962	10.5	18.7#
1972	1.021	11.3	−14.5
1973	.800	−1.0	−26.0
1974	.566	−17.4	36.9*
1975	.959	14.5	23.6*#
1976	.992	9.1	−7.2
1977	.890	4.4	6.4#
1978	.911	2.2	18.4#
1979	.992	−4.6	31.5*

TABLE 2.72 (concluded)

Year	December Down Ratio S&P Index[a] (1)	Percentage Change Leading Indicators Dec.–Dec. (2)	Following Year Financial Return S&P Index (3)
1980	.984	2.2	−4.8
1981	.913	−4.9	20.4*
1982	1.009	7.1	22.3
1983	.980	16.6	6.0*#
1984	.981	−1.6	31.1
1985	1.050	6.2	18.5
1986	1.013	6.9	5.7
1987	.732	1.8	16.6#
1988	.840	4.4	31.2#
1989	1.003	.0	−3.1
1990	.974	−4.1	?*

*Financial returns following years when the percentage change in the index of leading economic indicators was over 13 percent or under minus 1.8 percent.

#Financial returns following years when the percentage change in the index of leading indicators was positive and the December down ratio for the S&P index was less than .984.

[a]The down ratio is the average December value of the index expressed as a proportion of its previous average monthly cyclical high.

Source of basic data: BCI series 910 and Standard & Poor's *Security Price Index Record*.

TABLE 2.73

Changes in the Civilian Unemployment Rate and the Financial Returns from Holding Stock and Treasury Bills

Year	Civilian Unemployment Rate (1)	First Diff. Unemployment Rate (2)	Financial Return S&P Index (3)	Yield New 3-Month T-Bills (4)
1942	4.7	−5.2	19.2#	.3
1943	1.9	−2.8	25.7#	.4
1944	1.2	−.7	19.3#	.4
1945	1.9	.7	35.7	.4
1946	3.9	2.0	−7.8	.4**
1947	3.9	.0	5.5*	.6
1948	3.8	−.1	5.4	1.0
1949	5.9	2.1	17.8	1.1
1950	5.3	−.6	30.5*	1.2
1951	3.3	−2.0	23.4	1.6
1952	3.0	−.3	17.7#	1.8
1953	2.9	−.1	−1.2	1.9**
1954	5.5	2.6	51.2	1.0
1955	4.4	−1.1	31.0*	1.8
1956	4.1	−.3	6.4#	2.7
1957	4.3	.2	−10.4	3.3**
1958	6.8	2.5	42.4	1.8
1959	5.5	−1.3	11.8*	3.4
1960	5.5	.0	.3#	2.9**
1961	6.7	1.2	26.6	2.4
1962	5.5	−1.2	−8.8	2.8**
1963	5.7	.2	22.5#	3.2
1964	5.2	−.5	16.3	3.5
1965	4.5	−.7	12.3	4.0
1966	3.8	−.7	−10.0	4.9**
1967	3.8	.0	23.7	4.3
1968	3.6	−.2	10.8	5.3
1969	3.5	−.1	−8.3	6.7**
1970	4.9	1.4	3.5	6.5**
1971	5.9	1.0	14.1*	4.3
1972	5.6	−.3	18.7	4.1
1973	4.9	−.7	−14.5	7.0**
1974	5.6	.7	−26.0	7.9**
1975	8.5	2.9	36.9	5.8
1976	7.7	−.8	23.6*	5.0
1977	7.1	−.6	−7.2	5.3**
1978	6.1	−1.0	6.4	7.2**
1979	5.8	−.3	18.4#	10.0
1980	7.1	1.3	31.5	11.5
1981	7.6	.5	−4.8	14.0**

TABLE 2.73 (concluded)

Year	Civilian Unemployment Rate (1)	First Diff. Unemployment Rate (2)	Financial Return S&P Index (3)	Yield New 3-Month T-Bills (4)
1982	9.7	2.1	20.4	10.7
1983	9.6	−.1	22.3*	8.6
1984	7.5	−2.1	6.0	9.6**
1985	7.2	−.3	31.1#	7.5
1986	7.0	−.2	18.5	6.0
1987	6.2	−.8	5.7	5.8**
1988	5.5	−.7	16.3	6.7
1989	5.3	−.2	31.2	8.1
1990	5.5	.2	−3.1	7.5**

*Financial returns following years when the civilian unemployment rate increased 1.4 percentage points or more.
#Financial returns following years when the civilian unemployment rate declined by 1 percentage point or more.
**Years when the average yield on new three-month Treasury bills was greater than the financial return on the S&P stock price index in column (3).

Source of basic data: BCI series 43 and 114 and Standard & Poor's *Security Price Index Record.*

TABLE 2.74
Compound Average Annual Financial Returns Associated with Treasury Bills and the S&P Stock Price Index by Decade and the Returns That Could Have Been Obtained from Switching, 1930s–1980s

Decade	T-Bills (1)	S&P Index (2)	Perfect Switching[a] (3)	Practical Switching[b] (4)	Practical Difference[c] (5)
1930s	.5	.1	15.1	4.4	4.3
1940s	.5	8.9	12.3	5.0	−3.9
1950s	2.0	18.9	20.9	14.9	−4.0
1960s	4.0	7.4	12.4	10.2	2.8
1970s	6.3	5.8	11.0	9.6	3.8
1980s	8.8	17.2	19.8	19.8	2.6

[a]Assumes perfect switching on an end-of-the-year basis so as to always be in that asset, stocks, or T-bills which provides the highest return for the year.
[b]Assumes that one exits the stock market after two consecutive years of financial returns in excess of 10 percent and remains out of the stock market until after a yearly return of less than 10 percent.
[c]Column (4) minus column (2).

Source of basic data: BCI series 114 and Standard & Poor's *Security Price Index Record.*

TABLE 2.80

Record Earnings for the S&P Index, CPI Inflation, and the Financial Returns from Holding Common Stock

Year	Earnings ($) (1)	CPI (1982–84 = 100) (2)	Real Earnings[a] (3)	Financial Returns Current Year (4)	Financial Returns Following Year (5)
1929	1.61	17.3	9.31	−7.9	−23.9
1948	2.29	24.1	9.50	5.4P	17.8
1949	2.32	23.8	9.75	17.8	30.5
1950	2.84	24.1	11.78	30.5	23.4
1955	3.62	26.8	13.51	31.0	6.4
1962	3.67	30.2	12.15	−8.8	22.5
1963	4.02	30.6	13.14	22.5	16.3
1964	4.55	31.0	14.68	16.3	12.3
1965	5.19	31.5	16.48	12.3	−10.0
1966	5.55	32.4	17.13	−10.0	23.7
1968	5.76	34.8	16.55	10.8	−8.3
1969	5.78	36.7	15.75	−8.3P	3.5
1972	6.42	41.8	15.36	18.7	−14.5
1973	8.16	44.4	18.38	−14.5P	−26.0
1974	8.89	49.3	18.03	−26.0	36.9
1976	9.91	56.9	17.42	23.6	−7.2
1977	10.89	60.6	17.97	−7.2	6.4
1978	12.33	65.2	18.91	6.4	18.4
1979	14.86	72.6	20.47	18.4	31.5
1981	15.36	90.9	16.90	−4.8P	20.4
1984	16.64	103.9	16.02	6.0	31.1
1987	17.50	113.6	15.40	5.7	16.3
1988	23.76	118.3	20.08	16.3	31.2

[a]Column (1) divided by column (2).
P signifies a financial return associated with a year containing a peak in business activity.

Sources of basic data: BCI series 320 and Standard & Poor's *Security Price Index Record*.

TABLE 2.81
The Financial Returns Associated with Year-to-Year Declines in the
Earnings for the S&P Index of 6 Percent or More

Year	Earnings S&P Index (1)	% Decline in Earnings (2)	Financial Returns	
			Current Year (3)	Following Year (4)
1942	1.03	−11.2	19.2	25.7
1943	.94	−8.7	25.7	19.3
1951	2.44	−14.1	23.4	17.7
1958	2.89	−14.2	42.4	11.8
1970	5.13	−11.2	3.5	14.1
1975	7.96	−10.5	36.9	23.6
1982	12.64	−17.7	20.4	22.3
1985	14.61	−12.8	31.3	18.5
	Average return		25.4	19.1

Source of basic data: Standard & Poor's *Security Price Index Record.*

TABLE 2.82

Stock Market Bubbles Associated with an End-of-the-Quarter Price-Earnings Ratio for the S&P Index in Excess of 20.50

Quarter	Earnings per Share (4-Quarter Total)	S&P Index Values			Closing Price-Earnings Ratio
		High	Low	Close	
1933-4	.44	10.32	8.57	10.10*	22.95
1934-1	—	11.82	9.76	10.75	24.43
2	—	11.16	9.35	9.81	22.30
3	—	9.99	8.36L	9.10	20.68
1938-4	.64	13.79	12.32	13.21*	20.64
1939-1	.71	13.23	10.98L	10.98	15.46
1946-2	.84	19.25	18.03	18.43*	21.94
3	.89	18.54	14.33L	14.96	16.81
1961-1	3.09	65.06	57.57	65.06*	21.06
2	3.03	67.39	64.40	64.64	21.33
3	3.05	68.46	64.41	66.73	21.88
4	3.19	72.64	66.73	71.55	22.43
1962-1	3.37	71.13	67.90	69.55	20.64
2	3.47	69.37	52.32L	54.75	15.78
1987-2	14.42	309.65	279.16	304.00*	21.08
3	15.86	336.77	302.94	321.83	20.29
4	17.50	328.08	223.92L	247.06	14.12

*Closing value for the S&P index after the closing price-earnings ratio rises above 20.50.
L equals the cyclical low following P/E ratios in excess of 20.50.

Source of basic data: Standard & Poor's Security Price Index Record.

TABLE 2.83

The Earnings, Dividends, and Financial Returns Associated with the S&P Stock Price Index

Year	Earnings ($) (1)	Dividends ($) (2)	Payout Ratio (3)	% Change Dividends (4)	Difference[a] % Points (5)	Financial Return (6)
1942	1.03	.59	57.3	−16.9[@]	−22.9	19.2
1943	.94	.61	64.9[#]	3.4	20.3	25.7*
1944	.93	.64	68.8[#]	4.9	1.5	19.3
1945	.96	.66	68.8	3.1	−1.8	35.7
1946	1.06	.71	67.0	7.6	4.5	−7.8
1947	1.61	.84	52.2	18.3	10.7	5.5
1948	2.29	.93	40.6	10.7	−7.6	5.4
1949	2.32	1.14	49.1[#]	22.6	11.9	17.8*
1950	2.84	1.47	51.8[#]	28.9	6.3	30.5
1951	2.44	1.41	57.8[#]	−4.1[@]	−33.0	23.4
1952	2.40	1.41	58.8	.0	4.1	17.7*
1953	2.51	1.45	57.8	2.8	2.8	−1.2
1954	2.77	1.54	55.6	6.2	3.4	51.2
1955	3.62	1.64	45.3	6.5	.3	31.0
1956	3.41	1.74	51.0[#]	6.1	−.4	6.4
1957	3.37	1.79	53.1	2.9	−3.2	−10.4
1958	2.89	1.75	60.6[#]	−2.2[@]	−5.1	42.4*
1959	3.39	1.83	54.0	4.6	6.8	11.8*
1960	3.27	1.95	59.6[#]	6.6	2.0	.3
1961	3.19	2.02	63.3[#]	3.6	−3.0	26.6
1962	3.67	2.13	58.0	5.4	1.8	−8.8
1963	4.02	2.28	56.7	7.0	1.6	22.5
1964	4.55	2.50	54.9	9.6	2.6	16.3
1965	5.19	2.72	52.4	8.8	−.8	12.3
1966	5.55	2.87	51.7	5.5	−3.3	−10.0
1967	5.33	2.92	54.8[#]	1.7	−3.8	23.7*
1968	5.76	3.07	53.3	5.1	3.4	10.8*
1969	5.78	3.16	54.7	2.9	−2.2	−8.3
1970	5.13	3.14	61.2[#]	−.6[@]	−3.5	3.5
1971	5.70	3.07	53.9	−2.2[@]	−1.6	14.1*
1972	6.42	3.15	49.1	2.6	4.8	18.7
1973	8.16	3.38	41.4	7.3	4.7	−14.5
1974	8.89	3.60	40.5	6.5	−.8	−26.0
1975	7.96	3.68	46.2[#]	2.2	−4.3	36.9
1976	9.91	4.05	40.9	10.1	7.9	23.6*
1977	10.89	4.67	42.9	15.3	5.2	−7.2
1978	12.33	5.07	41.1	8.6	−6.7	6.4
1979	14.86	5.65	38.0	11.4	2.8	18.4*
1980	14.82	6.16	41.6[#]	9.0	−2.4	31.5
1981	15.36	6.63	43.2	7.6	−1.4	−4.8
1982	12.64	6.87	54.4[#]	3.6	−4.0	20.4
1983	14.03	7.10	50.6	3.3	−.3	22.3*
1984	16.64	7.53	45.3	6.1	2.8	6.0
1985	14.61	7.90	47.6[#]	4.9	−1.2	31.1
1986	14.48	8.28	57.2[#]	4.8	−.1	18.5

TABLE 2.83 (concluded)

Year	Earnings ($) (1)	Dividends ($) (2)	Payout Ratio (3)	% Change Dividends (4)	Difference[a] % Points (5)	Financial Return (6)
1987	17.50	8.81	50.3	6.4	1.6	5.7
1988	23.76	9.73	41.0	10.4	4.0	16.3
1989	22.87	11.05	48.3#	13.6	3.2	31.2
1990	21.60	12.10	56.0#	9.5	−4.1	−3.1
1991						?*

[a]The first differences in the growth rates for dividends in columnn (4).
#Years when the payout ratio increased by 2.3 percentage points or more. The financial returns in these years have usually been positive.
(@)Years when the dividend growth rate was negative. The financial returns in these years and the following year have been positive.
*Financial returns following negative differences in column (5) of 3.2 percentage points or more.

Source of basic data: Standard & Poor's *Security Price Index Record.*

TABLE 2.84
The Financial Returns Associated with the S&P Composite Stock Price Index Following Years When the Average Dividend Yield Increased 24 Basis Points or More

Year	Closing Value S&P Index (1)	Average Dividend Yield (2)	Increase Dividend Yield (3)	Financial Returns	
				Following Year (4)	2nd Following Year (5)
1941	8.69	6.82	1.23	19.2	25.7
1942	9.77	7.24	.42	25.7	19.3
1947	15.30	4.93	1.08	5.4	17.8
1948	15.20	5.54	.61	17.8	30.5
1949	16.76	6.59	1.05	30.5	23.4
1957	39.99	4.35	.26	42.4	11.8
1960	58.11	3.47	.24	26.6	−8.8
1962	63.10	3.37	.39	22.5	16.3
1966	80.33	3.40	.40	23.7	10.8
1970	92.15	3.83	.59	14.1	18.7
1974	68.56	4.47	1.41	36.9	23.6
1977	95.10	4.62	.85	6.4	18.4
1978	96.11	5.28	.66	18.4	31.5
1982	140.64	5.81	.61	22.3	6.0
1984	167.24	4.64	.24	31.1	18.5
1988	277.72	3.64	.56	31.2	−3.1

Source of basic data: Standard & Poor's *Security Price Index Record.*

TABLE 2.85
A Dividend Yield Strategy for Occasionally Getting Out of an Overvalued Stock Market and Back in at a More Attractive Price Based on the S&P Composite Stock Price Index, 1929–1990[a]

| Sell Month | Buy Month | Average Yield (%) | | Value of the S&P Index at End of the Month | | % Decline S&P Index |
		Sell Month (1)	Buy Month (2)	Sell Month (3)	Buy Month (4)	(5)
Sep. 1929	Nov. 1929	2.92	4.54	30.16	20.92	30.6
July 1933	Oct. 1933	2.95	3.59	9.95	8.96	9.9
Apr. 1961	June 1962	2.95	3.78	65.31	54.75	16.2
July 1964	Aug. 1966	2.96	3.60	83.18	77.10	7.3
Oct. 1968	Dec. 1969	2.94	3.52	103.41	92.06	11.0
Apr. 1971	Dec. 1973	2.99	3.70	103.95	97.55	6.2
Mar. 1987	Nov. 1987	2.93	3.66	291.70	230.30	21.0
			Average decline			14.6

[a]The strategy is to sell stock at the end of the first month that the average dividend yield falls below 3.0 percent and to buy back the S&P index at the end of the first month the average yield rises above 3.5 percent.

Source of basic data: Standard & Poor's *Security Price Index Record.*

TABLE 2.90

A Score Card for Some Conditional Stock Market Indicators and the Financial Returns Associated with the S&P Index

Year	(1)	(2)	(3)	(4)	(5)	(6)	(7)	(8)	(9)	(10)	Financial Return
1942	IPD		RM	DFD	HFD						19.2
1943	IPD		RM	DFD	HFD	PAY					25.7
1944			RM	DFD	HFD	PAY					19.3
1945			RM		HFD						35.7
1946											−7.8#
1947	IPD										5.5
1948	IPD			DFD							5.4
1949	IPD	OP	RM	DFD		PAY					17.8
1950		OP		DFD							30.5
1951				DFD		PAY					23.4
1952	IPD	OP	RM			PAY					17.7
1953											−1.2#
1954			RM								51.2
1955		OP	RM								31.0
1956						PAY					6.4
1957											−10.4#
1958	IPD	OP	RM	DFD		PAY					42.4
1959		OP									11.8
1960		OP	RM	DFD		PAY					.3
1961	IPD					PAY					26.6
1962											−8.8#
1963	IPD	OP	RM								22.5
1964	IPD	OP	RM								16.3
1965		OP	RM								12.3
1966											−10.0#
1967	IPD		RM	DFD		PAY					23.7
1968			RM								10.8

Year	IPD	OP	RM	DFD	HFD	PAY	
1969						PAY	−8.3#
1970	IPD						3.5
1971			RM				14.1
1972	IPD	OP	RM				18.7
1973							−14.7#
1974							−26.0#
1975				DFD	HFD	PAY	36.9
1976	IPD		RM				23.6
1977							−7.2#
1978							6.4#
1979							18.4#
1980				DFD		PAY	31.5
1981							−4.8#
1982	IPD	OP	RM	DFD	HFD	PAY	20.4
1983	IPD	OP	RM		HFD		22.3
1984	IPD	OP	RM		HFD		6.0
1985	IPD	OP	RM		HFD	PAY	31.1
1986	IPD	OP	RM		HFD	PAY	18.5
1987							5.7
1988		OP					16.3
1989						PAY	31.2
1990						PAY	−3.1

IPD represents years when the inflation rate for the implicit price deflator for real GNP declined. See Table 2.12.

OP represents years when the average first purchase or well head price for U.S. crude oil either remained the same or declined. See Table 2.12.

RM represents years when the real money supply increased by 1.6 percent or more. See Table 1.77.

DFD represents years when the federal budget surplus or deficit in the national income and product accounts deteriorated by at least 1 full percentage point. See Table 1.77.

HFD represents years when the federal budget deficit in the national income and product accounts was equal to at least (3.2) percent of nominal GNP. See Table 1.77.

PAY represents years when the divided payout ratio for the S&P index increased by 2.3 percentage points or more. See Table 2.83.

represents years when none of the conditional indicators in columns (1) through (6) were signaling a good year to own stock.

213

TABLE 2.91
A Score Card for Some "Perfect" Predictors of Good Years to Have Been in the Stock Market

Year	(1)	(2)	(3)	(4)	(5)	(6)	(7)	(8)	(9)	(10)	Following Year Return
1941	CPI		U		D	HLR					19.2
1942		M	U		D		E				25.7
1943	CPI		U			HLR	E				19.3
1944											35.7#
1945											−7.8#
1946			U								5.5
1947	CPI	M			D	HLR					5.4
1948	CPI	M		L	D						17.8
1949		M	U		D						30.5
1950				L		HLR					23.4
1951	CPI		U	L	D		E				17.7
1952				L							−1.2#
1953				L							51.2
1954	CPI		U	L							31.0
1955			U			HLR					6.4
1956											−10.4#
1957				L	D						42.4
1958		M	U	L	D						11.8
1959			U			HLR	E				.3
1960				L	D						26.6
1961				L							−8.8#
1962			U	L	D						22.5
1963						HLR					16.3
1964				L							12.3
1965					D						−10.0#
1966				L	D						23.7
1967		M				HLR					10.8
1968											−8.3#
1969				L		HLR					3.5

Year	CPI	M	U	L	D	HLR	E	
1970			U	L	D		E	14.1
1971				L		HLR		18.7
1972								−14.5*
1973								−26.0*
1974				L				36.9
1975	CPI	M	U	L	D	HLR	E	23.6
1976				L	D			−7.2*
1977				L	D			6.4
1978			U	L	D			18.4
1979				L		HLR		31.5
1980	CPI			L				−4.8*
1981	CPI			L		HLR		20.4
1982		M	U		D		E	22.3
1983			U	L	D	HLR		6.0
1984				L				31.1
1985		M				HLR		18.5
1986		M					E	5.7
1987				L		HLR		16.3
1988				L	D	HLR		31.2
1989								−3.1*
1990				L	D	HLR		?

CPI represents years when the Dec.-to-Dec. growth rate for the CPI was at least 1.4 percentage points less than the year-to-year growth rate in Table 2.15.

M represents years when the first differences in the Dec.-to-Dec. growth rates for the real money supply in Table 1.77 are equal to four percentage points.

U represents years when the unemployment rate in Table 2.73 either increased by 1.4 percentage points or declined by at least one percentage point.

L represents years when the index of leading indicators in Table 2.72 increased at least 13 percent, declined by at least 1.9 percent, or was positive when the December down ratio for the S&P index was less than .984.

D represents years when the dividend growth rate in Table 2.83 declined at least 3.2 percentage points or when the average dividend yield in Table 2.84 increased by at least 24 basis points.

HLR represents years when there was a downside reversal for the yearly high-low ratio in Table 3.30.

E represents years when the earnings for the S&P index in Table 2.81 declined by at least 6 percent.

identifies financial returns following years with no good year signals.

TABLE 2.92

Using Leading Indicators to Help Identify Stock Market Crashes before They Occur or Are Over

Crash Indicator, Date of Signal, the Value of the S&P Index and Its Down Ratio[a]

High P/E[b] (1)	Low Yield[c] (2)	Tight Money[d] (3)	Two Good Years[e] (4)	400 Trading Days[f] (5)	S&P Low (6)
—	—	12/31/56# 46.67 (.835)	12/30/55* 45.48 (.857)	4/19/55 38.22 (1.020)	10/22/57 38.98
—	—	7/31/59* 60.51 (.864)	12/31/59# 59.89 (.873)	5/27/59 58.19 (.899)	10/25/60 52.30
3/30/61 65.06 (8.04)	4/28/61* 65.31 (.801)	—	—	5/31/62# 59.63 (.877)	6/26/62 52.32
—	7/31/64* 83.18 (.880)	1/31/66 92.88 (.788)	12/31/64# 84.75 (.864)	1/29/64 76.63 (.955)	10/07/66 73.20
—	10/31/68* 103.41 (.670)	7/31/69 91.83 (.755)	12/31/68# 103.86 (.667)	5/14/68 98.12 (.706)	5/26/70 69.29
—	4/30/71 103.95 (.599)	7/31/73 108.22 (.575)	12/29/72# 118.05 (.528)	12/22/72* 101.18 (.616)	10/03/74 62.28
—	—	—	12/31/76* 107.46 (.809)	5/04/76 101.42 (.857)	3/06/78 86.90
—	—	10/31/79* 101.82 (.965)	—	10/03/79 109.59 (.896)	3/27/80 98.22
—	—	11/28/80	12/31/80*	10/27/81#	8/12/82

TABLE 2.92 (concluded)

Crash Indicator, Date of Signal, the Value of the S&P Index and Its Down Ratio[a]

High P/E[b] (1)	Low Yield[c] (2)	Tight Money[d] (3)	Two Good Years[e] (4)	400 Trading Days[f] (5)	S&P Low (6)
		140.52 (.729)	135.76 (.754)	119.29 (.859)	102.42
—	—	—	12/30/83 164.93 (.896)	3/12/84* 156.34 (.946)	7/24/84 147.82
6/30/87 304.00 (.737)	6/31/87# 291.70 (.768)	—	12/31/86* 242.17 (.925)	2/21/86 224.62 (.997)	12/04/87 223.92
—	—	—	12/29/89* 353.40 (.836)	7/06/89 321.55 (.919)	10/11/90 295.46

[a]The figures in parentheses are down ratios obtained by dividing the value of the S&P index into the cyclical low in column (6).

[b]Date, closing value, and down ratio associated with the first end of the quarter price-earnings ratio in excess of 20.50 in Table 2.82.

[c]Date, closing value, and down ratio associated with the first month that the average dividend yield falls below 3.0 percent in Table 2.85.

[d]Date, closing value, and down ratio associated with the first month that the three-year Treasury note yield is 4.5 percent higher than the 10-year Treasury bond yield in Table 1.86.

[e]Date, closing value, and down ratio after the first two annual double-digit financial returns for the S&P index in Table 3.22.

[f]Date, closing value, and down ratio 400 trading days after the preceding cyclical low for the S&P index in Table 3.21.

*Date after second crash signal.

#Date after third crash signal.

TABLE 2.93

A Chronology of Trades Based on Buy (B) and Sell (S) Signals in This Almanac[a]

Indicator	B or S	Signal Date	Closing Value S&P Index	% Change
P/E ratio over 20.5	S	12/31/38	13.21	
S&P index down 19.4%	B	11/28/41	9.21	−31.0
P/E ratio over 20.5	S	6/28/46	18.43	
S&P index down 19.4%	B	9/04/46	15.46	−16.1
Prime rate increase of 11%	S	8/31/48	15.97	
Unemployment claims up 16%	B	11/30/48	14.75	−7.6
January to August gain of 15.5%	S	8/31/55	43.18	
One day S&P decline of 6%	B	9/26/55	42.61	−1.3
Highly inverted yield curve	S	12/31/56	46.67	
S&P index down 19.4%	B	10/21/57	39.15	−16.1
Highly inverted yield curve	S	7/31/59	60.51	
Average unemployment rate down 1% point	B	12/31/59	59.89	−1.0
P/E ratio over 20.5	S	3/30/61	65.06	
S&P index down 19.4%	B	5/28/62	55.50	−14.3
Dividend yield under 3.0%	S	7/31/64	83.18	
December and January effect signals	B	1/29/65	87.56	5.3
Highly inverted yield curve	S	1/31/66	92.88	
Record volume NYSE and lower S&P	B	5/06/66	87.84	−5.4
Dividend yield under 3.0%	S	10/31/68	103.41	
Dividend yield over 3.5%	B	12/31/69	92.06	−11.0
Dividend yield under 3.0 percent	S	4/30/71	103.95	
NYSE advances over 1300 and S&P up 2.8%	B	8/16/71	98.76	−5.0
Two good years in a row	S	12/29/72	118.05	
S&P index down 19.4%	B	11/26/73	96.58	−18.2
January to August gain of 15.5%	S	8/31/78	103.29	
August to October decline of 4.8%	B	10/31/78	93.15	−9.8

TABLE 2.93 (*concluded*)

Indicator	B or S	Signal Date	Closing Value S&P Index	% Change
Highly inverted yield curve	S	10/31/79	101.82	
Unemployment claims up 16%	B	11/30/79	106.16	4.3
Prime rate increase of 11%	S	10/31/80	127.47	
S&P index down 19.4%	B	9/25/81	112.77	−11.5
January to August gain of 15.5%	S	8/29/86	252.93	
Record volume NYSE and lower S&P	B	9/11/86	230.67	−8.8
Dividend yield under 3.0 percent	S	3/31/87	291.70	
S&P index down 19.4 percent and others	B	10/19/87	224.84	−22.9
January to August gain of 15.5 percent	S	8/31/89	351.45	
One day decline of six percent	B	10/13/89	333.62	−5.5
Two good years in a row	S	12/29/89	353.40	
NYSE advances over 1300 and S&P up 2.8%	B	8/27/90	321.44	−9.0

[a]These signals are from the chronology of buy and sell signals at the end of the basic tables section. The 400 trading day exit signals are ignored in compiling these trades. Equal weight is given to all of the other buy and sell signals in the chronology.

TABLE 3.00

Major Fluctuations in the Daily Closing Values of the S&P Composite Stock Price Index since 1946

Date of		Value of S&P Index		Duration (months)		% Change Index		Following Appreciation[a]	
Peak	Trough	Peak (1)	Trough (2)	Rise (3)	Decline (4)	Rise (5)	Decline (6)	1st Yr (7)	2nd Yr (8)
5/29/46	5/17/47	19.25	13.71*	—	12	—	28.8	6.6	−14.2
6/15/48	6/13/49	17.06	13.55	13	12	24.4	20.6	21.3	24.2
1/05/53	9/14/53	26.66	22.71	43	8	96.8	14.8	41.1	21.2
8/02/56	10/22/57	49.74	38.98	35	15	119.0	21.6	27.0	.6
8/03/59	10/25/60	60.71	52.30	21	15	55.7	13.9	13.3	−3.9
12/12/61	6/26/62	72.64	52.32*	14	7	38.9	28.0	20.0	18.9
2/09/66	10/07/66	94.06	73.20*	43	8	79.8	22.2	14.4	3.8
11/29/68	5/26/70	108.37	69.29	26	18	48.0	36.1	24.0	10.6
1/11/73	10/03/74	120.24	62.28	31	21	73.5	48.2	22.7	13.0
9/21/76	3/06/78	107.83	86.90*	24	18	73.1	19.4	.7	12.1
2/13/80	3/27/80	118.44	98.22	23	2	36.3	17.1	16.8	−16.9
11/28/80	8/12/82	140.52	102.42	8	21	43.1	27.1	36.8	3.3
8/25/87	12/04/87	336.77	223.92*	60	3	228.8	33.5	8.3	25.8
7/16/90	10/11/90	368.95	295.46	31	3	64.8	19.9	?	?

[a]Price appreciation in percent following a 15 percent recovery from the trough value in column (2).

*Large declines in stock prices that were not associated with economic recessions.

Source of basic data: Standard & Poor's *Security Price Index Record.*

TABLE 3.01
Percentage Changes in the Daily Closing Values of the S&P Composite Stock Price Index Following Major Bear Markets since 1946

Date of Trough	Decline (%) (1)	1st Q (2)	2nd Q (3)	3rd Q (4)	4th Q (5)	1st Yr. (6)	2nd Yr. (7)
		Quarterly % Changes Following Trough				*Annual % Changes Following Trough*	
		Recessionary Bear Markets					
6/13/49	−20.6	16.2	5.7	2.9	12.4	42.1	11.9
9/14/53	−14.8	8.7	8.1	7.2	9.3	37.1	43.8
10/22/57	−21.6	5.7	3.9	8.4	10.0	31.0	9.7
10/25/60	−13.6	15.7	7.9	−.1	4.8	30.7	−20.0
5/26/70	−36.1	17.2	4.8	13.7	2.9	43.7	11.1
10/03/74	−48.2	13.5	15.3	15.8	−8.9	38.0	21.2
3/27/80	−17.1	18.1	8.9	8.1	−1.4	37.1	−16.9
8/12/82	−27.1	36.2	5.8	11.3	−1.3	58.3	2.0
10/11/90	−19.9	6.7	19.8	−.2			
Averages	−24.3	15.3	8.9	7.5	3.5	39.8	7.8
		Bear Markets in the Midst of Prosperity					
5/17/47	−28.8	13.6	−2.5	−7.6	18.3	21.2	−10.1
6/26/62	−28.0	7.3	12.2	5.4	4.5	32.7	17.4
10/07/66	−22.2	12.3	8.7	2.6	6.1	32.9	6.6
3/06/78	−19.4	15.4	5.0	−7.5	.4	12.6	11.0
7/24/84	−14.4	13.1	5.7	3.1	5.1	29.6	24.2
12/04/87	−33.5	19.4	−.3	−.3	2.6	21.4	29.3
Averages	−24.4	13.5	4.8	−.7	6.2	25.1	13.1

Source of basic data: Standard & Poor's *Security Price Index Record.*

TABLE 3.02

Annual Price Appreciation for the S&P Composite Stock Price Index after Cumulative Declines Amounting to 19.4 Percent or More since 1928

Downside Purchase Date	Closing Value S & P (1)	Following Year Price Appreciation (%) First Year (2)	Second Year (3)
10/28/29	22.74	−21.5	−43.6*
6/16/30	20.56	−33.6	−62.5*
4/29/31	14.37	−59.4	42.7*
9/12/31	12.37	−34.1	35.7*
11/28/31	9.17	−25.8	42.6*
4/01/32	7.18	−18.1	82.8*
9/14/32	7.35	51.1	−23.9
2/18/33	6.19	87.2	−19.4
7/21/33	9.65	−2.2	12.4*
5/12/34	9.42	4.0	41.4*
9/07/37	14.69	−15.5	.7*
3/31/39	10.98	11.6	−18.7
5/14/40	10.28	−7.7	−17.9*
11/28/41	9.12	2.4	19.1*
9/04/46	15.46	−2.1	7.4*
6/13/49	13.55	42.1	11.9
10/21/57	39.15	31.0	10.3
5/28/62	55.50	26.1	14.8
8/29/66	74.53	24.6	6.3
1/28/70	86.79	9.7	9.4*
11/26/73	96.58	−28.1	30.9*
3/06/78	86.90	12.6	11.0
9/25/81	112.77	9.4	37.5*
10/19/87	224.84	23.2	25.3
10/11/90	295.46	?	?

*Price appreciation following first year gains under 10 percent.

Source of basic data: Standard & Poor's *Security Price Index Record.*

TABLE 3.03
Price Appreciation Associated with a Policy of Buying the S&P Index after a Two-Quarter Decline of 14 Percent or More

Date of Purchase	Value of S&P Index (1)	Preceding 6-Month % Change in S&P Index (2)	Following Percentage Change in S&P Index 1st Qtr. (3)	1st Year (4)	2nd Year (5)
9/30/46	14.96	−17.3	2.3	1.0	2.5
12/31/57	39.99	−15.6	5.3	38.1	8.5
6/29/62	54.75	−23.5	2.8	26.7	17.8
9/30/66	76.56	−14.2	4.9	26.3	6.2
6/30/70	72.72	−21.0	15.8	37.1	7.5
9/30/74	63.54	−32.4	7.9	32.0	25.5
9/30/81	116.18	−14.6	5.5	3.6	37.9
12/31/87	247.08	−15.3	4.8	12.4	27.3

Source of basic data: Standard & Poor's *Security Price Index Record.*

TABLE 3.04
Closing Values and Related Information for One-Day Declines in the S&P Composite Stock Index of 6 Percent or More

Date of Decline	Closing Values for the Index Intervening High Day (1)	Decline Day (2)	Intervening Low Day (3)	% Change Decline Day[a] (4)	Next 6% Move[b] (5)
Oct. 28, 1929	31.92	22.74	22.74	−12.3(2)	−10.2
Oct. 29, 1929	22.74	20.43	20.43	−10.2(3)	12.5*
Nov. 6, 1929	24.15	20.61	20.61	−9.9(4)	−9.1
Nov. 11, 1929	21.37	19.86	17.67	−6.2	−11.1*
Sep. 24, 1931	25.92	10.68	8.82	−7.3	−9.1
May 31, 1932	11.52	4.47	4.40	−7.8	9.4
Aug. 12, 1932	7.65	7.00	6.94	−8.0	6.3*
Sep. 12, 1932	9.31	8.15	7.34	−7.2	−9.8
Oct. 5, 1932	8.52	7.39	5.53	−8.2	−8.4
June 15, 1933	10.89	9.74	9.74	−7.0	9.6*
July 20, 1933	12.20	10.57	10.57	−8.9(6)	−8.7
July 21, 1933	10.57	9.65	9.65	−8.7(7)	8.8*
Sep. 21, 1933	11.28	10.03	9.62	−6.2	−8.2
Oct. 16, 1933	10.32	9.21	8.57	−6.8	−6.5*
July 26, 1934	11.82	8.36	8.06	−7.8	7.1
Oct. 18, 1937	18.68	10.76	8.50	−9.3(5)	10.9
May 14, 1940	13.79	10.28	10.28	−7.5	−11.1
May 21, 1940	10.48	9.14	7.47	−6.6	8.2
Sep. 3, 1946	19.25	15.53	13.55	−6.7	−6.1

TABLE 3.04 (concluded)

Date of Decline	Closing Values for the Index Intervening High Day (1)	Decline Day (2)	Intervening Low Day (3)	% Change Decline Day[a] (4)	Next 6% Move[b] (5)
Sep. 26, 1955	45.63	42.61	38.98	−6.6	6.2*
May 28, 1962	72.62	55.50	52.32	−6.7	7.4
Oct. 19, 1987	336.77	224.84	224.84	−20.5(1)	14.9
Oct. 26, 1987	258.38	227.67	223.92	−8.3(8)	7.5
Jan. 8, 1988	261.07	243.40	242.63	−6.8	6.8*
Oct. 13, 1989	359.80	333.62	332.61	−6.1	7.8*

[a]The numbers in parentheses identify the eight largest one-day declines since 1927.
[b]The cumulative change in the S&P index until it has closed either 6 percent above or below the decline day close in column (2).
*Moves following intervening high to decline day closes of 11 percent or less.

Source of basic data: Standard & Poor's *Security Price Index Record.*

TABLE 3.05

Declines of 3 Percent or More in the S&P 500 Stock Price Index after It Has Achieved a New All-Time High since September 7, 1929

Date of Peak	Trough	Value S&P Index at Peak (1)	Trough (2)	% Change in Index Peak to Trough (3)	Peak to Peak (4)
9/7/29	6/1/32	31.92	4.50**	−86.2	—
9/28/54	10/29/54	32.69	31.68	−3.1	2.4
1/3/55	1/17/55	36.75	34.58	−5.9	12.4
3/4/55	3/14/55	37.52	34.96	−6.8	2.1
4/21/56	5/17/55	38.32*	36.97	−3.5	2.1
7/27/55	8/10/55	43.76	41.74	−4.6	14.2
9/23/55	10/11/55	45.63	40.80	−10.6	4.3
11/14/55	1/23/56	46.41	43.11	−7.1	1.7
3/20/56	5/28/56	48.87	44.10	−9.8	5.3
8/2/56	10/22/57	49.74	38.98**	−21.6	1.8
11/17/58	11/25/58	53.24	51.02	−4.2	7.0
1/21/59	2/9/59	56.04	53.58	−4.4	5.3
5/29/59	6/10/59	58.68	56.36	−4.0	4.7
8/3/59	10/25/60	60.71*	52.30**	−13.9	3.5
4/17/61	4/24/61	66.68	64.40	−3.4	9.8
5/17/61	7/18/61	67.39	64.41	−4.4	1.1
9/6/61	9/25/61	68.46	65.77	−3.9	1.6
12/12/61	6/26/62	72.64*	52.32**	−28.0	6.1
10/28/63	11/22/63	74.48	69.61	−6.5	2.5
5/12/64	6/8/64	81.16	78.64	−3.1	9.0
7/17/64	8/26/64	84.01	81.32	−3.2	3.5
11/20/64	12/15/64	86.28*	83.22	−3.5	2.7

TABLE 3.05 (concluded)

Date of		Value S&P Index at		% Change in Index	
Peak	Trough	Peak (1)	Trough (2)	Peak to Trough (3)	Peak to Peak (4)
5/13/65	6/28/65	90.27	81.60	−9.6	4.6
2/9/66	10/7/66	94.06	73.20**	−22.2	4.2
5/8/67	6/5/67	94.58	88.43	−6.5	.6
8/4/67	8/28/67	95.83	92.64	−3.3	1.3
9/25/67	3/5/68	97.59	87.72	−10.1	1.8
9/11/68	8/2/68	102.39*	96.63	−5.6	4.9
11/29/68	5/26/70	108.37	69.29**	−36.1	5.8
4/12/72	5/9/72	110.18	104.74	−4.9	1.7
5/26/72	7/20/72	110.66	105.81	−4.4	.4
8/14/72	10/16/72	112.55	106.77	−5.1	1.7
12/11/72	12/21/72	119.12*	115.11	−3.3	5.8
1/11/73	10/3/74	120.24	62.28**	−48.2	.9
8/22/80	8/28/80	126.02	122.08	−3.1	4.8
9/22/80	9/29/80	130.40	123.54	−5.3	3.5
10/15/80	10/30/80	133.70	126.29	−5.5	2.5
11/28/80	8/12/82	140.52*	102.42**	−27.1	5.1
11/9/82	11/23/82	143.02	132.93	−7.1	1.8
1/10/83	1/24/83	146.78	139.97	−4.6	2.6
6/22/83	8/9/83	170.99	159.18	−6.9	16.5
10/10/83	7/24/84	172.65*	147.82**	−14.4	1.0
2/13/85	3/15/85	183.35	176.53	−3.7	6.2
6/6/85	6/13/85	191.06	185.33	−3.0	4.2
7/17/85	9/25/85	195.65	180.66	−7.8	2.4
1/7/86	1/22/86	213.80*	203.49	−4.8	9.3
3/27/86	4/7/86	238.97	228.63	−4.3	11.8
4/21/86	5/16/86	244.74	232.76	−4.9	2.4
5/29/86	6/10/86	247.98	239.58	−3.4	1.3
7/2/86	7/15/86	252.70	233.66	−7.5	1.9
9/4/86	9/12/86	253.83	230.67	−9.1	.5
12/2/86	12/29/86	254.00	242.17	−4.7	.1
3/24/87	3/30/87	301.64	289.20	−4.1	18.8
4/6/87	4/14/87	301.95	279.16	−7.5	.1
8/25/87	12/4/87	336.77	223.92**	−33.5	11.5
9/1/89	9/14/89	353.73	343.16	−3.0	5.0
10/9/89	1/30/90	359.80	322.98	−10.2	1.7
6/4/90	6/26/90	367.40	352.06	−4.2	2.1
7/16/90	10/11/90	368.95*	295.46**	−19.9	.4
4/17/91	5/15/91	390.45	368.57	−5.6	5.8

*Fourth new high to be followed by a 3 percent decline for the bull market in question.
**A major bear market low.

Source of basic data: Standard & Poor's *Security Price Index Record*.

TABLE 3.06
Three Strategies for Acquiring a Portfolio Similar to the S&P Index

	Average Daily Closing Values for the S&P Index			Number of Days	
Year	All Days (1)	Days Index Up 1% (2)	Days Index Down 1% (3)	Up 1% (4)	Down 1% (5)
1968	98.37H	95.43	94.37L	10	9
1969	97.75H	94.81L	96.25	9	18
1970	83.17H	81.47	79.53L	30	33
1971	98.32H	97.80	95.77L	18	14
1972	109.13	109.29H	108.48L	4	6
1973	107.44H	105.56	104.70L	35	43
1974	82.78H	82.15	79.46L	47	67
1975	86.18H	84.36L	85.58	45	35
1976	102.04H	101.26L	101.32	25	14
1977	98.18H	96.56L	97.33	5	12
1978	96.11	97.31H	95.58L	19	24
1979	103.00H	102.84	102.11L	17	13
1980	118.71	119.71H	117.70L	43	37
1981	128.04	128.47H	126.88L	24	30
1982	119.65L	123.33H	120.92	44	39
1983	160.47H	158.30	158.29L	29	26
1984	160.46	161.61H	157.08L	25	16
1985	186.81H	186.32	186.07L	23	8
1986	236.39H	235.16	234.61L	35	26
1987	287.00H	277.30	276.03L	53	42
1988	265.79H	264.58	261.06L	37	32
1989	322.83	326.27H	319.72L	27	14
1990	334.63H	331.27	327.26L	33	42

H is the high cost strategy for the year.
L is the low cost strategy for the year.

Source of basic data: Standard & Poor's *Security Price Index Record.*

TABLE 3.10
First-Year Price Appreciation Following One-Day Gains of 3.5 Percent or More for the S&P 500 Stock Price Index

Date of 3.5% Advance	Closing Value S&P Index (1)	First Day Price Appreciation (%) (2)	Following Year Price Appreciation (%) (3)
Dec. 30, 1941	8.74	4.4	11.7
Oct. 15, 1946	15.30	4.0	1.9
Oct. 31, 1946	14.84	3.6	4.0
July 6, 1955	43.18	3.6	11.3
Oct. 23, 1957	40.73	4.5	25.1
May 29, 1962	58.08	4.6	21.1
Nov. 26, 1963	72.38	4.0	18.0
May 27, 1970	72.77	5.0	36.6
July 12, 1974	83.15	4.1	13.8
Sep. 19, 1974	70.09	3.5	22.5
Oct. 7, 1974	64.95	4.2	33.6
Oct. 9, 1974	67.82	4.6	30.3
Oct. 29, 1974	72.83	3.9	22.7
Nov. 1, 1978	96.85	4.0	5.9
Apr. 22, 1980	103.43	3.6	29.7
Aug. 17, 1982	109.04	4.8	51.6
Aug. 20, 1982	113.02	3.5	45.1
Nov. 3, 1982	142.87	3.9	14.4
Oct. 20, 1987	236.83	5.3	19.4
Oct. 21, 1987	258.38	9.1	9.8
Oct. 29, 1987	244.77	4.9	13.8
Jan. 4, 1988	255.94	3.6	9.2
Jan. 17, 1991	327.97	3.7	?

Source of basic data: Standard & Poor's *Security Price Index Record*.

TABLE 3.11

Record Point Increases for the Dow Jones Industrial Average

Date of Record	The Dow Jones Average			% Changes		
	Preceding High (1)	Closing Value (2)	Point Increase (3)	DJIA (4)	S&P 500 (5)	Value Line (6)
Oct. 30, 1929	381.17	258.47	28.40	12.3	12.5	—
Nov. 26, 1963	760.50	743.52*	32.03	4.5	4.0	—
May 27, 1970	985.21	663.20*	32.04	5.1	5.0	—
Aug. 16, 1971	950.82	888.95*	32.93	3.8	3.2	—
Nov. 1, 1978	907.74	827.79*	35.34	4.5	4.0	—
Aug. 17, 1982	1000.17	831.24	38.81	4.9	4.8	3.0
Nov. 3, 1982	1036.98	1065.49	43.41	4.2	3.9	3.0
Jan. 5, 1987	1955.57	1971.32	44.01	2.3	2.3	2.8
Jan. 22, 1987	2104.47	2145.67	51.60	2.5	2.3	1.1
Feb. 17, 1987	2201.49	2237.49	54.14	2.5	2.1	1.1
Apr. 3, 1987	2372.59	2390.34	69.89	3.0	2.3	1.4
Sep. 22, 1987	2722.42	2568.05	75.23	3.0	2.9	.9
Oct. 20, 1987	2722.42	1841.01*	102.27	5.9	5.3	−5.5
Oct. 21, 1987	2722.42	2027.85*	186.84	10.1	9.1	8.7

*Cases since the stock market crash of 1929 when the closing value was at least 6 percent less than the preceding high in column (1). The following year price appreciation for the S&P index in theses six cases was 36.6, 13.1, 5.9, 51.6, 19.4, and 9.8 percent and can be compared to percentage changes of −24.6, 18.0, 14.4, 2.6, −8.7, −9.2, −13.8, and −15.7 percent for the eight other cases.

Source of basic data: *The Wall Street Journal.*

TABLE 3.12

A Comparison of Year-End Closing Values and Annual Price Appreciation for the S&P Composite Stock Price Index and the DJIA

Year	Year-End Closing Values		Percentage Changes	
	S&P (1)	DJIA (2)	S&P (3)	DJIA (4)
1959	59.89	679.36	8.5	16.4*
1960	58.11	615.89	−3.0	−9.3
1961	71.55	731.14	23.1	18.7
1962	63.10	652.10	−11.8	−10.8*
1963	75.02	762.95	18.9	17.0
1964	84.75	874.13	13.0	14.6*
1965	92.43	969.26	9.1	10.9*
1966	80.33	785.69	−13.1	−18.9
1967	96.47	905.11	20.1	15.2
1968	103.86	943.75	7.7	4.3
1969	92.06	800.36	−11.4	−15.2
1970	92.15	838.92	.1	4.8*
1971	102.09	890.20	10.8	6.1
1972	118.05	1020.02	15.6	14.6
1973	97.55	850.86	−17.4	−16.6*
1974	68.56	616.24	−29.7	−27.6*
1975	90.19	852.41	31.5	38.3*
1976	107.46	1004.65	19.1	17.9
1977	95.10	831.17	−11.5	−17.3
1978	96.11	805.01	1.1	−3.1
1979	107.94	838.74	12.3	4.2
1980	135.76	963.99	25.8	14.9
1981	122.55	875.00	−9.7	−9.2*
1982	140.64	1046.54	14.8	19.6*
1983	164.93	1258.64	17.3	20.3*
1984	167.24	1211.57	1.4	−3.7
1985	211.28	1546.67	26.3	27.7*
1986	242.17	1895.95	14.6	22.6*
1987	247.06	1983.83	2.0	4.6*
1988	277.72	2168.57	12.4	9.3
1989	353.40	2753.20	27.3	27.0
1990	330.22	2633.66	−6.6	−4.3*

*Years when the DJIA outperformed the S&P composite stock price index.

Source of basic data: *The Wall Street Journal.*

TABLE 3.13

Days When the Number of Advances on the NYSE Was over 1,300 and the S&P Composite Stock Index Increased over 2 Percent

Date	Number Advancing Issues (1)	Closing Value S&P Index (2)	Percentage Change in S&P Stock Price Index	
			Same Day (3)	Following Year (4)
5/27/70	1312	72.77	5.0	36.6#
8/16/71	1503	98.76	3.2	13.1#
12/07/73	1339	96.51	2.2	−32.6
1/03/74	1565	99.80	2.2	−29.1
7/12/74	1364	83.15	4.1	13.8#
10/07/74	1301	64.95	4.2	33.6#
10/10/74*	1338	69.79	2.9	26.4*#
1/02/75	1450	70.23	2.4	29.4
1/10/75*	1417	72.61	2.0	30.8*
1/27/75	1476	75.37	3.3	31.4#
11/01/78	1506	96.85	4.0	5.9#
11/26/79	1460	106.80	2.0	31.2
4/22/80	1402	103.43	3.6	29.7#
1/28/82	1339	118.92	2.8	21.5#
8/17/82	1564	109.04	4.8	51.6#
8/20/82*	1384	113.02	3.5	45.1*#
8/23/82*	1352	116.11	2.7	40.2*
10/06/82	1344	125.97	3.3	35.2#
10/07/82*	1384	128.80	2.2	32.6*
10/11/82*	1504	134.47	2.6	26.7*
11/03/82	1518	142.87	3.9	14.4#
7/20/83	1391	169.29	2.7	−11.7
2/24/84	1336	157.51	2.1	13.9
8/01/84	1370	154.08	2.3	24.7
8/02/84*	1477	157.99	2.5	21.2*
8/03/84*	1490	162.35	2.8	17.9*#
8/09/84*	1316	165.54	2.3	13.8*
12/18/84	1433	168.11	2.8	24.8#
1/21/85	1331	175.23	2.3	17.4
3/11/86	1363	231.69	2.3	25.3
4/08/86	1392	233.52	2.1	27.3
1/05/87	1613	252.19	2.3	2.6
5/26/87	1325	289.11	2.5	−11.9
10/21/87	1756	258.38	9.1	9.8#
10/29/87*	1405	244.77	4.9	13.8*#
10/30/87*	1611	251.79	2.9	10.6*#
1/04/88	1592	255.94	3.6	9.2#
1/15/88*	1406	252.05	2.5	12.6*

TABLE 3.13 (concluded)

Date	Number Advancing Issues (1)	Closing Value S&P Index (2)	Percentage Change in S&P Stock Price Index	
			Same Day (3)	Following Year (4)
6/08/88	1306	271.52	2.4	20.3
8/27/90	1453	321.44	3.2	?#
1/17/91	1519	327.97	3.7	?#
2/11/91	1433	368.58	2.6	?

*Second or more case during a 15-day period.
#Cases where the same day gain was equal to 2.8 percent or more.

Source of basic data: *The Wall Street Journal.*

TABLE 3.14
Record Daily Stock Sales on the New York Stock Exchange since World War II and the Following Annual Percentage Change in the S&P Composite Stock Price Index

Date	Millions of Shares Traded (1)	S&P Index Closing Values (2)	% Change in the S&P Index	
			Record Day (3)	Following Year (4)
6/28/45	2.94	15.04	−2.0	22.5
1/18/46	3.23	18.30	−.2	−16.8
1/28/46	3.49	18.62	2.9	−16.9
9/04/46	3.62	15.46**	−.5	−2.1**
5/14/48	3.84	16.39	2.4	−9.0
6/26/50	3.95*	18.11	−5.4	17.6
6/27/50	4.86*	17.91**	−1.1	19.3**
12/18/50	4.50	19.85	1.1	18.3
1/03/55	4.57	36.75	2.1	22.9
1/05/55	4.64	35.52**	−2.5	26.5**
1/06/55	5.30	35.04**	−1.4	28.8**
9/26/55	7.72*	42.61	−6.6	7.5
10/17/58	5.37	51.46	1.0	11.4
2/09/61	5.59	62.02	−.3	13.6
1/23/61	5.62	62.59	.4	12.1
1/28/61	5.83	63.44	.2	10.3
3/08/61	5.91	63.44	−.1	10.6
3/09/61	6.01	63.50	.1	10.9
4/03/61	6.47	65.60	.8	4.9
4/04/61	7.08	65.66	.1	4.3

TABLE 3.14 (continued)

| | Millions of Shares Traded (1) | S&P Index Closing Values (2) | % Change in the S&P Index | |
Date			Record Day (3)	Following Year (4)
5/28/62	9.35*	55.50**	−6.7	26.1**
5/29/62	14.75*	58.08	4.6	21.1
6/15/62	7.13	55.89**	2.9	25.7**
9/06/63	7.16	72.84	−.3	13.6
11/26/63	9.32	72.38**	4.0	18.0**
2/10/65	7.22	86.46	−.9	8.5
3/04/65	7.30	86.98	−.3	2.6
6/10/65	7.47	84.73**	−.4	2.0**
6/15/65	8.47	84.49**	.6	2.7**
6/29/65	10.45	82.41**	1.0	3.0**
9/29/65	10.61	90.02	−.5	−15.2
12/06/65	11.43	90.59	−.8	−10.8
4/14/66	12.99	91.87	.4	−1.6
5/06/66	13.12	87.84**	−.1	7.5**
1/11/67	13.24	83.47**	.8	15.8**
3/10/67	14.90	88.89	.4	.2
12/29/67	14.95	96.47	.6	8.6
4/01/68	17.73	92.48**	2.5	9.7**
4/03/68	19.29	93.47	.9	7.7
4/10/68	20.41	95.67	.8	6.1
6/13/68	21.35	101.25	−.4	−2.6
9/24/70	21.35	83.91**	1.3	17.0**
1/22/71	21.68	94.88	.7	9.2
2/02/71	22.03	96.43	.0	8.6
2/08/71	25.60	97.45	.5	7.5
2/09/71	28.25	97.51	.1	8.2
8/16/71	31.73	98.76	3.2	13.1
1/27/75	32.13	75.37**	3.3	31.4**
2/13/75	35.16	81.01	1.4	23.0
1/15/76	38.45	96.61	−.5	7.7
1/30/76	38.51	100.86	.7	1.1
2/19/76	39.21	101.41	1.6	−.9
2/20/76	44.51	102.10	3.3	−1.6
4/14/78	52.28	92.92**	2.1	9.8**
4/17/78	63.49	94.45	1.6	7.2
8/03/78	66.37	103.51	.6	.5
10/10/79	81.62	105.30	−1.2	23.7
11/05/80	84.08	131.33	1.8	−5.9
1/07/81	92.89	135.08	−2.2	−12.0
8/18/82	132.70	108.53**	−.5	50.7**
8/26/82	137.30	118.55	.8	36.8
10/07/82	147.07	128.80	2.2	32.6
11/04/82	149.40	141.85	−.7	14.5
1/05/84	160.00	168.81	1.2	−3.0
8/02/84	172.80	157.99**	2.5	21.2**
8/03/84	236.60	162.35	2.8	17.9
9/11/86	237.60	235.18	−4.8	36.9
9/12/86	240.50	230.67**	−1.9	39.6**

TABLE 3.14 (*concluded*)

Date	Millions of Shares Traded (1)	S&P Index Closing Values (2)	% Change in the S&P Index	
			Record Day (3)	Following Year (4)
12/19/86	244.70	249.73	1.2	−.2
1/15/87	253.10	265.49	1.1	−5.1
1/23/87	302.40	270.10	−1.4	−8.7
10/16/87	338.50*	282.70	−5.2	−2.5
10/19/87	604.30*	224.84**	−20.5	23.2**
10/20/87	608.10*	236.83	5.3	19.4
6/08/88	310.03	271.52	2.4	20.3
6/17/88	342.92	270.58**	.3	18.7**
10/16/89	416.29*	342.85	2.8	−12.8

*Volumes that may have been distorted upward by panic selling.
**Indicates those cases where the S&P index has a lower closing value than for the preceding record trading day.

Source of basic data: *The Wall Street Journal.*

TABLE 3.15
Using December and January Gains in the S&P Composite Stock Price Index to Signal Good Years to Own Common Stock

Year	% Change S&P Index		Full Year Financial Return for the S&P Index (3)
	Preceding December (1)	January (2)	
1947	4.3	2.4*	5.5*#
1948	2.1	−4.0	5.4
1949	3.1	.1	17.8#
1950	4.4	1.7*	30.5*#
1951	4.6	6.1*	23.4*#
1952	3.9	1.6*	17.7*#
1953	3.5	−.7	−1.2
1954	.2	5.1*	51.2*#
1955	5.1	1.8*	31.0*#
1956	−.1	−3.6	6.4
1957	3.5	−4.2	−10.4
1958	−4.4	4.3*	42.4*
1959	5.2	.4	11.8#
1960	2.8	−7.1	.3
1961	4.6	6.3*	26.6*#
1962	.3	−3.8	−8.8

TABLE 3.15 (*concluded*)

Year	% Change S&P Index Preceding December (1)	January (2)	Full Year Financial Return for the S&P Index (3)
1963	1.4	4.9*	22.5*#
1964	2.4	2.7*	16.3*#
1965	.4	3.3*	12.3*#
1966	.9	.5	−10.0
1967	−.2	7.8*	23.7*#
1968	2.6	−4.4	10.8
1969	−4.2	−.8	−8.3
1970	−1.9	−7.6	3.5
1971	5.7	4.0*	14.1*#
1972	8.6	1.8*	18.7*#
1973	1.2	−1.7	−14.5
1974	1.7	−1.0	−26.0
1975	−2.0	12.3*	36.9*#
1976	−1.2	11.8*	23.6*#
1977	5.2	−5.1	−7.2
1978	.3	−6.2	6.4
1979	1.5	4.0*	18.4*#
1980	1.7	5.8*	31.5*#
1981	−3.4	−4.6	−4.8
1982	−3.0	−1.8	20.4
1983	1.5	3.3*	22.3*#
1984	−.9	−.9	6.0
1985	2.2	7.4*	31.1*#
1986	4.2	.5	18.5#
1987	−2.8	13.2*	5.7*#
1988	7.3	4.0*	16.6*#
1989	1.5	7.1*	31.2*#
1990	2.1	−6.9	−3.1
1991	2.5	4.2*	?*#

*Years when the January gain for the S&P index was more than 1 percent.
#Years when the combined gain for both Dec. and Jan. was over 3 percent.

Source of basic data: Standard & Poor's *Security Price Index Record.*

TABLE 3.16
Percentage Changes in the End-of-the-Month Closing Values for the
S&P Stock Price Index, August to October, October to January, and
January to August

| | | % Change in End-of-the-Month Closing Values | | |
Year	August S&P Close (1)	August to October (2)	October to January (3)	January to August (4)
1928	20.87	3.9	18.7	23.2$^{\#}$
1929	31.71	$-23.8^{@}$	-4.9^{*}	-7.0
1930	21.37	-20.7	-5.0^{*}	-13.9
1931	13.86	-24.0	-25.1^{*}	6.3
1932	8.39	-17.0	$-.3^{*}$	59.8
1933	11.09	$-19.2^{@}$	24.7*	$-18.1^{\#}$
1934	9.15	-3.7	3.3	24.4
1935	11.32	10.1$^{@}$	14.8**	11.7$^{\#}$
1936	15.99	7.6	3.6**	-10.0
1937	16.04	-22.9	-13.5^{*}	12.8
1938	12.06	9.2	-6.6^{**}	-9.1
1939	11.18	14.8	-6.1^{**}	-12.4
1940	10.56	4.9	-9.1	2.3
1941	10.30	-7.8	-7.3^{*}	-2.2
1942	8.62	9.3	11.1**	12.7$^{\#}$
1943	11.80	1.0	$-.6$	8.2
1944	12.82	$-.3$	5.4	15.1
1945	15.51	7.4	11.5**	$-10.3^{\#}$
1946	16.65	-10.9	5.5*	-2.2
1947	15.32	.7	-4.8	8.7
1948	15.97	3.6	-8.0	.0
1949	15.22	5.4	6.3**	8.0
1950	18.42	6.0	10.9**	7.5$^{\#}$
1951	23.28	-1.5	5.2	3.7
1952	25.03	-2.0	7.6	-11.6
1953	23.32	5.2	6.3**	14.4
1954	29.83	6.2	15.6**	17.9$^{\#}$
1955	43.18	$-1.9^{@}$	3.5	8.4
1956	47.51	-4.1	-1.9	1.1
1957	45.22	-9.2	1.6*	14.5
1958	47.75	7.5	8.0**	7.5$^{\#}$
1959	59.60	-3.5	-3.3	2.1
1960	56.96	-6.3	15.7*	10.2$^{\#}$
1961	68.07	.8	.3	-14.1
1962	59.12	-4.4	17.1	9.5$^{\#}$
1963	72.50	2.1	4.1	6.2
1964	81.83	3.7	3.2	$-.4$

TABLE 3.16 (concluded)

Year	August S&P Close (1)	% Change in End-of-the-Month Closing Values		
		August to October (2)	October to January (3)	January to August (4)
1965	87.17	6.0	.5**	−17.0
1966	77.10	4.0	8.0	8.1#
1967	93.64	.3	−1.8	7.2
1968	98.86	4.6	−.4	−7.3
1969	95.51	1.8	−12.6	−4.1
1970	81.52	2.1	15.2	3.3#
1971	99.03	−4.8	10.3*	6.9#
1972	111.09	.4	4.0	−10.2
1973	104.25	3.9	−10.8	−25.3
1974	72.15	2.4	4.2	12.9
1975	86.88	2.5	13.3	2.0#
1976	102.91	−.0	−.8	−5.2
1977	96.77	−4.6	−3.3	15.7
1978	103.29	−9.8@	7.3*	9.4#
1979	109.32	−6.9	12.1*	7.2#
1980	122.38	4.2	1.6	−5.2
1981	122.79	−.7	−1.2	−.7
1982	119.51	11.8	8.8**	13.1#
1983	164.40	−.5	−.1	2.0
1984	166.68	−.4	8.2	5.0#
1985	188.63	.6	11.6	19.4#
1986	252.93	−3.6@	12.4	20.3#
1987	329.80	−23.7@	2.1*	1.7
1988	261.52	6.7	6.6**	18.1
1989	351.45	−3.2@	−3.3	−2.0
1990	322.56	−5.8	13.1*	?#

	Average Price Appreciation (%)		
1928–41	−6.3	−.9	4.8
1942–62	.4	5.4	5.3
1963–75	2.2	2.9	−1.4
1976–89	−2.2	5.0	7.8
1928–89	−1.3	3.3	4.3

@Price appreciation following January-to-August gains of 15.5 percent or more in column (4).

*Price appreciation associated with August-to-October declines in the S&P index in column (2) of 4.8 percent or more.

**Price appreciation following August-to-October gains of 5 percent or more in column (2).

#Price appreciation associated with October-to-January gains of 8 percent or more in column (3).

Source of basic data: Standard & Poor's *Security Price Index Record*.

TABLE 3.20
Gains and Losses for the S&P Index during September and October after Spectacular Advances of 15.5 Percent or More from February through August

	% Changes	
Year	Feb. to Aug.	Sept. to Oct.
1933	59.8	−19.2
1935	24.4	10.1
1929	23.2	−23.8
1987	20.3	−23.7
1986	19.4	−3.6
1989	18.1	−3.2
1955	17.9	−1.9
1978	15.7	−9.8

Source of basic data: Standard & Poor's *Security Price Index Record.*

TABLE 3.21
Major Bull Markets and the Law of Diminishing Returns as Exemplified by the 400 Trading Day Exit

Date of			Closing Value S&P Index			400 Day Exit to Next Trough (% Change)
Trough	400 Day Exit	Peak	Trough	400 Day Exit	Peak	
5/17/47	10/26/48	6/15/48*	13.71	16.59	17.06*	−18.3
6/13/49	11/21/50	1/05/53	13.55	19.88	26.66	14.2
9/14/53	4/19/55	8/02/56	22.71	38.22	49.74	2.0
10/22/57	5/27/59	8/03/59	38.98	58.19	60.71	−10.1
10/25/60	5/31/62	12/12/61*	52.30	59.63	72.64*	−12.3
6/26/62	1/29/64	2/09/66	52.32	76.63	94.06	−4.5
10/07/66	5/14/68	11/29/68	73.20	98.12	108.37	−29.4
5/26/70	12/22/71	1/11/73	69.29	101.18	120.24	−38.4
10/03/74	5/04/76	9/21/76	62.28	101.42	107.83	−14.3
3/06/78	10/03/79	2/13/80	86.90	109.59	118.44	−10.4
3/27/80	10/27/81	11/28/80*	98.22	119.29	140.52	−14.1
8/12/82	3/12/84	10/10/83*	102.42	156.34	172.65*	−5.4
7/24/84	2/21/86	8/25/87	147.82	224.62	336.77	−.3
12/04/87	7/06/89	7/16/90	223.92	321.55	368.95	−8.1
10/11/90			295.46			

*Cases where the stock market peak occurred before the 400 day trading exit.

Source of basic data: Standard & Poor's *Security Price Index Record.*

TABLE 3.22
Stock Market Bubbles Associated with Two Years of Double-Digit Returns for the S&P Composite Stock Price Index

Year	Financial Return (%) (1)	S&P Index Values High (2)	S&P Index Values Low (3)	S&P Index Values Close (4)	% Decline after Two Double-Digit Returns[a] (5)
1953	−1.2	26.66	22.71	24.81	—
1954	51.2	35.98	24.80	35.98	—
1955	31.0	46.41	34.58	45.48*	—
1956	6.4	49.74	43.11	46.67	—
1957	−10.4	49.13	38.98L	39.99	−14.3
1958	42.4	55.21	40.33	55.21	—
1959	11.8	60.71	53.58	59.89*	—
1960	.3	60.39	52.30L	58.11	−12.7
1961	26.6	72.64	57.57	71.55	—
1962	−8.8	71.13	52.32	63.10	—
1963	22.3	75.02	62.69	75.02	—
1964	16.3	86.28	75.43	84.75*	—
1965	12.3	92.63	81.60	92.43	—
1966	−10.0	94.06	73.20L	80.33	−13.6
1967	23.7	97.59	80.38	96.47	—
1968	10.8	108.37	87.72	103.86*	—
1969	−8.3	106.16	89.20	92.06	—
1970	3.5	93.46	69.29L	92.15	−33.3
1971	14.1	104.77	90.16	102.09	—
1972	18.7	119.12	101.87	118.05*	—
1973	−14.5	120.24	92.16	97.55	—
1974	−26.0	99.80	62.28L	68.56	−47.2
1975	36.9	95.61	70.04	90.19	—
1976	23.6	107.63	90.90	107.46*	—
1977	−7.2	107.00	90.71	95.10	—
1978	6.4	106.99	86.90L	96.11	−19.1
1979	18.4	111.27	96.13	107.94	—
1980	31.5	140.52	98.22	135.76*	—
1981	−4.8	138.12	112.77	122.55	—
1982	20.4	143.02	102.42L	140.64	−24.6
1983	22.3	172.65	138.34	164.93*	—
1984	6.0	170.41	147.82L	167.24	−10.4
1985	31.1	212.02	163.68	211.28	—
1986	18.5	254.00	203.49	242.17*	—
1987	5.7	336.77	223.92L	247.08	−7.5
1988	16.6	283.66	242.63	277.72	—
1989	31.2	359.80	275.31	353.40*	—
1990	−3.1	368.95	295.46L	330.22	−16.4

*Closing value for second year of double-digit return in column (1).
L equals subsequent bear market low.
[a]Percentage decline from the double-digit close in column (4) to the subsequent bear market low.

Source of basic data: Standard & Poor's *Security Price Index Record.*

TABLE 3.23
Common Stock Offered for Cash by Underwriters

Year	Offerings Millions of Dollars (1)	% Changes in Stock Offerings (2)	% Changes in S&P Stock Index (3)
1957	2,516**	9.3	−14.3
1958	1,334	−47.0	38.1
1959	2,027	51.9	8.5#
1960	1,664	−17.9	−3.0
1961	3,294**	98.0	23.1
1962	1,314	−60.1	−11.8*
1963	1,011	−23.1	18.9#
1964	2,679	165.0	13.0#
1965	1,473	−45.0	9.1
1966	1,901	29.1	−13.1
1967	1,927	1.4	20.1
1968	3,885**	101.6	7.7
1969	7,640**	96.7	−11.4*
1970	7,037	−7.9	.1*
1971	9,485**	34.8	10.8
1972	10,707**	12.9	15.6
1973	7,642	−28.6	−17.4
1974	4,050	−47.0	−29.7
1975	7,414	83.1	31.5#
1976	8,305	12.0	19.1
1977	8,047	−3.1	−11.5
1978	7,865	−2.3	1.1
1979	9,106	15.5	12.3
1980	19,443**	113.5	25.8
1981	25,505**	31.2	−9.7*
1982	23,707	−7.0	14.8
1983	45,335**	91.2	17.3
1984	22,248	−50.9	1.4*
1985	36,718	65.0	26.0#
1986	59,002**	60.7	14.9
1987	66,508**	12.7	2.0*
1988	57,802	−13.1	12.4
1989	57,870	.1	27.3

*Indicates price appreciation after new stock offerings increase 50 percent or more and set new dollar records.
**Indicates years when stock offerings set new dollar records.
#Indicates price appreciation after cumulative declines in new offerings of more than 45 percent.

Sources: *Federal Reserve Bulletin*, Table 1.46 and Standard & Poor's *Security Price Index Record*.

TABLE 3.24
Old-Fashioned Risk Premiums for the S&P Composite Stock Price Index Based on Past Earnings and Nominal Interest Rates

Year	Closing Value S&P Index (1)	Associated Earnings (2)	Three-Year Average Earnings to Closing Value Ratio (%) (3)	Moody's December Aaa Corporate Bond Yield (4)	End-of-Year Risk Premium[a] (5)	% Change S&P Index (6)
1957	39.99	3.37	8.68	3.81	4.87	—
1958	55.21	2.89	5.83	4.08	1.75	38.1
1959	59.89	3.39	5.38	4.58	.80	8.5
1960	58.11	3.27	5.47	4.35	1.12	−3.0
1961	71.55	3.19	4.58	4.42	.16	23.1
1962	63.10	3.67	5.36	4.24	1.12	−11.8*
1963	75.02	4.02	4.84	4.35	.49	18.9
1964	84.75	4.55	4.81	4.44	.37	13.0
1965	92.43	5.19	4.97	4.68	.29	9.1
1966	80.33	5.55	6.35	5.39	.96	−13.1*
1967	96.47	5.33	5.56	6.19	−.63	20.1
1968	103.86	5.76	5.34	6.45	−1.11	7.7*
1969	92.06	5.78	6.10	7.72	−1.62	−11.4*
1970	92.15	5.13	6.03	7.64	−1.61	.1*
1971	102.09	5.70	5.43	7.25	−1.82	10.8*

1972	118.05	6.42	4.86	7.08	-2.22	15.6*
1973	97.55	8.16	6.93	7.68	-.75	-17.4*
1974	68.56	8.89	11.41	8.89	2.52	-29.7*
1975	90.19	7.96	9.25	8.79	.46	31.5
1976	107.46	9.91	8.30	7.98	.32	19.1
1977	95.10	10.89	10.08	8.19	1.89	-11.5*
1978	96.11	12.33	11.49	9.16	2.33	1.1
1979	107.94	14.86	11.76	10.74	1.02	12.3
1980	135.76	14.82	10.31	13.21	-2.90	25.8
1981	122.55	15.36	12.25	14.23	-1.98	-9.7*
1982	140.64	12.64	10.15	11.83	-1.68	14.8
1983	164.93	14.03	8.49	12.57	-4.08	17.3
1984	167.24	16.64	8.63	12.13	-3.50	1.4
1985	211.28	14.61	7.14	10.16	-3.02	26.3
1986	242.17	14.48	6.29	8.49	-2.20	14.6
1987	247.08	17.50	6.29	10.11	-3.82	2.0
1988	277.72	23.76	6.69	9.57	-2.88	12.4
1989	353.40	22.87	6.05	8.86	-2.81	27.3
1990	330.22	21.60	6.89	9.05	-2.16	-6.6

aColumn (3) minus column (4).

*Price appreciation following years with a risk premium less than .35 percentage points for the period 1957–1980 only.

Sources of basic data: Standard & Poor's Security Price Index Record and the finance section of SCB.

TABLE 3.25
Modern Risk Premiums for the S&P Composite Stock Price Index Based on Earnings, Nominal Interest Rates, and the Inflation Rate for the Consumer Price Index

Year	Closing Value S&P Index (1)	Earnings for the S&P Index (2)	High Earnings Price Ratio[a] (3)	Moody's December Aaa Corp. Bond Yield (4)	CPI Inflation Rate (5)	Real Risk Premium[b] (6)	% Change S&P Index (7)
1957	39.99	3.37	9.05	3.81	3.02	8.26	−14.3
1958	55.21	2.89	6.56	4.08	1.76	4.24	38.1
1959	59.89	3.39	6.04	4.58	1.50	2.96	8.5
1960	58.11	3.27	6.23	4.35	1.48	3.36	−3.0
1961	71.55	3.19	5.06	4.42	.67	1.31	23.1
1962	63.10	3.67H	5.82	4.24	1.22	2.80	−11.8*
1963	75.02	4.02H	5.36	4.35	1.65	2.66	18.9
1964	84.75	4.55H	5.37	4.44	1.19	2.12	13.0
1965	92.43	5.19H	5.62	4.68	1.92	2.86	9.1
1966	80.33	5.55H	6.91	5.39	3.35	4.87	−13.1
1967	96.47	5.33	5.75	6.19	3.04	2.60	20.1
1968	103.86	5.76H	5.55	6.45	4.72	3.82	7.7
1969	92.06	5.78H	6.28	7.72	6.11	4.67	−11.4
1970	92.15	5.13	6.27	7.64	5.49	4.12	.1
1971	102.09	5.70	5.66	7.25	3.36	1.77	10.8
1972	118.05	6.42H	5.44	7.08	3.41	1.77	15.6

Year							
1973	97.55	8.16H	8.36	7.68	8.80	9.48	−17.4
1974	68.56	8.89H	12.97	8.89	12.20	16.28	−29.7
1975	90.19	7.96	9.86	8.79	7.01	8.08	31.5
1976	107.46	9.91H	9.22	7.98	4.81	6.05	19.1
1977	95.10	10.89H	11.45	8.19	6.77	10.03	−11.5
1978	96.11	12.33H	12.83	9.16	9.03	12.70	1.1
1979	107.94	14.86H	13.77	10.74	13.31	16.34	12.3
1980	135.76	14.82	10.95	13.21	12.40	10.14	25.8
1981	122.55	15.36H	12.53	14.23	8.94	7.24	−9.7
1982	140.64	12.64	10.92	11.83	3.87	2.96	14.8
1983	164.93	14.03	9.31	12.57	3.80	.54	17.3
1984	167.24	16.64H	9.95	12.13	3.95	1.77	1.4*
1985	211.28	14.61	7.88	10.16	3.77	1.49	26.3
1986	242.17	14.48	6.87	8.49	1.13	−.49	14.6
1987	247.08	17.50H	7.08	10.11	4.41	1.38	2.0*
1988	277.72	23.76H	8.56	9.57	4.42	3.41	12.4
1989	353.40	22.87	6.72	8.86	4.65	2.51	27.3
1990	330.22	21.60	7.20	9.05	6.11	4.26	−6.6

aThe highest earnings for the current year or any previous year expressed as a percent of the closing value for the S&P index in column (1).
bColumn (3) minus column (4) plus column (5).
H indicates the record earnings that are used to compute the high earnings price ratios in column (3).
*Price appreciation for the S&P index following real risk premiums in column (6) that are less than 1.35 percentage points.

Sources: Standard & Poor's *Security Price Index Record* and the finance section of *SCB*.

TABLE 3.30

Stock Market Volatility and the Financial Returns Associated with the S&P Index

Year	Values for the S&P Index High (1)	Low (2)	Close (3)	High-Low Ratio (4)	Financial Return (5)
1928	24.35	16.95	24.35	1.437	41.9
1929	31.92	17.66	21.45	1.807	−7.9
1930	25.92	14.44	15.34	1.795	−23.9
1931	18.17	7.72	8.12	2.354	−41.7*
1932	9.31	4.40	6.89	2.116	−9.0
1933	12.20	5.53	10.10	2.206	53.0*
1934	11.82	8.36	9.50	1.414	−1.5
1935	13.46	8.06	13.43	1.670	46.3*
1936	17.69	13.40	17.18	1.320	33.3
1937	18.68	10.17	10.55	1.837	−33.9*
1938	13.79	8.50	13.21	1.622	30.0
1939	13.23	10.18	12.49	1.300	−.8*
1940	12.77	8.99	10.58	1.420	−9.9
1941	10.86	8.37	8.69	1.297	−11.2
1942	9.77	7.47	9.77	1.308	19.2*
1943	12.64	9.84	11.67	1.285	25.7
1944	13.29	11.56	13.28	1.150	19.3*
1945	17.68	13.21	17.36	1.338	35.7
1946	19.25	14.12	15.30	1.363	−7.8
1947	16.20	13.71	15.30	1.182	5.5
1948	17.06	13.84	15.20	1.233	5.4*
1949	16.79	13.55	16.76	1.239	17.8
1950	20.43	16.65	20.41	1.227	30.5
1951	23.85	20.69	23.77	1.153	23.4*
1952	26.59	23.09	26.57	1.152	17.7
1953	26.66	22.71	24.81	1.174	−1.2
1954	35.98	24.80	35.98	1.451	51.2
1955	46.41	34.58	45.48	1.342	31.0
1956	49.74	43.11	46.67	1.154	6.4*
1957	49.13	38.98	39.99	1.260	−10.4
1958	55.21	40.33	55.21	1.369	42.4
1959	60.71	53.58	59.89	1.133	11.8
1960	60.39	52.30	58.11	1.155	.3*
1961	72.64	57.57	71.55	1.262	26.6
1962	71.13	52.32	63.10	1.360	−8.8
1963	75.02	62.69	75.02	1.197	22.5
1964	86.28	75.43	84.75	1.144	16.3*
1965	92.63	81.60	92.43	1.135	12.3
1966	94.06	73.20	80.33	1.285	−10.0

TABLE 3.30 (concluded)

Year	Values for the S&P Index			High-Low Ratio (4)	Financial Return (5)
	High (1)	Low (2)	Close (3)		
1967	97.59	80.38	96.47	1.214	23.7
1968	108.37	87.72	103.86	1.235	10.8*
1969	106.16	89.20	92.06	1.190	−8.3
1970	93.46	69.29	92.15	1.349	3.5*
1971	104.77	90.16	102.09	1.162	14.1
1972	119.12	101.67	118.05	1.172	18.7*
1973	120.24	92.16	92.55	1.305	−14.5
1974	99.80	62.28	68.56	1.602	−26.0
1975	95.61	70.04	90.19	1.365	36.9
1976	107.83	90.90	107.46	1.186	23.6*
1977	107.00	90.71	95.10	1.180	−7.2
1978	106.99	86.90	96.11	1.231	6.4
1979	111.27	96.13	107.94	1.157	18.4
1980	140.52	98.22	135.76	1.431	31.5*
1981	138.12	112.77	122.55	1.225	−4.8
1982	143.02	102.42	140.64	1.396	20.4*
1983	172.65	138.34	164.93	1.248	22.3
1984	170.41	147.82	167.24	1.153	6.0*
1985	212.02	163.68	211.28	1.295	31.1
1986	254.00	203.49	242.17	1.248	18.5
1987	336.77	223.92	247.08	1.504	5.7*
1988	283.66	242.63	277.72	1.169	16.3
1989	359.80	275.31	353.40	1.307	31.2*
1990	368.95	295.46	330.22	1.249	−3.1
1991					?*

*Financial return following a downside reversal for the yearly high-low ratio in column (4).

Source of basic data: Standard & Poor's *Security Price Index Record*.

TABLE 3.31
Residual Volatility and the S&P Index

Year	Annual High-Low Range[a] (% Points) (1)	Current Financial Return (%) (2)	Residual Volatility[b] (3)	Following Year Financial Return (%) (4)
1941	29.7	−11.2	18.5	19.2
1946	36.3	−7.8	28.5	5.5
1948	23.3	5.4	17.9	17.8
1953	17.4	−1.2	16.2	51.2
1962	36.0	−8.8	27.2	22.5
1966	28.5	−10.0	18.5	23.7
1970	34.9	3.5	31.4	14.1
1974	60.2	−26.0	34.2	36.9
1978	23.1	6.4	16.7	18.4
1981	22.5	−4.8	17.7	20.4
1982	39.6	20.4	19.2	22.3
1987	50.4	5.7	44.7	16.3
1990	24.9	−3.1	21.8	?

[a]The high-low range is obtained by subtracting one from the ratios in column (4) of Table 3.30 and multiplying the remainder by 100.
[b]Column (1) minus the absolute value of column (2) to remove the yearly trend in stock prices. The following year financial returns since the beginning of World War II have so far always been positive when this difference has been in excess of 16 percentage points.

Source of basic data: Standard & Poor's *Security Price Index Record.*

TABLE 3.32
New Historic Highs for the S&P Composite Stock Price, Selected Years and Decades

Years	Total Number of New Highs (1)	% Occurring on a Daily Gain of More Than 1% (2)
1928–29	106	27.4
1950s	135	3.8
1960s	220	3.7
1970s	35	.0
1980s	188	38.3
1986–87	78	39.7
1989	13	46.2
1990	6	33.3
1991p	11	36.4

p equals a preliminary estimate as of May 31, 1991.

Source of basic data: Standard & Poor's *Security Price Index Record.*

TABLE 3.33
December-to-December Declines in the Volume of Shares Traded on the NYSE of 10 Percent or More and the Following Year Financial Returns for the S&P Stock Price Index

Year	% Decline	Following Year Financial Return
1941	−17.9	19.2
1942	−46.9	25.7
1946	−12.7	5.5
1951	−49.7	17.7
1953	−10.8	51.2
1955	−33.3	6.4
1966	−13.4	23.7
1974	−18.0	36.9
1977	−15.6	6.4
1988	−27.6	31.2

Sources of basic data: Blue page financial section of the *Survey of Current Business* and Standard & Poor's *Security Price Index Record*.

TABLE 3.40
A Chronology of Buy (+) and Sell (−) Signals for the S&P Index

Indicator	Basic Table	Signal Date	Closing Value S&P Index
NBER business trough		6/30/38	11.56
P-E ratio over 20.5	2.82	12/31/38	13.21(−)
S&P index down 19.4%	3.02	11/28/41	9.12(+)
One-day S&P gain of 3.5%	3.10	12/30/41	8.74(+)
Fed. share of GNP up .6% points	1.77	12/31/41	8.69(+)
Average unemployment rate down 1% point	2.73	12/31/41	8.69(+)
Dividend yield up 24 basis points	2.84	12/31/41	8.69(+)
High-low ratio decline signal	3.30	12/31/41	8.69(+)
Residual volatility signal	3.31	12/31/41	8.69(+)
August-to-October S&P gain of 5%	3.16	10/31/42	9.42(+)
Weak propensity to spend	1.31	12/31/42	9.77(+)
Real M1 growth acceleration of 4% points	1.77	12/31/42	9.77(+)
Fed. share of GNP up .6% points	1.77	12/31/42	9.77(+)
CPI deceleration of 1.4% points	2.15	12/31/42	9.77(+)
Average unemployment rate down 1% point	2.73	12/31/42	9.77(+)

TABLE 3.40 (*continued*)

Indicator	Basic Table	Signal Date	Closing Value S&P Index
S&P earnings down 6%	2.81	12/31/42	9.77(+)
Negative dividend growth rate	2.83	12/31/42	9.77(+)
Dividend growth rate decline of 3.2% pts.	2.83	12/31/42	9.77(+)
Dividend yield up 24 basis points	2.84	12/31/42	9.77(+)
October-to-January gain of 8%	3.16	1/30/43	10.47(+)
Fed. share of GNP up .6% points	1.77	12/31/43	11.67(+)
CPI deceleration of 1.4% points	2.15	12/31/43	11.67(+)
Average unemployment rate down 1% point	2.73	12/31/43	11.67(+)
S&P earnings down 6%	2.81	12/31/43	11.67(+)
High-low ratio decline signal	3.30	12/31/43	11.67(+)
Weak propensity to spend	1.31	12/30/44	13.28(+)
NBER business peak		2/28/45	14.30
NBER business trough		10/31/45	16.65
August-to-October S&P gain of 5%	3.16	10/31/45	16.65(+)
October-to-January gain of 8%	3.16	1/31/46	18.57(+)
Major S&P peak		5/29/46	HHH19.25
P-E ratio over 20.5	2.82	6/28/46	18.43(−)
S&P index down 19.4%	3.00	9/04/46	15.46(+)
Record volume NYSE and lower S&P	3.14	9/04/46	15.46(+)
Two-quarter S&P decline of 14%	3.03	9/30/46	14.96(+)
One-day S&P gain of 3.5%	3.10	10/15/46	15.30(+)
One-day S&P gain of 3.5%	3.10	10/31/46	14.84(+)
August-to-October decline of 4.8%	3.16	10/31/46	14.84(+)
Accelerator residual 2.2% points	1.32	12/31/46	15.30(+)
Real GNP down .3% or more	1.32	12/31/46	15.30(+)
Average unemployment rate up 1.4% points	2.73	12/31/46	15.30(+)
Residual volatility signal	3.31	12/31/46	15.30(+)
December and January effect signals	3.15	1/31/47	15.66(+)
Major S&P low		5/17/47	LLL13.71
S&P index up 15%	3.00	7/11/47	15.87(+)
Accelerator residual 2.2% points	1.32	12/31/47	15.30(+)
Real GNP down .3% or more	1.32	12/31/47	15.30(+)
Real M1 growth acceleration of 4% points	1.77	12/31/47	15.30(+)
CPI deceleration of 1.4% points	2.15	12/31/47	15.30(+)
Dividend yield up 24 basis points	2.84	12/31/47	15.30(+)
High-low ratio decline signal	3.30	12/31/47	15.30(+)

TABLE 3.40 (continued)

Indicator	Basic Table	Signal Date	Closing Value S&P Index
Major S&P peak		6/15/48	HHH17.06
Prime rate increase of 11%	1.87	8/31/48	15.97(−)
400 trading day exit	3.21	10/26/48	16.59(−)
Unemployment claims up 16%	1.41	11/30/48	14.75(+)
NBER business peak		11/30/48	14.75
Accelerator residual 2.2% points	1.32	12/31/48	15.20(+)
Leading indicators down 1.9%	1.17	12/31/48	15.20(+)
Real M1 growth acceleration of 4% points	1.77	12/31/48	15.20(+)
Fed. share of GNP up .65% points	1.77	12/31/48	15.20(+)
CPI deceleration of 1.4% points	2.15	12/31/48	15.20(+)
Dividend growth rate decline of 3.2% pts.	2.83	12/31/48	15.20(+)
Dividend yield up 24 basis points	2.84	12/31/48	15.20(+)
Residual volatility signal	3.31	12/31/48	15.20(+)
December and January effect signal	3.15	1/31/49	15.22(+)
Unemployment rate up .9% points	1.28	2/28/49	14.62(+)
Unemployment rate up 1.2% points	1.28	3/31/49	15.06(+)
Unemployment rate up 1.5% points	1.28	4/30/49	14.74(+)
Unemployment rate up 1.8% points	1.28	5/31/49	14.19(+)
S&P index down 19.4%	3.02	6/13/49	13.55(+)
Major S&P low		6/13/49	LLL13.55
Wages and salaries down 6%	1.36	6/30/49	16.92(+)
Two months after two-quarter recession	2.71	8/31/49	15.22(+)
S&P index up 15%	3.00	9/13/49	15.74(+)
August-to-October S&P gain of 5%	3.16	10/31/49	16.04(+)
NBER business trough		10/31/49	16.04
Unemployment claims up 16%	1.41	11/30/49	16.06(+)
Housing starts up 25%	1.41	11/30/49	16.06(+)
Leading indicators up 3.5%	1.17	12/31/49	16.76(+)
Durable goods production down 2%	1.35	12/31/49	16.76(+)
Real M1 growth acceleration of 4% points	1.77	12/31/49	16.76(+)
Fed. share of GNP up .6% points	1.77	12/31/49	16.76(+)
Average unemployment rate up 1.45% points	2.73	12/31/49	16.76(+)
Dividend yield up 24 basis points	2.84	12/31/49	16.76(+)
December and January effect signals	3.15	1/31/50	17.05(+)

TABLE 3.40 (*continued*)

Indicator	Basic Table	Signal Date	Closing Value S&P Index
Record volume NYSE and lower S&P	3.14	6/27/50	17.91(+)
August-to-October S&P gain of 5%	3.16	10/31/50	19.53(+)
400 trading day exit	3.21	11/21/50	19.88(−)
Leading indicators up 13%	1.17	12/30/50	20.41(+)
High-low ratio decline signal	3.30	12/30/50	20.41(+)
December and January effect signals	3.15	1/31/51	21.66(+)
October-to-January gain of 8%	3.16	1/31/51	21.66(+)
Leading indicators down 1.9%	1.17	12/31/51	23.77(+)
Fed. share of GNP up .6% points	1.77	12/31/51	23.77(+)
CPI deceleration of 1.4% points	2.15	12/31/51	23.77(+)
Average unemployment rate down 1% point	2.73	12/31/51	23.77(+)
S&P earnings down 6%	2.81	12/31/51	23.77(+)
Negative dividend growth rate	2.83	12/31/51	23.77(+)
Dividend growth rate decline of 3.2% pts.	2.83	12/31/51	23.77(+)
December and January effect signals	3.15	1/31/52	24.14(+)
Weak propensity to spend	1.31	12/31/52	26.57(+)
Fed. share of GNP up .6% points	1.77	12/31/52	26.57(+)
Major S&P high		1/05/53	HHH26.66
NBER business peak		7/31/53	24.75
Major S&P low		9/14/53	LLL22.71
T-bill yield down 20%	2.19	10/30/53	24.54(+)
August-to-October S&P gain of 5%	3.16	10/30/53	24.54(+)
Unemployment claims up 16%	1.41	11/30/53	24.76(+)
Weak propensity to spend	1.31	12/31/53	24.81(+)
Leading indicators down 1.9%	1.17	12/31/53	24.81(+)
Unemployment rate up .9% points	1.28	12/31/53	24.81(+)
Durable goods production down 2%	1.35	12/31/53	24.81(+)
Fed. share of GNP up .6% points	1.77	12/31/53	24.81(+)
Dec.–Dec. T-bill yield down 10%	2.18	12/31/53	24.81(+)
Residual volatility signal	3.31	12/31/53	24.81(+)
Unemployment rate up 1.2% points	1.28	1/29/54	26.08(+)
Unemployment rate up 1.5% points	1.28	1/29/54	26.08(+)
Unemployment rate up 1.8% points	1.28	1/29/54	26.08(+)
December and January effect signals	3.15	1/29/54	26.08(+)
S&P index up 15%	3.00	2/04/54	26.20(+)
Wages and salaries down 6%	1.36	2/26/54	26.15(+)
Two months after two-quarter recession	2.71	2/26/54	26.15(+)
NBER business trough		5/28/54	29.19

TABLE 3.40 (continued)

Indicator	Basic Table	Signal Date	Closing Value S&P Index
August-to-October S&P gain of 5%	3.16	10/29/54	31.68(+)
Housing starts up 25%	1.41	11/30/54	34.24(+)
Weak propensity to spend	1.31	12/31/54	35.98(+)
Leading indicators up 13%	1.17	12/31/54	35.98(+)
Real GNP down .3% or more	1.32	12/31/54	35.98(+)
Accelerator residual 2.2% points	1.32	12/31/54	35.98(+)
CPI deceleration of 1.4% points	2.15	12/31/54	35.98(+)
Dec.–Dec. T-bill yield down 10%	2.18	12/31/54	35.98(+)
Average unemployment rate up 1.4% points	2.73	12/31/54	35.98(+)
Record volume NYSE and lower S&P	3.14	1/05/55	35.52(+)
Record volume NYSE and lower S&P	3.14	1/06/55	35.04(+)
December and January effect signals	3.15	1/31/55	36.63(+)
October to January gain of 8%	3.16	1/31/55	36.63(+)
400 trading day exit	3.21	4/21/55	38.22(−)
One-day S&P gain of 3.5%	3.10	7/06/55	43.18(+)
January-to-August gain of 15.5%	3.16	8/31/55	43.18(−)
One-day S&P decline of 6%	3.04	9/26/55	42.61(+)
Average unemployment rate down 1% point	2.73	12/30/55	45.48(+)
Two good years in a row	3.22	12/30/55	45.48(−)
High-low ratio decline signal	3.30	12/30/55	45.48(+)
Major S&P high		8/02/56	HHH49.74
Highly inverted yield curve	1.86	12/31/56	46.67(−)
NBER business peak		8/30/57	45.22
S&P index down 19.4%	3.02	10/21/57	39.15(+)
Major S&P low		10/22/57	LLL38.98
One-day S&P gain of 3.5%	3.10	10/23/57	40.73(+)
August-to-October decline of 4.8%	3.16	10/31/57	41.06(+)
Unemployment claims up 16%	1.41	11/29/57	41.72(+)
Leading indicators down 1.9%	1.17	12/31/57	39.99(+)
Unemployment rate up .9% points	1.28	12/31/57	39.99(+)
Unemployment rate up 1.2% points	1.28	12/31/57	39.99(+)
Durable goods production down 2%	1.35	12/31/57	39.99(+)
Dividend growth rate decline of 3.2% pts.	2.83	12/31/57	39.99(+)
Dividend yield up 24 basis points	2.84	12/31/57	39.99(+)
Two-quarter S&P decline of 14%	3.03	12/31/57	39.99(+)
Unemployment rate up 1.5% points	1.28	1/31/58	41.70(+)
Wages and salaries down 6%	1.36	1/31/58	41.70(+)
T-bill yield down 20%	2.19	1/31/58	41.70(+)

TABLE 3.40 (*continued*)

Indicator	Basic Table	Signal Date	Closing Value S&P Index
January effect signal	3.15	1/31/58	41.70(+)
Unemployment rate up 1.8% points	1.28	2/28/58	40.28(+)
NBER business trough		4/30/58	43.44
Two months after two-quarter recession	2.71	5/29/58	44.09(+)
S&P index up 15%	3.00	6/17/58	44.94(+)
August-to-October S&P gain of 5%	3.16	10/31/58	51.33(+)
Housing starts up 25%	1.41	11/28/58	52.48(+)
Weak propensity to spend	1.31	12/31/58	55.21(+)
Leading indicators up 13%	1.17	12/31/58	55.21(+)
Real GNP down .3% or more	1.32	12/31/58	55.21(+)
Real M1 growth acceleration of 4% points	1.77	12/31/58	55.21(+)
Fed. share of GNP up .6% points	1.77	12/31/58	55.21(+)
Average unemployment rate up 1.4% points	2.73	12/31/58	55.21(+)
S&P earnings down 6%	2.81	12/31/58	55.21(+)
Negative dividend growth rate	2.83	12/31/58	55.21(+)
Dividend growth rate decline of 3.2% points	2.83	12/31/58	55.21(+)
December and January effect signal	3.15	1/30/59	55.42(+)
October-to-January gain of 8%	3.16	1/30/59	55.42(+)
400 trading day exit	3.21	5/27/59	58.19(−)
Highly inverted yield curve	1.86	7/31/59	60.51(−)
Major S&P high		8/30/59	HHH60.71
Prime rate increase of 11%	1.87	9/30/59	56.88(−)
Average unemployment rate down 1% point	2.73	12/31/59	59.89(+)
Two good years in a row	3.22	12/31/59	59.89(−)
High-low ratio decline signal	3.30	12/31/59	59.89(+)
T-bill yield down 20%	2.19	3/31/60	55.34(+)
NBER business peak		4/29/60	54.37
Major S&P low		10/25/60	LLL52.30
August-to-October decline of 4.8%	3.16	10/31/60	53.39(+)
Unemployment rate up .9% points	1.28	11/30/60	55.54(+)
Unemployment rate up 1.2% points	1.28	11/30/60	55.54(+)
Two months after two-quarter recession	2.71	11/30/60	55.54(+)

TABLE 3.40 (*continued*)

Indicator	Basic Table	Signal Date	Closing Value S&P Index
Leading indicators down 1.9%	1.17	12/30/60	58.11(+)
Durable goods production down 2%	1.35	12/30/60	58.11(+)
Dec.–Dec. T-bill yield down 10%	2.18	12/30/60	58.11(+)
Dividend yield up 24 basis points	2.84	12/30/60	58.11(+)
S&P index up 15%	3.00	1/23/61	60.29(+)
Unemployment rate up 1.5% points	1.28	1/31/61	61.78(+)
Unemployment rate up 1.8% points	1.28	1/31/61	61.78(+)
Wages and salaries down 6%	1.36	1/31/61	61.78(+)
December and January effect signals	3.15	1/31/61	61.78(+)
October-to-January gain of 8%	3.16	1/31/61	61.78(+)
NBER business trough		2/28/61	63.44
P-E ratio over 20.5	2.82	3/30/61	65.06(−)
Dividend yield under 3.0%	2.85	4/28/61	65.31(−)
Major S&P high		12/12/61	HHH72.64
Record stock offering signal	3.23	12/29/61	71.55(−)
S&P index down 19.4%	3.02	5/28/62	55.50(+)
One-day S&P decline of 6%	3.04	5/28/62	55.50(+)
Record volume NYSE and lower S&P	3.14	5/28/62	55.50(+)
One day S&P gain of 3.5%	3.10	5/29/62	58.08(+)
400 trading day exit	3.21	5/31/62	59.63(−)
Record volume NYSE and lower S&P	3.14	6/15/62	55.89(+)
Major S&P low		6/26/62	LLL52.32
Dividend yield over 3.5%	2.85	6/29/62	54.75(+)
Two-quarter S&P decline of 14%	3.03	6/29/62	54.75(+)
S&P index up 15%	3.00	11/20/62	60.45(+)
Leading indicators up, stocks down 1.7%	2.72	12/31/62	63.10(+)
Average unemployment rate down 1% point	2.73	12/31/62	63.10(+)
Dividend yield up 24 basis points	2.84	12/31/62	63.10(+)
Residual volatility signal	3.31	12/31/62	63.10(+)
December and January effect signals	3.15	1/31/63	66.20(+)
October-to-January gain of 8%	3.16	1/31/63	66.20(+)
One-day S&P gain of 3.5%	3.10	11/26/63	72.38(+)
Record volume NYSE and lower S&P	3.14	11/26/63	72.38(+)
High-low ratio decline signal	3.30	12/31/63	75.02(+)
400 trading day exit	3.21	1/29/64	76.63(−)
December and January effect signals	3.15	1/31/64	77.04(+)
Dividend yield under 3.0%	2.85	7/31/64	83.18(−)

TABLE 3.40 (*continued*)

Indicator	Basic Table	Signal Date	Closing Value S&P Index
Leading indicators up, stocks down 1.7%	2.72	12/31/64	84.75(+)
Two good years in a row	3.22	12/31/64	84.75(−)
December and January effect signals	3.15	1/29/65	87.56(+)
Record volume NYSE and lower S&P	3.14	6/10/65	84.73(+)
Record volume NYSE and lower S&P	3.14	6/15/65	84.49(+)
Record volume NYSE and lower S&P	3.14	6/29/65	82.41(+)
August-to-October S&P gain of 5%	3.16	10/29/65	92.42(+)
Highly inverted yield curve	1.86	1/31/66	92.88(−)
Major S&P high		2/09/66	HHH94.06
Record volume NYSE and lower S&P	3.14	5/06/66	87.84(+)
S&P index down 19.4%	3.02	8/29/66	74.53(+)
Dividend yield over 3.5%	2.85	8/31/66	77.10(+)
Two-quarter S&P decline of 14%	3.03	9/30/66	76.56(+)
Major S&P low		10/07/66	LLL73.20
Leading indicators down 1.9%	1.17	12/30/66	80.33(+)
Weak propensity to spend	1.31	12/30/66	80.33(+)
Fed. share of GNP up .6% points	1.77	12/30/66	80.33(+)
Dividend growth rate decline of 3.2% points	2.83	12/30/66	80.33(+)
Dividend yield up 24 basis points	2.84	12/30/66	80.33(+)
Residual volatility signal	3.31	12/30/66	80.33(+)
Record volume NYSE and lower S&P	3.14	1/11/67	83.47(+)
S&P index up 15%	3.00	1/13/67	84.53(+)
December and January effect signals	3.15	1/31/67	86.61(+)
October-to-January gain of 8%	3.16	1/31/67	86.61(+)
T-bill yield down 20%	2.19	3/31/67	90.20(+)
Housing starts up 25%	1.41	11/30/67	94.00(+)
Weak propensity to spend	1.31	12/29/67	96.47(+)
Real M1 growth acceleration of 4% points	1.77	12/29/67	96.47(+)
Fed. share of GNP up .6% points	1.77	12/29/67	96.47(+)
Dividend growth rate decline of 3.2% pts.	2.83	12/29/67	96.47(+)
High-low ratio decline signal	3.30	12/29/67	96.47(+)
Record volume NYSE and lower S&P	3.14	4/01/68	92.48(+)
400 trading day exit	3.21	5/14/68	98.12(−)
Dividend yield under 3.0	2.85	10/31/68	103.41(−)

TABLE 3.40 (*continued*)

Indicator	Basic Table	Signal Date	Closing Value S&P Index
Major S&P high		11/29/68	HHH108.37
Two good years in a row	3.22	12/31/68	103.86(−)
Record stock offering signal	3.23	12/31/68	103.86(−)
Highly inverted yield curve	1.86	7/31/69	91.83(−)
Leading indicators down 1.9%	1.17	12/31/69	92.06(+)
Accelerator residual 2.2% points	1.32	12/31/69	92.06(+)
Dividend yield over 3.5%	2.85	12/31/69	92.06(+)
Record stock offering signal	3.23	12/31/69	92.06(−)
High-low ratio decline signal	3.30	12/31/69	92.06(+)
NBER business peak		12/31/69	92.06
S&P index down 19.4%	3.02	1/28/70	86.79(+)
Unemployment rate up .9% points	1.28	4/30/70	81.52(+)
Major S&P low		5/26/70	LLL69.29
One-day S&P gain of 3.5%	3.10	5/27/70	72.77(+)
NYSE advances over 1300 & S&P up 2.8%	3.13	5/27/70	72.77(+)
Unemployment rate up 1.2% points	1.28	5/29/70	76.55(+)
Two months after two-quarter recession	2.71	5/29/70	76.55(+)
Two-quarter S&P decline of 14%	3.03	6/30/70	72.72(+)
Unemployment rate up 1.5% points	1.28	7/31/70	78.05(+)
S&P index up 15%	3.00	8/24/70	80.99(+)
Record volume NYSE and lower S&P	3.14	9/24/70	83.91(+)
T-bill yield down 20%	2.19	9/30/70	84.21(+)
Unemployment rate up 1.8% points	1.28	10/30/70	83.25(+)
Wages and salaries down 6%	1.36	10/30/70	83.25(+)
Unemployment claims up 16%	1.41	11/30/70	87.20(+)
Housing starts up 25%	1.41	11/30/70	87.20(+)
NBER business trough		11/30/70	87.20
Leading indicators down 1.9%	1.17	12/31/70	92.15(+)
Real GNP down .3% or more	1.32	12/31/70	92.15(+)
Accelerator residual 2.2% points	1.32	12/31/70	92.15(+)
Weak propensity to spend	1.31	12/31/70	92.15(+)
Durable goods production down 2%	1.35	12/31/70	92.15(+)
Dec.–Dec. T-bill yield down 10%	2.18	12/31/70	95.15(+)
Average unemployment rate up 1.4% points	2.73	12/31/70	92.15(+)
S&P earnings down 6%	2.81	12/31/70	92.15(+)
Negative dividend growth rate	2.83	12/31/70	92.15(+)

TABLE 3.40 (*continued*)

Indicator	Basic Table	Signal Date	Closing Value S&P Index
Dividend growth rate decline of 3.2% pts.	2.83	12/31/70	92.15(+)
Dividend yield up 24 basis points	2.84	12/31/70	92.15(+)
Residual volatility signal	3.31	12/31/70	92.15(+)
December and January effect signals	3.15	1/29/71	95.88(+)
October-to-January gain of 8%	3.16	1/29/71	95.88(+)
Dividend yield under 3.0%	2.84	4/30/71	103.95(−)
NYSE advances over 1300 and S&P up 2.8%	3.13	8/16/71	98.76(+)
August-to-October decline of 4.8%	3.16	10/29/71	94.23(+)
Housing starts up 25%	1.41	11/30/71	93.99(+)
T-bill yield down 20%	2.19	11/30/71	93.99(+)
400 trading day exit	3.21	12/22/71	101.18(−)
Leading indicators up 3.5%	1.17	12/31/71	102.09(+)
Weak propensity to spend	1.31	12/31/71	102.09(+)
Accelerator residual 2.2% points	1.32	12/31/71	102.09(+)
Dec.–Dec. T-bill yield down 10%	2.18	12/31/71	102.09(+)
Leading indicators up, stocks down 1.7%	2.72	12/31/71	102.09(+)
Negative dividend growth rate	2.83	12/31/71	102.09(+)
High-low ratio decline signal	3.30	12/31/71	102.09(+)
December and January effect signals	3.15	1/31/72	103.94(+)
October-to-January gain of 8%	3.16	1/31/72	103.94(+)
Two good years in a row	3.22	12/29/72	118.05(−)
Major S&P high		1/11/73	HHH120.24
Highly inverted yield curve	1.86	7/31/73	108.22(−)
Prime rate increase of 11%	1.87	8/31/73	104.25(−)
S&P index down 19.4%	3.02	11/26/73	96.58(+)
NBER business peak		11/30/73	95.96
Dividend yield over 3.5%	2.85	12/31/73	97.55(+)
One-day S&P gain of 3.5%	3.10	7/12/74	83.15(+)
NYSE advances over 1300 and S&P up 2.8%	3.13	7/12/74	83.15(+)
Unemployment rate up .9% points	1.28	8/30/74	72.15(+)
Two months after two-quarter recession	2.71	8/30/74	72.15(+)
One-day S&P gain of 3.5%	3.10	9/19/74	70.09(+)
Two-quarter S&P decline of 14%	3.03	9/30/74	63.54(+)
Major S&P low		10/03/74	LLL62.28

TABLE 3.40 (*continued*)

Indicator	Basic Table	Signal Date	Closing Value S&P Index
One-day S&P gain of 3.5%	3.10	10/07/74	64.95(+)
NYSE advances over 1300 and S&P up 2.8%	3.13	10/07/74	64.95(+)
One-day S&P gain of 3.5%	3.10	10/09/74	67.82(+)
NYSE advances over 1300 and S&P up 2.8%	3.13	10/10/74	69.79(+)
Two NYSE advances over 1300 in 15 days	3.13	10/10/74	69.79(+)
S&P index up 15%	3.00	10/14/74	72.74(+)
One-day S&P gain of 3.5%	3.10	10/29/74	72.83(+)
Unemployment rate up 1.2% points	1.28	10/31/74	73.90(+)
Unemployment claims up 16%	1.41	11/29/74	69.97(+)
Unemployment rate up 1.5% points	1.28	12/31/74	68.56(+)
Weak propensity to spend	1.31	12/31/74	68.56(+)
Real GNP down .3% or more	1.32	12/31/74	68.56(+)
Unemployment rate up 1.8% points	1.28	12/31/74	68.56(+)
Leading indicators down 1.9%	1.17	12/31/74	68.56(+)
Durable goods production down 2%	1.35	12/31/74	68.56(+)
Wages and salaries down 6%	1.36	12/31/74	68.56(+)
Dividend yield up 24 basis points	2.84	12/31/74	68.56(+)
Residual volatility signal	3.31	12/31/74	68.56(+)
Two NYSE advances over 1300 in 15 days	3.13	1/10/75	72.61(+)
NYSE advances over 1300 and S&P up 2.8%	3.13	1/27/75	75.37(+)
Record volume NYSE and lower S&P	3.14	1/27/75	75.37(+)
T-bill yield down 20%	2.19	1/31/75	76.98(+)
December and January effect signals	3.15	1/31/75	76.98(+)
NBER business trough		3/31/75	83.36
Housing starts up 25%	1.41	11/28/75	91.24(+)
Leading indicators up 13%	1.17	12/31/75	90.19(+)
Weak propensity to spend	1.31	12/31/75	90.19(+)
Real GNP down .3% or more	1.32	12/31/75	90.19(+)
Durable goods production down 2%	1.35	12/31/75	90.19(+)
Real M1 growth acceleration of 4% points	1.77	12/31/75	90.19(+)
CPI deceleration of 1.4% points	2.15	12/31/75	90.19(+)
Dec.–Dec. T-bill yield down 10%	2.18	12/31/75	90.19(+)
Leading indicators up, stocks down 1.7%	2.72	12/31/75	90.19(+)
Average unemployment rate up 1.4% points	2.73	12/31/75	90.19(+)
S&P earnings down 6%	2.81	12/31/75	90.19(+)

TABLE 3.40 (*continued*)

Indicator	Basic Table	Signal Date	Closing Value S&P Index
Dividend growth rate decline of 3.2% pts.	2.83	12/31/75	90.19(+)
High-low ratio decline signal	3.30	12/31/75	90.19(+)
T-bill yield down 20%	2.19	1/30/76	100.86(+)
December and January effect signals	3.15	1/30/76	100.86(+)
October-to-January gain of 8%	3.16	1/30/76	100.86(+)
400 trading day exit	3.21	5/04/76	101.42(−)
Major S&P high		9/21/76	HHH107.83
Dec.–Dec. T-bill yield down 10%	2.18	12/31/76	107.46(+)
Two good years in a row	3.22	12/31/76	107.46(−)
Accelerator residual 2.2% points	1.32	12/30/77	95.10(+)
Leading indicators up, stocks down 1.7%	2.72	12/30/77	95.10(+)
Dividend yield up 24 basis points	2.84	12/30/77	95.10(+)
S&P index down 19.4%	3.02	3/06/78	86.90(+)
Major S&P low		3/06/78	LLL86.90
Record volume NYSE and lower S&P	3.14	4/14/78	92.92(+)
S&P index up 15%	3.00	6/05/78	99.95(+)
January-to-August gain of 15.5%	3.16	8/31/78	103.29(−)
August-to-October decline of 4.8%	3.16	10/31/78	93.15(+)
One-day S&P gain of 3.5%	3.10	11/01/78	96.85(+)
NYSE advances over 1200 and S&P up 2.8%	3.13	11/01/78	96.85(+)
Weak propensity to spend	1.31	12/29/78	96.11(+)
Leading indicators up, stocks down 1.7%	2.72	12/29/78	96.11(+)
Average unemployment rate down 1% point	2.73	12/29/78	96.11(+)
Dividend growth rate decline of 3.2% pts.	2.83	12/29/78	96.11(+)
Dividend yield up 24 basis points	2.84	12/29/78	96.11(+)
Residual volatility signal	3.31	12/29/78	96.11(+)
December and January effect signals	3.15	1/31/79	99.93(+)
October-to-January gain of 8%	3.16	1/31/79	99.93(+)
400 trading day exit	3.21	10/03/79	109.59(−)
Highly inverted yield curve	1.86	10/31/79	101.82(−)
Prime rate increase of 11%	1.87	10/31/79	101.82(−)
August-to-October decline of 4.8%	3.16	10/31/79	101.82(+)
Unemployment claims up 16%	1.41	11/30/79	106.16(+)

TABLE 3.40 (continued)

Indicator	Basic Table	Signal Date	Closing Value S&P Index
Leading indicators down 1.9%	1.17	12/31/79	107.94(+)
Accelerator residual 2.2% points	1.32	12/31/79	107.94(+)
Weak propensity to spend	1.31	12/31/79	107.94(+)
High-low ratio decline signal	3.30	12/31/79	107.94(+)
December and January effect signals	3.15	1/31/80	114.16(+)
October-to-January gain of 8%	3.16	1/31/80	114.16(+)
NBER business peak		1/31/80	114.16
Major S&P high		2/13/80	HHH118.44
Major S&P low		3/27/80	LLL98.22
One-day S&P gain of 3.5%	3.10	4/22/80	103.43(+)
NYSE advances over 1300 and S&P up 2.8%	3.13	4/22/80	103.43(+)
Wages and salaries down 6%	1.36	4/30/80	106.29(+)
Unemployment rate up .9% points	1.28	5/30/80	111.24(+)
Unemployment rate up 1.2% points	1.28	5/30/80	111.24(+)
T-bill yield down 20%	2.19	5/30/80	111.24(+)
S&P index up 15%	3.00	6/06/80	113.20(+)
Unemployment rate up 1.5% points	1.28	6//30/80	114.24(+)
Unemployment rate up 1.8% points	1.28	6/30/80	114.24(+)
NBER business trough		7/31/80	121.67
Prime rate increase of 11%	1.87	10/31/80	127.47(−)
Highly inverted yield curve	1.86	11/28/80	140.52(−)
Major S&P high		11/28/80	HHH140.52
Two good years in a row	3.22	12/31/80	135.76(−)
Record stock offering signal	3.23	12/31/80	135.76(−)
NBER business peak		7/31/81	130.91
S&P index down 19.4%	3.02	9/25/81	112.77(+)
400 trading day exit	3.21	10/27/81	119.29(−)
Unemployment claims up 16%	1.41	11/30/81	126.35(+)
T-bill yield down 20%	1.19	11/30/81	126.35(+)
Leading indicators down 1.9%	1.17	12/31/81	122.55(+)
Unemployment rate up .9% points	1.28	12/31/81	122.55(+)
Durable goods production down 2%	1.35	12/31/81	122.55(+)
CPI deceleration of 1.4% points	2.15	12/31/81	122.55(+)
Dec.–Dec. T-bill rate down 10%	2.18	12/31/81	122.55(+)
High-low ratio decline signal	3.30	12/31/81	122.55(+)
Residual volatility signal	3.31	12/31/81	122.55(+)

TABLE 3.40 (*continued*)

Indicator	Basic Table	Signal Date	Closing Value S&P Index
NYSE advances over 1300 and S&P up 2.8%	3.13	1/28/82	118.92(+)
Unemployment rate up 1.2% points	1.28	1/30/82	129.55(+)
Unemployment rate up 1.5% points	1.28	3/31/82	136.00(+)
Unemployment rate up 1.8% points	1.28	4/30/82	132.81(+)
Two months after two-quarter recession	2.71	5/28/82	111.88(+)
Wages and salaries down 6%	1.36	6/30/82	109.61(+)
Major S&P low		8/12/82	LLL102.42
One-day S&P gain of 3.5%	3.10	8/17/82	109.04(+)
NYSE advances over 1300 and S&P up 2.8%	3.13	8/17/82	109.04(+)
Record volume NYSE and lower S&P	3.14	8/18/82	108.53(+)
One-day S&P gain of 3.5%	3.10	8/20/82	113.02(+)
Two NYSE advances over 1300 in 15 days	3.13	8/20/82	113.02(+)
NYSE advances over 1300 and S&P up 2.8%	3.13	8/20/82	113.02(+)
Two NYSE advances over 1300 in 15 days	3.13	8/23/82	116.11(+)
S&P index up 15%	3.00	8/26/82	118.55(+)
T-bill yield down 20%	2.19	8/31/82	119.51(+)
NYSE advances over 1300 and S&P up 2.8%	3.13	10/06/82	125.97(+)
Two NYSE advances over 1300 in 15 days	3.13	10/07/82	128.80(+)
Two NYSE advances over 1300 in 15 days	3.13	10/11/82	134.47(+)
August-to-October S&P gain of 5%	3.16	10/28/82	133.59(+)
One-day S&P gain of 3.5%	3.10	11/03/82	142.87(+)
NYSE advances over 1300 and S&P up 2.8%	3.13	11/03/82	142.87(+)
Housing starts up 25%	1.41	11/30/82	138.54(+)
NBER business trough		11/30/82	138.54
Leading indicators up 3.5%	1.17	12/31/82	140.64(+)
Accelerator residual 2.2% points	1.32	12/31/82	140.64(+)
Real GNP down .3% or more	1.32	12/31/82	140.64(+)
Weak propensity to spend	1.31	12/31/82	140.64(+)
Durable goods production down 2%	1.35	12/31/82	140.64(+)
Real M1 growth acceleration of 4% points	1.77	12/31/82	140.64(+)
Fed. share of GNP up .6% points	1.77	12/31/82	140.64(+)

TABLE 3.40 (*continued*)

Indicator	Basic Table	Signal Date	Closing Value S&P Index
CPI deceleration of 1.4% points	2.15	12/31/82	140.64(+)
Dec.–Dec. T-bill yield down 10%	2.18	12/31/82	140.64(+)
Average unemployment rate up 1.4% points	2.73	12/31/82	140.64(+)
S&P earnings down 6%	2.81	12/31/82	140.64(+)
Dividend growth rate decline of 3.2% points	2.83	12/31/82	140.64(+)
Dividend yield up 24 basis points	2.84	12/31/82	140.64(+)
Residual volatility signal	3.31	12/31/82	140.64(+)
December and January effect signals	3.15	1/31/83	145.30(+)
October-to-January gain of 8%	3.16	1/31/83	145.30(+)
Housing starts up 25%	1.41	11/30/83	166.40(+)
Leading indicators up 13%	1.17	12/30/83	164.93(+)
Accelerator residual 2.2% points	1.32	12/30/83	164.93(+)
Leading indicators up, stocks down 1.7%	2.72	12/30/83	164.93(+)
Two good years in a row	3.22	12/30/83	164.93(−)
Record stock offering signal	3.23	12/30/83	164.93(−)
High-low ratio decline signal	3.30	12/30/83	164.93(+)
400 trading day exit	3.21	3/12/84	156.34(−)
Two NYSE advances over 1300 in 15 days	3.13	8/02/84	157.99(+)
Record volume NYSE and lower S&P	3.14	8/02/84	157.99(+)
NYSE advances over 1300 and S&P up 2.8%	3.13	8/03/84	162.35(+)
Two NYSE advances over 1300 in 15 days	3.13	8/03/84	162.35(+)
Two NYSE advances over 1300 in 15 days	3.13	8/09/84	165.54(+)
NYSE advances over 1300 and S&P up 2.8%	3.13	12/18/84	168.11(+)
Weak propensity to spend	1.31	12/31/84	167.24(+)
Accelerator residual 2.2% points	1.32	12/31/84	167.24(+)
T-bill yield down 20%	2.19	12/31/84	167.24(+)
Average unemployment rate down 1% point	2.73	12/31/84	167.24(+)
Dividend yield up 24 basis points	2.84	12/31/84	167.24(+)
December and January effect signals	3.15	1/31/85	179.63(+)
October-to-January gain of 8%	3.16	1/31/85	179.63(+)
Weak propensity to spend	1.31	12/30/85	210.68(+)
Real M1 growth acceleration of 4% points	1.77	12/30/85	210.68(+)

TABLE 3.40 (*continued*)

Indicator	Basic Table	Signal Date	Closing Value S&P Index
Fed. share of GNP up .6% points	1.77	12/30/85	210.68(+)
Dec.–Dec. T-bill yield down 10%	2.18	12/30/85	210.68(+)
S&P earnings down 6%	2.81	12/30/85	210.68(+)
December and January effect signal	3.15	1/31/86	211.78(+)
October-to-January gain of 8%	3.16	1/31/86	211.78(+)
400 trading day exit	3.21	2/21/86	224.62(−)
January to August gain of 15.5%	3.16	8/29/86	252.93(−)
Record volume NYSE and lower S&P	3.14	9/11/86	230.67(+)
Weak propensity to spend	1.31	12/31/86	242.17(+)
Real M1 growth acceleration of 4% points	1.77	12/31/86	242.17(+)
Dec.–Dec. T-bill yield down 10%	2.18	12/31/86	242.17(+)
Two good years in a row	3.22	12/31/86	242.17(−)
Record stock offering signal	3.23	12/31/86	242.17(−)
High-low ratio decline signal	3.30	12/31/86	242.17(+)
December and January effect signals	3.15	1/30/87	274.08(+)
October-to-January gain of 8%	3.16	1/30/87	274.08(+)
Dividend yield under 3.0%	2.83	3/31/87	291.70(−)
P-E ratio over 20.5	2.82	6/30/87	304.00(−)
Major S&P high		8/25/87	HHH336.77
January-to-August gain of 15.5%	3.16	8/31/87	329.80(−)
S&P index down 19.4%	3.02	10/19/87	224.84(+)
One-day S&P decline of 6%	3.04	10/19/87	224.84(+)
Record volume NYSE and lower S&P	3.14	10/19/87	224.84(+)
One-day S&P gain of 3.5%	3.10	10/20/87	236.83(+)
One-day S&P gain of 3.5%	3.10	10/21/87	258.38(+)
NYSE advances over 1300 and S&P up 2.8%	3.13	10/21/87	258.38(+)
One-day S&P decline of 6%	3.04	10/26/87	227.67(+)
One-day S&P gain of 3.5%	3.10	10/29/87	244.77(+)
Two NYSE advances over 1300 in 15 days	3.13	10/29/87	244.77(+)
NYSE advances over 1300 and S&P up 2.8%	3.13	10/29/87	244.77(+)
NYSE advances over 1300 and S&P up 2.8%	3.13	10/30/87	251.79(+)
Two NYSE advances over 1300 in 15 days	3.13	10/30/87	251.79(+)
August-to-October decline of 4.8%	3.16	10/30/87	251.79(+)
Dividend yield over 3.5%	2.85	11/30/87	230.30(+)
Major S&P low		12/04/87	LLL223.92
Leading indicators down 1.9%	1.17	12/31/87	247.08(+)
Leading indicators up, stocks down 1.7%	2.72	12/31/87	247.08(+)
Two-quarter S&P decline of 14%	3.03	12/31/87	247.08(+)

TABLE 3.40 (*continued*)

Indicator	Basic Table	Signal Date	Closing Value S&P Index
Residual volatility signal	3.31	12/31/87	247.08(+)
One-day S&P gain of 3.5%	3.10	1/04/88	255.94(+)
NYSE advances over 1300 and S&P up 2.8%	3.13	1/04/88	255.94(+)
S&P index up 15%	3.00	1/05/88	258.63(+)
One-day S&P decline of 6%	3.04	1/08/88	243.40(+)
Two NYSE advances over 1300 in 15 days	3.13	1/15/88	252.05(+)
December and January effect signals	3.15	1/29/88	257.07(+)
Record volume NYSE and lower S&P	3.14	6/17/88	270.58(+)
August-to-October S&P gain of 5%	3.16	10/31/88	278.97(+)
Leading indicators up, stocks down 1.7%	2.72	12/30/88	277.72(+)
Dividend yield up 24 basis points	2.84	12/30/88	277.72(+)
High-low ratio decline signal	3.30	12/30/88	277.72(+)
December and January effect signals	3.15	1/31/89	297.47(+)
400 trading day exit	3.21	7/06/89	321.55(−)
January-to-August gain of 15.5%	3.16	8/31/89	351.45(−)
One-day S&P decline of 6%	3.04	10/13/89	333.62(+)
Two good years in a row	3.22	12/29/89	353.40(−)
Major S&P high		7/16/90	HHH368.95
NBER business peak		7/31/90	356.15
NYSE advances over 1300 & S&P up 2.8%	3.13	8/27/90	321.44(+)
Wages and salaries down 6%	1.36	9/28/90	306.05(+)
S&P index down 19.4%	3.02	10/11/90	295.46(+)
Major S&P low		10/11/90	LLL295.46
August-to-October decline of 4.8%	3.16	10/31/90	304.00(+)
Unemployment claims up 16%	1.41	11/30/90	322.22(+)
Leading indicators down 1.9%	1.17	12/31/90	330.22(+)
Accelerator residual 2.2% points	1.32	12/31/90	330.22(+)
Durable goods production down 2%	1.35	12/31/90	330.22(+)
Dec.–Dec. T-bill yield down 10%	2.18	12/31/90	330.22(+)
T-bill yield down 20%	2.19	12/31/90	330.22(+)
Dividend growth rate decline of 3.2% pts.	2.83	12/31/90	330.22(+)
High-low ratio decline signal	3.30	12/31/90	330.22(+)
Residual volatility signal	3.31	12/31/90	330.22(+)

TABLE 3.40 (concluded)

Indicator	Basic Table	Signal Date	Closing Value S&P Index
One-day S&P gain of 3.5%	3.10	1/17/91	327.97(+)
NYSE advances over 1300 and S&P up 2.8%	3.13	1/17/91	327.97(+)
S&P index up 15%	3.00	1/30/91	340.91(+)
Unemployment rate up .9% points	1.28	1/31/91	343.93(+)
December and January effect signals	3.15	1/31/91	343.93(+)
October-to-January gain of 8 percent	3.16	1/31/91	343.93(+)
Unemployment rate up 1.2% points	1.28	3/28/91	375.22(+)
Unemployment rate up 1.5% points	1.28	4/30/91	375.35(+)
Two months after two-quarter recession	2.71	5/31/91	389.83(+)
Unemployment rate up 1.8% points	1.28	6/28/91	371.16(+)

HHH flags the major highs identified in Table 3.00.
LLL flags the major lows identified in Table 3.00.

INDEX

A

Accelerator principle, 33, 335
Aggregate accelerator model, 34–35
Average weekly hours of production
  workers, 28–30; *see also* Special
  features tables

B

Bad Octobers, 100
  prediction of, 101–2
Baumol, William, 60, 62n
Bear markets, 43
  recoveries in, 93
Black, Robert, 51
Blue Chip Economic Indicators, 8, 54
  economic recessions and, 22
  on GNP growth, 61
  predicting yearly growth, 56–57
  recessionary surprise and, 14
Bond markets, 49
Bull markets, 45
  law of diminishing returns and, 102
Bureau of Economic Analysis (BEA), 20,
  57
Business cycles, 2; *see also* Special
  features tables
  cycles within, 94–95
  dating peaks/troughs, 21–22
  expansions and contractions of, 20–22
  stock market and, 45–47
Buy-hold policy, 91
Buy/sell signals, 17, 91, 247–63

C

Civilian unemployment rate, 31; *see also*
  Special features tables
Cohn, Richard, 104
Coincident indicators, 23–24, 56
Commerce Department, U.S., 1, 26
  leading economic indicators of, 2–3, 5,
  15
Common stock, 10
  bull markets and, 45
  Federal Reserve forecasts and, 67–68
  as inflationary hedge, 63
  predictors of good periods for, 90
Composites, 2
Computerized programmed trading, 107
Consensus forecasting, 4–5
Consumer expectation index, 22
Consumer price index (CPI), 27, 63; *see*
  also Special features tables
  inflation rate of, 66
  volatile components of, 70–71
Corporate bonds, 10; *see also* Special
  features tables
  high-grade issues, 50
  inflation and, 66
Corporate earnings, 86–88
  declines in, 86–87
Cowles Commission, 43
CPI; *see* Consumer price index (CPI)
CPI inflation indicators, 66–67
Crash indicators, 10
  review of, 101–5
Credit, 49–51

Crude oil; *see also* Special features tables
  disposition of world production, 77
  extra-U.S. world reserves, 75
  OPEC production of, 76–77
  price of imported, 72–73
  in the United States, 74–75
Cyclical indicators, 7, 22
Cyclical work week, 28–29

D

Dating peaks/troughs, 21–22
Deficit, federal, 48
  stock market and, 89
Diffusion index, 58
Diversity, 15–16
Dividends, corporate, 86–88
  associated with S&P index, 87–88
  growth of, 18
"Double bottoms," 42
Double-digit inflation, 72
Durable manufactures, 36
Dow Jones Industrial Average (DJIA), 17;
  see also Special features tables
  bad Octobers and, 102
  record point increases in, 96–97
  versus S&P index, 97

E

Economic indicators, 3–5
  using, 7–9
Economic Recovery Tax Act of 1981, 34, 48
  tax-deferred retirement accounts, 84
Economic Report of the President, 8
Economy, United States, 1
Efficient markets, 4
Eisenhower market, 98
Employed labor force, 29
Employment, 15
Employment cost index, 69–70
Employment recession, 30; *see also*
  Special features tables
  forecasting length of, 56–57

F

Fama, Eugene, 68n
Federal Reserve
  index of industrial production, 3, 21, 35
  and inflation, 24
  inflationary reaction function of, 52–53, 64
  money supply and, 27
  recession and, 18
  recessionary reaction function of, 51–52
Feldstein, Paul, 4
Financial Analysts Journal, 90
Financial return cycles, 102–3
Fiscal policy, 33
  stock market and, 47–48
Forecasting, 1, 9
  business economists and, 25
  consensus approach to, 3
Freidman, Milton, 33

G

*General Theory of Employment, Interest
  and Money, The*, 41
GNP
  accelerator principle and, 34–35
  economic recession and, 33
  forecasting nominal GNP, 78–79
  inventory recessions and, 42
Gordon, Robert, 62
Great Depression (1930s), 17
  S&P index and, 19
Greenspan, Alan, 106
Growth, economic, 25–27

H

Hedging against inflation, 63–64
  gold versus stock as, 64
Housing starts, 39–40, 137
Hubbert, M. King, 75

I

Implicit price deflator, 65–66
  wage-price inflation and, 69
Income expenditure multiplier model, 33–
  36
Indexes, 22–24
Index of industrial production, 3
  NBER's recessionary troughs and, 21
  recessionary surprise and, 14
Index of leading indicators, 3, 7, 15, 56;
  see also Special features tables
  oil prices and, 26
  recessionary surprise and, 14
  revision of index, 22–23
  safety in stock market and, 82–83
Indicator approach, 1
  criticism of, 16
Industrial production, 35–36
Inflation, 18
  causes of, 69–73
  Federal Reserve action and, 24
  Federal Reserve's reaction to, 52–53
  predicting changes in, 65
Institutional investors, 32
Interest rates, 24
  IRA investors and, 50
  yield curves and, 50–51
Inventory, 14
Inventory recessions, 41
  duration of, 41–42
IRA investors, 50

J

January effect, 98–99
Johnson's Charts, 10
Just-in-time delivery, 41

K

Kaufman, Henry, 44
Keynes, John Maynard, 33, 41
Keynesian economics, 21, 34

L

Labor force, 60–61
Lagging indicators, 24
Law of diminishing returns, 102
Leading economic indicators; see Index of
  leading indicators

M

Macroeconomic forecasts, 25
Macroeconomics, 62
Market Chronicle, 16
McNees, Stephen, 61, 62n, 68n
Michigan index of consumer expectation,
  22, 37; see also Special features
  tables
  in poor growth years, 37–38
Mill, John Stuart, 59
Mitchell, Wesley, 20
Modigliani, Franco, 104
Molnar, David, 36
Monetary policy, 47–48
Money markets, 49
Money supply M1/M2, 22, 27; see also
  Special features tables
  implementation of M2, 49
  M2 versus M3, 78
  stock prices and, 47
  using, 48–49
Moody's indexes, 8
Moore, Geoffrey, 45
Moran, Alfred, 81–82

N

National Bureau of Economic Research
  (NBER), 3, 27, 56
  recessionary troughs and, 21, 24
  on stock prices, 45
National income, 22
NBER; see National Bureau of Economic
  Research (NBER)
Nominal GNP, 78–79, 197, 199
Nonagricultural payrolls, 29–30

Nonrandom stock price theory, 83
NYSE (New York Stock Exchange), 97, 107
record trading on, 97–98

O

Oil; *see* Crude oil
Oil/gas resources in United States, 74–77
Oil price shocks, 26–27
Okun, Arthur, 61
Okun's Law, 18, 61
OPEC, 72–73

P

Payroll employment, 15, 30
Peaks, business, 21–22
cyclical work week and, 28
stock market after, 46
Personal computers, 1
Personal income, 35
Political business cycle, 18–19
Presidential election years; *see also*
Special features tables
effect on inflation, 71–72
effect on S&P composite index, 18–19
S&P composite index and, 18–19
Price-earnings ratios, 87
Prime rate, 51
Producer price acceleration, 59–60
Product accounting, 22

Q-R

Quantity theory of money, 78, 197
Real currency, 60
Real GNP, 60–61, 79
Recession, economic, 1; *see also* Special
features tables
announcing, 22
composite indexes and, 23–24
effect on GNP, 33
identifying, 54–55
institutional investors and, 32
leading indicators and, 1

Recession, economic—*Cont.*
personal income and, 35
taking advantage of, 81–82
Recessionary buy signal, 36
Recessionary indicators, 81–85
Recessionary surprise, 13–14
Recessionary troughs, 56
stock returns in, 81
Recovery indicators, 30, 160
for recessionary troughs, 56
Renshaw, Edward, 62n
Residential building permits, 39
Residual volatility, 106
Risk premiums, 104–5

S

Samuelson, Paul, 33
SCB; *see Survey of Current Business (SCB)*
Security Price Index Record, 9
Short-term interest rates, 49–50
Slow growth indicators, 57
Slow growth rates
identifying 59–60, 59
stock returns and, 59
Smith, Vernon, 88
Sommers, Albert, 1
Special features tables, 109–263
average weekly hours of production
workers (1990–91), 121
BEA's composite index, 117
business cycles
expansions/contractions (1854–1991), 113–14
fluctuations in unemployment of .6%, 126
buy/sell signals, 218–19
chronology for S&P index, 247–63
common stock offered by underwriters, 239
composite index of lagging indicators
declines of 4% or more, 117
fluctuations of 2.5 % or more, 117
consumer price index (CPI), 186

Special features tables—*Cont.*
consumer price inflation indicators,
180–81
corporate bonds and stocks
cyclical increases in yield, 150
financial returns from holding, 179
crude oil
disposition of world production, 196
non-OPEC production of, 194
OPEC production of, 195
production by United States, 192
world reserves of, 193
crude oil import cost
fluctuations in, 191
relationship to CPI inflation rate, 190
(DJIA) Dow Jones industrial average
compared to S&P composite index,
229
record point increases in, 228
employment by major U.S. industry
(1947–90), 122
employment declines, 125
employment recessions
monthly duration indicators, 158
and monthly production lead time,
125
of nonagricultural payrolls, 124
index of leading indicators
delineating unhealthy expansions
with, 165–66
fluctuations of 2.5% or more, 116
identifying poor growth years with,
118–19
increases and recessions in
production, 118
lead times for (1953–90), 110
inflation rates with consensus forecasts,
176
interest rates
and FED's reaction to various
indicators, 155
good years for stock ownership and,
182–83
inventory investments post World War
II, 138
major bull markets, 237

Special features tables—*Cont.*
Michigan index of expectations and
S&P changes, 135
money and bond market, 149
money supply M1/M2
fluctuations in M1 of 3% or more,
148
fluctuations in M2 of 1.5% or more,
148
new housing permits/starts
cyclical fluctuations in, 137
recessionary peaks and, 137
nominal GNP
with consensus forecast, 199
and quantity theory of money, 197
nonagricultural payroll fluctuations, 123
NYSE daily record sales, 230–33
oil and gas resource estimates, 191
payroll employment and recessionary
decline, 110
peak-trough months for industrial
production, 115
personal income in recessionary
declines, 133
presidential election years
predicting outcomes, 187–88
and S&P composite (1928–89), 113
prime rate average and various
indicators, 153
propensity to spend and stock returns,
130–31
quantity theory of money and nominal
GNP, 197
real GNP growth
civilian unemployment rate changes
(1967–90), 171
consumer oriented-indicators and,
135–36
forecasting methods, 161–62
forecasting with producer price
index, 167
hourly earnings of production
workers and, 184–85
implicit price deflator for, 177
and labor force, 170
recessionary declines and, 128–29

Special features tables—*Cont.*
real GNP growth—*Cont.*
slow rates in, 166
using civilian unemployment rate, 169
using currency rates and CPI, 168
recessionary indicators, 156
recessionary reaction of FED, 154
recessions in GNP, 139
recessions in industrial production, 118
recovery indicators, 160
returns on combinations of S&P and
T-bills, 205
return strategies for $2000 investment,
151
S&P composite stock index; *see* S&P
composite stock index, special
feature tables
stock indexes of various countries, 200
stock market
bubbles associated with double-digit
returns, 238
bubbles associated with PE ratios
over 20.5, 208
perfect predictors for, 214–15
using CPI to forecast good years, 178
stock market crashes
identifying with leading indicators,
216–17
at 10% of average monthly S&P
index, 140–41
stock market declines post WWII, 143
stock market fluctuations, 142
stock prices
growth rates for real GNP and, 144–
45
monthly lead times at peaks/troughs,
143
stock returns
accelerator relationships and, 131–32
and shifting propensity to spend, 130
treasury securities
comparative average yields, 151–52
T-bills (91–day) discount rates, 150
unemployment insurance increases, 127
unemployment rate
and financial returns on stock/T-bills,
204–5

Special features tables—*Cont.*
unemployment rate—*Cont.*
inflation rates for CPI and, 185
U S. crude oil prices, 120
U.S. economy
forecasting poor growth years for, 157
forecasting slow growth rate, 163–64
growth rate based on Okun's Law,
172
U.S. industrial production
cumulative declines over 2%, 133
recessions in payroll employment
and, 159
Sprinkle, Beryl, 47
Standard & Poor's (S&P) composite
index, 6, 8, 43–44
buying strategies for, 93–94
civilian unemployment rate and, 31
cloning a portfolio like, 95
closing value fluctuations in, 92–95
diversity and, 16
dividends and, 87
durable manufactures and, 36
election years and, 18–19
historic highs of, 106–7
inflation of, 64–65
recessionary surprise and, 14
recessionary troughs and, 81
record earnings for, 86
and residual propensity to spend, 34
residual volatility and, 106
returns on, 17
Standard & Poor's (S&P) composite stock
index, special feature tables
annual declines in NYSE volume and,
247
appreciation after 19.4% declines, 222
appreciation after one-day gains, 227
appreciation two-quarter declines of
14%, 223
buy signals associated with recession
(1990–91), 111
chronology of buy/sell signals for, 247–
63
closings during bear markets, 221
closing values for one-declines of 6%,
223–24

Standard & Poor's (S&P) composite stock index, special features tables—*Cont.*
combining with leading indicators, 202–3
compared to DJIA, 229
compound GNP growth rates associated with (1889–1989), 112
conditional market indicators and, 212–13
cumulative increases in unemployment, 127
declines in real GNP and, 201
declines of 3% or more following highs, 224–25
and discount on 91–day T-bills, 183
earnings, dividends, returns associated with, 209–10, 210
end of decade values (1879–1989), 141
fluctuations amounting to 10%, 139–40
fluctuations in daily closings of, 220
fluctuations in inflation and, 173
gains and losses after advances, 237
gold price appreciation and, 173–74
historic highs for, 246
inflation indicators associated with, 174–75
in/out strategies for (1929–90), 211
market volatility associated, 244–45
Michigan index of expectations and, 135
modern risk premiums for, 242–43
NYSE advances and increases over 2% in, 230–31
old-fashioned risk premiums for, 240–41
percentage changes in closing values, 235–336
positive returns using monetary-fiscal policy variables, 146–47
presidential elections associated with (1928–89), 113
purchasing during recessionary decline, 134
rates of return (1929–90), 112
residual volatility and, 246
returns for holding, 201

Standard & Poor's (S&P) composite stock index, special features tables—*Cont.*
returns in periods of declining production, 134
returns with declines in earnings, 207
strategies for cloning the index, 226
using December/January gains, 233–34
Statistical models, 25
Stock, James, 15
Stock issues, new, 103
Stock market, 8–9
business cycles and, 45–47
employment/unemployment statistics and, 28
indicators affecting, 89–90
January effect and, 98–99
performance of, 10–11
recessionary indicators and, 81–85
unemployment rate and, 31–32
volatility of, 106–7
Stock market crashes, 43–45
indicators of, 90
low dividend yield and, 88
Stock market indexes, foreign, 80
Stock price indexes, 4–5
Stock prices, 45
economic growth and, 47
major fluctuations in, 92
monthly lead times for, 46–47
Surplus-liquidity indicators, 89
Survey of Current Business (SCB), 8, 20

T

Tinbergen, Jan, 53
Trade and Securities Statistics, 8
Troughs, business, 21–22
lagging indicators and, 24
Truman market, 98
Turning points, 22

U

Unemployment rate, 31
stock market and, 83–84
Unhealthy expansion periods, 58

Unused labor capacity, 60
"UP-ticks," 42

W

Wage-price inflation, 69–73
Wall Street
  one-day gains on, 96
  panic days on, 94
Wall Street Journal, 8

Watson, Mark, 15
Weak recovery hypothesis, 14–15
Wilson, Woodrow, 71
Winning on Wall Street, 48

Y–Z

Year-end basis, switching, 84–85
Zarnowitz, Victor, 68n
Zweig, Martin, 48